INTERFACES

Series Editor: Barbara Green, O.P.

D1636613

James of Jerusalem

Heir to Jesus of Nazareth

Patrick J. Hartin

A Michael Glazier Book

LITURGICAL PRESS

Collegeville, Minnesota

www.litpress.org

A Michael Glazier Book published by the Liturgical Press

Cover design by Ann Blattner. Watercolor by Ethel Boyle.

1	2	3	4	5	6	7	8

Library of Congress Cataloging-in-Publication Data

Hartin, P. J. (Patrick J.)
    James of Jerusalem : heir to Jesus of Nazareth / Patrick J. Hartin.
        p.   cm. — (Interfaces)
    "A Michael Glazier book."
    Includes bibliographical references and index.
    ISBN 0-8146-5152-6 (pbk. : alk. paper)
    1. James, Brother of the Lord, Saint.   I. Title.   II. Series: Interfaces
(Collegeville, Minn.).

BS2454.J3H37   2004
225.9'2—dc22
[B]   2004006462

CONTENTS

PREFACE

The book you hold in your hand is one of ten volumes in a new set. This series, called INTERFACES, is basically a curriculum adventure, a creative opportunity in teaching and learning, presented at this moment in the long story of how the Bible has been studied, interpreted, and appropriated.

The INTERFACES project was prompted by a number of experiences that you, perhaps, share. When I first taught undergraduates, the college had just received a substantial grant from the National Endowment for the Humanities, and one of the recurring courses designed within the grant was called Great Figures in Pursuit of Excellence. Three courses would be taught, each centering on a figure from some academic discipline, with a common seminar section to provide occasion for some integration. Some triads were more successful than others, as you might imagine. But the opportunity to concentrate on a single individual—whether historical or literary—to team teach, to make links to another pair of figures, and to learn new things about other disciplines was stimulating and fun for all involved. A second experience that gave rise to the present series came at the same time, connected as well with undergraduates. It was my frequent experience to have Roman Catholic students feel quite put out about taking "more" biblical studies, since, as they confidently affirmed, they had already been there many times and done it all. That was, of course, not true; as we well know, there is always more to learn. And often those who felt most informed were the least likely to take on new information when offered it.

A stimulus as primary as my experience with students was the familiarity of listening to friends and colleagues at professional meetings talking about the research that excites us most. I often wondered: Do her undergraduate students know about this? Or how does he bring these ideas— clearly so energizing to him—into the college classroom? Perhaps some of us have felt bored with classes that seem wholly unrelated to research, that rehash the same familiar material repeatedly. Hence the idea for this series of books to bring to the fore and combine some of our research interests with our teaching and learning. Accordingly, this series is not so much about creating texts *for* student audiences but rather about *sharing* our scholarly passions with them. Because these volumes are intended each as a piece of original scholarship, they are geared to be stimulating to both students and established scholars, perhaps resulting in some fruitful collaborative learning adventures.

The series also developed from a widely shared sense that all academic fields are expanding and exploding, and that to contemplate "covering" even a testament (let alone the whole Bible or Western monotheistic religions) needs to be abandoned in favor of something with greater depth and fresh focus. At the same time, the links between our fields are becoming increasingly obvious as well, and the possibilities for study that draw together academic realms that had once seemed separate is exciting. Finally, the spark of enthusiasm that almost always ignited when I mentioned to students and colleagues the idea of single figures in combination—interfacing—encouraged me that this was an idea worth trying.

And so with the leadership and help of Liturgical Press Academic Editor Linda Maloney, as well as with the encouragement and support of Editorial Director Mark Twomey, the series has begun to take shape.

Each volume in the INTERFACES series focuses clearly on a biblical character (or perhaps a pair of them). The characters from the first set of volumes are in some cases powerful—King Saul, Pontius Pilate—and familiar—John the Baptist, the patriarch Joseph; in other cases they will strike you as minor and little-known—the Cannibal Mothers, Herodias. The second "litter" emerging adds notables of various ranks and classes: Jezebel, queen of the Northern Israelite realm; James of Jerusalem, "brother of the Lord"; Simon the Pharisee, dinner host to Jesus; Legion, the Gerasene demoniac encountered so dramatically by Jesus. In any case, each of them has been chosen to open up a set of worlds for consideration. The named (or unnamed) character interfaces with his or her historical-cultural world and its many issues, with other characters from biblical literature; each character has drawn forth the creativity of the author, who has taken on the challenge of engaging many readers. The books are designed for college students (though we think they are suitable for seminary courses and for serious Bible study), planned to provide young adults with relevant information and at a level of critical sophistication that matches the rest of the undergraduate curriculum. In fact, the expectation is that what students are learning of historiography, literary theory, and cultural anthropology in other classes will find an echo in these books, each of which is explicit about at least two relevant methodologies. It is surely the case that biblical studies is in a methodology-conscious moment, and the INTERFACES series embraces it enthusiastically. Our hope is for students to continue to see the relationship between their best questions and their most valuable insights, between how they approach texts and what they find there. The volumes go well beyond familiar paraphrase of narratives to ask questions that are relevant in our era. At the same time, the series authors also have each dealt with the notion of the Bible as Scripture in a way condign for them. None of the books is preachy or hortatory, and yet the self-implicating aspects of working with the revelatory text are handled frankly. The assumption is, again, that college can be a good time for people to reexamine and rethink their beliefs and assumptions, and they need to do so in good company. The INTERFACES volumes all challenge teachers to re-vision radically the scope of a course, to allow the many connections among characters to serve as its warp and weft. What would emerge fresh if a Deuteronomistic History class were organized around King Saul, Queen Jezebel, and the two women who petitioned their nameless monarch? How is Jesus' ministry thrown into fresh relief when structured by shared concerns implied by a demoniac, a Pharisee, James—a disciple, and John the Baptist—a mentor? And for those who must "do it all" in one semester, a study of Genesis' Joseph, Herodias, and Pontius Pilate might allow for a timely foray into postcolonialism.

The INTERFACES volumes are not substitutes for the Bible. In every case they are to be read with the text. Quoting has been kept to a minimum for that very reason. The series is accompanied by a straightforward companion, *From Earth's Creation to John's Revelation: The INTERFACES Biblical Storyline Companion,* which provides a quick overview of the whole storyline into which the characters under special study fit. The companion is available gratis for those using two or more of the INTERFACES volumes. Already readers of diverse proficiency and familiarity have registered satisfaction with this slim overview narrated by biblical Sophia.

The series' challenge—for publisher, writers, teachers, and students— is to combine the volumes creatively, to INTERFACE them well so that the vast potential of the biblical text continues to unfold for us all. These ten volumes offer a foretaste of other volumes currently on the drawing board. It has been a pleasure to work with the authors of these first volumes as well as with the series consultants: Carleen Mandolfo for Hebrew Bible and Catherine Murphy for New Testament. It is the hope of all of us that you will find the series useful and stimulating for your own teaching and learning.

Barbara Green, O.P.
INTERFACES Series Editor
May 16, 2004
Berkeley, California

ACKNOWLEDGMENTS

James of Jerusalem has intrigued me throughout my years of college teaching. I welcome this opportunity of synthesizing my reflections upon the person of James of Jerusalem not simply as an isolated individual but rather in interface with other great Christian leaders, Paul and Peter, as well as with his "brother" Jesus. I hope that this study will infuse in those who read it my passion for this subject. Its importance lies in the way in which it sheds new light upon those early decades of nascent Christianity, helping us rediscover dimensions either lost or glossed over in its transmission.

All biblical quotations are taken from the *New Revised Standard Version Bible* except for those instances where I note that I have translated the text myself.

I wish to acknowledge my gratitude to Kevin Eiler for his meticulous assistance with the bibliographical material and his painstaking checking of the manuscript in the various stages of development. I also wish to thank Barbara Green, the editor of INTERFACES, for inviting me to do this study on James of Jerusalem as well as for her invaluable comments and suggestions that have enhanced this manuscript. Finally, I should like to thank all the editors of Liturgical Press for bringing this project to fruition: Linda Maloney, Colleen Stiller, Mark Twomey, and Polly Chappell.

I dedicate this book to my students past and present whose questions and insights have contributed toward my understanding of James of Jerusalem as true heir to the legacy of Jesus of Nazareth.

ABBREVIATIONS

Biblical Books and Apocrypha

Gen	Nah	1–2–3–4 Kgdms	John
Exod	Hab	Ad Esth	Acts
Lev	Zeph	Bar	Rom
Num	Hag	Bel	1–2 Cor
Deut	Zech	1-2 Esdr	Gal
Josh	Mal	4 Ezra	Eph
Judg	Ps (*pl.*: Pss)	Jdt	Phil
1–2 Sam	Job	Ep Jer	Col
1–2 Kgs	Prov	1–2–3–4 Macc	1–2 Thess
Isa	Ruth	Pr Azar	1–2 Tim
Jer	Cant	Pr Man	Titus
Ezek	Eccl (*or* Qoh)	Sir	Phlm
Hos	Lam	Sus	Heb
Joel	Esth	Tob	Jas
Amos	Dan	Wis	1–2 Pet
Obad	Ezra	Matt	1–2–3 John
Jonah	Neh	Mark	Jude
Mic	1–2 Chr	Luke	Rev

Other Ancient Texts, Periodicals, Reference Works

AB   Anchor Bible

ABD   *Anchor Bible Dictionary.* Edited by David Noel Freedman. 6 vols. New York: Doubleday, 1992.

ABRL   Anchor Bible Reference Library

ACW   Ancient Christian Writers. Edited by Walter J. Burghardt, John J. Dillon, and Dennis D. McManus.

A.J.   Josephus, *Antiquitates judaicae (Jewish Antiquities)*

ANRW   *Aufstieg und Niedergang der römischen Welt: Geschichte und Kultur Roms im Spiegel der neueren Forschung.* Edited by Wolfgang Haase and Hildegard Temporini. Berlin and New York: Walter De Gruyter, 1972–

Ap. Jas.	*The Apocryphon of James*
1 Apoc. Jas.	*The (First) Apocalypse of James*
2 Apoc. Jas.	*The (Second) Apocalypse of James*
BHT	Beiträge zur historischen Theologie
Bib	*Biblica*
BNTC	Black's New Testament Commentaries
BTB	*Biblical Theology Bulletin*
CBQ	*Catholic Biblical Quarterly*
CurTM	*Currents in Theology and Mission*
GBS	Guides to Biblical Scholarship
GLB	De-Gruyter-Lehrbuch
Gos. Thom.	*The Gospel of Thomas*
Hist. eccl.	Eusebius, *Historia ecclesiastica (Ecclesiastical History)*
HvTSt	*Hervormde teologiese studies*
HR	*History of Religions*
Int	*Interpretation*
JSNT	*Journal for the Study of the New Testament*
JSNTSup	Journal for the Study of the New Testament: Supplement Series
JSOT	*Journal for the Study of the Old Testament*
JTS	*Journal of Theological Studies*
JTSA	*Journal of Theology for Southern Africa*
LCL	Loeb Classical Library
LSJ	*A Greek-English Lexicon,* compiled by Henry George Liddell and Robert Scott, revised and augmented by Henry Stuart Jones and Roderick McKenzie (9th edition with revised supplement) Oxford: Clarendon Press, 1996.
LXX	Septuagint (The Greek Translation of the Old Testament)
MPL	*Patrologia latina [= Patrologiae cursus completus: Series latina].* Edited by J.-P. Migne. 217 vols. Paris, 1844–64.
NIGTC	*New International Greek Testament Commentary*
NovTSup	Supplements to Novum Testamentum
NovT	*Novum Testamentum*
NTS	*New Testament Studies*
NRSV	*New Revised Standard Version*
Prot. Jas.	*The Protevangelium of James*
RB	*Revue biblique*
ResQ	*Restoration Quarterly*
RHR	*Revue de l'histoire des religions*
RevQ	*Revue de Qumran*
SBLDS	Society of Biblical Literature Dissertation Series

SBLSP	Society of Biblical Literature Seminar Papers
SJLA	Studies in Judaism in Late Antiquity
Semeia	*Semeia*
SNTSMS	Society for New Testament Studies Monograph Series
SP	Sacra Pagina
Vita	Josephus, *Vita (The Life)*
WBC	Word Biblical Commentary
ZNW	*Zeitschrift für die neutestamentliche Wissenschaft und die Kunde der älteren Kirche*

INTRODUCTION

Through the Looking Glass

> The Walrus and the Carpenter
> Walked on a mile or so,
> And then they rested on a rock
> Conveniently low:
> And all the little Oysters stood
> And waited in a row.
>
> "The time has come," the Walrus said,
> "To talk of many things:
> Of shoes – and ships – and sealing-wax –
> Of cabbages – and kings – "[1]

Our major access to the world of the first century is through the writings of the New Testament. Much like Alice who stood before the "Looking-Glass House,"[2] we stand before the text and with excitement mixed with trepidation we jump into the text to discover a whole new world that lies before us. Just as Alice discovered a world that was very different from her own and what she was used to, so we discover as well a world that challenges our assumptions and helps us to view reality in ways that are new, exciting, strange, and challenging. When we return from the world of the text we will emerge as people whose outlook, understanding, and experience of the first Christian centuries has been dramatically changed. This change is not simply on the intellectual level. It affects our whole being

---

[1] Lewis Carroll, *Through the Looking-Glass and What Alice Found There,* Books of Wonder (New York: William Morrow & Co., [1872] 1993) 75.
[2] Ibid. 1–25.

since we have interacted with texts whose rhetorical purpose is to communicate with the reader. This communication reaches out to engage the reader and through this interaction produces a transformation at some level.

Why James?

To enter the world of the first century C.E. following James of Jerusalem as a guide is much like Alice's adventure in being led by the White Rabbit into Wonderland. The character of James enables us to look upon the birth and characters of Christianity differently. Through James' interface with his world and the other leaders of the movement we discover a new world that lies beneath the surface, with interactions that seem to have been muffled either deliberately or unintentionally. With the character of James of Jerusalem as center and guide we have a valuable way of approaching anew the origins and growth of the early Christian movement, not just during the first century, but over the course of the next three centuries as well.

The impression gained initially by those who have read the New Testament is that there are many more influential figures from the New Testament world such as Peter, Paul, John, Thomas, Mary Magdalene; so the question naturally arises, "Why focus on James?" A close reading of the texts and an interpretation that follows critical methodologies of interpretation reveal a different picture. James of Jerusalem, otherwise referred to as "James, the brother of the Lord" in the New Testament writings, or as "James the Righteous One," or simply "James the Just" in subsequent writings beyond the New Testament, appears in a number of different traditions both within the New Testament and beyond. This clearly testifies to the influential position his character exercised within early Christian thought. However, our eyes, like those of Alice, will be opened in the course of this study when we discover how his leadership role has been glossed over in much of the New Testament tradition. The New Testament writings tended to approach James' interface with Peter and Paul from the perspective of Peter or Paul rather than from James' perspective. This naturally led to the relegation of James to the sidelines. Our study will endeavor to rehabilitate James by discovering the influential role he did play within that early first century.

The aim of this study is to unearth James' role within the early Christian movement. As we examine James' interface with the different traditions and characters, the true diversity of early Christianity emerges. The Acts of the Apostles presents a beautiful and harmonious picture of the spread of Christianity to Rome, "the ends of the earth" (Acts 1:8), largely through a focus on the characters of Peter and Paul. But nothing is said about the spread of the Christian movement to other areas, such as North

Africa and Syria, which were to become important and thriving Christian centers in the following centuries. The objective of our study will be to situate James within his own world, and through our historical-critical examination of the traditions relating to James we will endeavor to take him seriously as a character in his own right.

By paying attention to those passages where James appears (directly or indirectly), this study tries to flesh out aspects of the development of early Christianity, particularly through its struggle to define itself in interface both with its roots in Judaism and with the ever increasing numbers of believers joining the movement from the wider Greek and Roman worlds. James of Jerusalem will place in the forefront the Jewish matrix of the Jesus movement. As Jews faithful to their traditions, both Jesus and James endeavored to preserve their Jewish heritage not in a legalistic way, but in a way that appropriated God's will faithfully in new contexts and situations. This was always the spirit of the Torah that was meant to convey God's will for the present. That will continually need to be examined and appropriated as the centuries passed and the world changed. This conforms to Jesus' understanding of his role and relationship to the Jewish Torah: "Do not think that I have come to abolish the law or the prophets: I have come not to abolish but to fulfill" (Matt 5:17). This study will demonstrate that James saw his task as continuing this mission of Jesus. In fact, James is the true heir to the message and way of life of Jesus. On him the mantle of Jesus truly rests.

I have had a scholarly passion for James, and in particular the letter of James, for the past twenty years. This interest arose from the context of a college classroom and was in large part initiated by my students. I began my teaching career in South Africa at the University of the Witwatersrand, where I taught a semester course on the letter of James to upper-division students. In the course of that study the students raised insightful questions regarding the Jewish matrix for the birth of Christianity and at the same time the puzzling similarities between the message of James and the sayings of Jesus, especially those found in Matthew's Sermon on the Mount. These questions lie at the heart of the letter of James and concern its interface with both its Jewish heritage and with the person of Jesus and the world of nascent Christianity. These have been issues I have struggled with for two decades. It is my sincere wish to share my scholarly passion for James of Jerusalem, and I hope that with this monograph and its focus on the character of James students will also be excited and challenged to wrestle with these issues anew. Hopefully this interaction will awaken a deeper awareness of the richness and the diversity of traditions that underpin the New Testament world.

While many important insights will emerge from this investigation, there are two that are paramount. The first arises from the challenge posed by the harmonious and peaceful picture the Acts of the Apostles paints of the early Christian communities (Acts 2:44-47).

Contrary to this picture, this study will show that tension and conflict lie at the heart of the interface between the main leaders of the Christian movement. This was a healthy tension, for it enabled the followers of Jesus to evaluate their own perspectives and come to terms with what were the essentials of Jesus' message to which believers, new and old, must adhere. Further, the tensions reveal the beauty of the diversity of early Christianity. Tensions within the different Christian groups were healthy signs of growth. After all, it is only through an honest acknowledgment and a wrestling with tensions that clarity can later emerge.

The second insight that arises from this study concerns respecting the difference and distinction between the *textual world* that emerges from the documents of the New Testament and beyond, and the *historical and actual world* behind those documents. There is an important need for recognizing and honoring this distinction. In the world of any narrative one cannot simply jump from the world of the story to the world of reality and history. Not to respect these two worlds when reading Alice in Wonderland would result in some really strange and fantastic conclusions! To read it as a historical record of the journeys of a young girl, the people and creatures she encounters, and the strange experiences that come her way would raise questions that would distract from its beauty and the rhetorical purpose of the author. The same is true of the New Testament documents and other writings we examine. Their primary concern was not to produce a historical record. Rather, they have a different rhetorical function in mind. One of the basic approaches in this study is the attempt to remain faithful and true to the author's rhetorical intent. A discovery of the text's rhetorical function will enable us to see the writing with new eyes. To read the New Testament narratives (the gospels and the Acts of the Apostles) with a twenty-first-century historical concern that wishes to mine these writings for a historical discovery of the person and character of James would ultimately be unproductive and would distort the texts themselves. The writers of these texts were not intent on writing a historical account as we understand history today. This was not their rhetorical intent. Instead, the intent was to construct a narrative that would speak to their own communities and communicate to them insights that the writers felt were vital for the lives of their communities. The writer would construct his own world in the narrative and use that to communicate and teach Jesus' message. This will emerge more clearly when we examine references to the family of Jesus within the

Gospel of Mark. The failure to respect this distinction between the textual world and the historical world is characteristic of fundamentalist interpretations of the Scriptures and in reality distorts the message.

This does not lead to the opposite conclusion, namely that the narratives are unhistorical. There is undoubtedly a relationship between the text itself and the historical reality behind the text. The way to access that historical event behind the text is twofold. The starting point is the conscious realization of the rhetorical function of the narrative itself. By examining the author's intent the reader endeavors to remain true to the author's purpose in producing the narrative. Second, examining independent and diverse traditions helps to point toward a commonly reflected historical reality. This is a fundamental principle of the historical critical method that is called "the criterion of multiple attestation."[3] When a theme, fact, saying, or event appears in a number of independent literary sources and genres, they all independently point to the same historical reality behind the text. The agreement of two or more independent traditions helps to bridge the literary and historical divide. We will illustrate this approach more fully in Chapter Two when we examine the Acts of the Apostles and the letter to the Galatians. They both in their own rhetorical way refer to the events surrounding the acceptance of Gentiles into the Christian movement as illustrated in the Apostolic Decree and the issue of table fellowship.

What Maps Are Needed for This Journey?

I approach this examination of the character of James from a canonical perspective. This means that I begin with an initial analysis of the gospels (Matthew, Mark, Luke, and John). Then I proceed to examine the Acts of the Apostles and the writings of Paul. Finally, I look at the letter of James. This is the canonical order in which they appear in the New Testament. One could have approached this investigation using a chronological map that would have commenced with the letters of Paul and then progressed into the gospels and other New Testament writings. However, such an approach would have made the journey confusing and repetitious.

At the same time this investigation uses a number of methodological interpretive approaches that enable us to be responsible readers of the text. Each chapter uses methods that are appropriate to the material as well as to the aim of the investigation.

---

[3] See John P. Meier, *A Marginal Jew: Rethinking the Historical Jesus.* Vol. One: *The Roots of the Problem and the Person* (New York: Doubleday, 1991), 174–75.

Chapter One focuses on the interface between Jesus and his family in the gospels. The four gospels are examined by using two appropriate methodologies, narrative criticism and source criticism. It will be clear that I adopt the generally accepted solution to the Synoptic Problem: that Mark is the first gospel to have been written and that Matthew and Luke both used Mark independently in the composition of their gospels. At the same time Matthew and Luke drew upon a second document, the Sayings Source Q, for the sayings of Jesus. The examination of passages relating to Jesus and his family reveals the distinctiveness and focus of each of the traditions and how and why they have presented the interface in their own distinctive way.

Chapter Two examines the Acts of the Apostles and the letters of Paul (especially the letter to the Galatians) to focus on James as leader of the Jerusalem community. The methodological starting point for this examination is the understanding of genre. The genres of the Acts of the Apostles and Paul's letters are decidedly different. Each has its own rhetorical function. By remaining true to the genre of narrative (Acts of the Apostles) and letters (Paul's writings) and their rhetorical function, the interpreter is able to walk a path through the apparent contradictions presented by these different writings. The investigation will show that in fact there is no real contradiction. Social-scientific methodology will also be used to illustrate the importance of purity laws and the role they played within the context of a group or religion at that time. This examination provides the opportunity to interface with the relationship between Jewish and Gentile Christianity. Acts 15 and Gal 2:1-10 are examined to show how Christianity was defining itself with regard to its roots within Judaism and the wider world. James emerges in the leadership role in Jerusalem, holding authority over all Jewish Christian centers in the Diaspora. James' interface with Peter and Paul is such that he retains leadership of the Jewish community while Peter is entrusted with the mission to the Jews and Paul with the mission to the Gentiles. This study gives an opportunity to reflect on the diversity that made up early Christianity.

Chapter Three looks at the letter of James. The examination of the genre of the letter provides the methodological starting point for the interpretation of this writing. In examining the letter of James, we focus exclusively on the question, "What can the letter reveal about the character of James?" Once again the letter shows James in interface with the world of Judaism and his Jewish heritage, as well as with Jesus and his Christian heritage.

Chapter Four gives attention to the picture of James as he emerges in documents beyond the New Testament. Writings emanating from the Jewish historian Josephus and the Christian historian Eusebius, as well as

Gnostic and Jewish Christian writings, form the center of consideration. From a methodological perspective this chapter is a study in tradition history and shows how a tradition develops and is influenced by the socio-cultural context in which it is used.

Finally, *Chapter Five* attempts to bring together the legacy James of Jerusalem left behind and his relevance for our world of the twenty-first century. This investigation again reveals how close James remains to the voice of Jesus; particularly in concern for the poor they both offer a decidedly vital challenge for our world.

This book is about James and the heritage of Judaism to which he endeavors to remain true. In passing through the Looking Glass, our examination will reveal a picture of James very different from traditional understandings. Like Alice we will wonder at it all in surprise. James was a giant of the early Christian church, the residential leader of the Jerusalem community and other Jewish Christian centers. His vision was to remain true to his roots within Judaism and to his brother Jesus. As time went on his vision lost out to Paul. It is both important and exciting to be able to unearth from the documents of the first three centuries the character of someone who indeed played an extremely important role. This study provides new insight into the world we call early Christianity.

CHAPTER ONE

Who Is James?
The Family of Jesus in the Gospels

"Don't stand chattering to yourself like that,"
Humpty Dumpty said, looking at her for the first time,
"but tell me your name and your business."
"My *name* is Alice, but—"
"It's a stupid name enough!" Humpty Dumpty interrupted impatiently.
"What does it mean?"
"*Must* a name mean something?" Alice asked doubtfully.
"Of course it must," Humpty Dumpty said with a short laugh:
"*my* name means the shape I am—
and a good handsome shape it is too.
With a name like yours, you might be any shape, almost."[1]

The letters of Paul contain chronologically the earliest New Testament evidence for the figure of James. The gospels, on the other hand, present a more detailed understanding of James and his relationship to Jesus. For this reason I begin with the gospels to examine the interface between Jesus and his family. The study in this chapter of passages relating to Jesus and his family will embrace two distinct methodologies, namely narrative criticism and source criticism, and will show the beauty, distinctiveness, and focus of each tradition and how and why they have presented the relationship in their own distinctive ways. As a result, a much more positive picture should emerge of Jesus' relationship to James and family than is generally presented by scholarship.

---

[1] Lewis Carroll, *Through the Looking-Glass and What Alice Found There,* Books of Wonder (New York: William Morrow, [1872] 1993) 115–16.

1

References to James in the New Testament

The name James is the English translation of the Greek *Iakōbos,* which in turn reproduces the Hebrew *ya'aqōb* ("Jacob"). The English names *James* and *Jacob* originate from one common name, not two as is often thought. The variation on the same name *Iakōbos* is also observable in other languages: in Latin, for example, both *Jacobus* and *Jacomus* occur, while in Italian we have *Giacobbe* and *Giacomo,* and in Spanish there are *Iago* and *Jaime.*

The Hebrew name "Jacob" was clearly very popular in the Jewish world of the first century, given that Jacob was the patriarch and the father from whom the twelve tribes of Israel traced their origin. The New Testament itself mentions a number of people who bear the name of *Iakōbos:*

- James, son of Zebedee, and brother of John (Mark 1:19); they were both among the twelve apostles; Jesus gave them the nickname "Boanerges" or "Sons of Thunder" (Mark 3:17; see also Matt 10:3; Luke 6:14; Acts 1:13).

- James, son of Alphaeus, another of the twelve apostles (Matt 10:3; Mark 3:18; Luke 6:15; Acts 1:13).

- James, the "brother" of Jesus (Matt 13:55; Mark 6:3; Acts 12:17; 15:13; 21:18; Gal 1:19; 2:9, 12; 1 Cor 15:7).

- James, "the younger" or "the small one" or "the less" *(Iakōbos ho mikros)* (Mark 15:40; 16:1; Matt 27:56; Luke 24:10).

- James, the father of Jude, who was also one of the Twelve (Luke 6:16; Acts 1:13).

- The author of the letter of James (1:1).

- James, the brother of the author of the letter of Jude (1:1).

Some of these references could be to the same person. In the course of Christian tradition many of these references were combined to refer to one man: for example, the early Scripture scholar, Jerome, viewed James the son of Alphaeus, James the Less, and James the brother of the Lord as one and the same person. On May 3 the Roman Catholic Church celebrates a feastday of James that embraces all three references.

The two most prominent people bearing the name James are the brother of John (who was put to death by Herod Agrippa I in 44 C.E.; see Acts 12:2) and James "the brother of the Lord" (see Gal 1:19). It is interesting to note that after Acts 12:2 had mentioned the death of James, the brother of John,

Acts 12:17 refers to another James without identifying exactly who he is. The author of Acts felt no need to identify him since the readers would immediately know from the context that he was referring to the best-known James in the early church, namely James "the brother of the Lord." It is this James who forms the center of consideration in this study. He was often referred to in other ways, such as "James the Just." This designation is not one found in the New Testament, but originates from later tradition. For example, Hegesippus refers to James in this way: "He was called 'the Just' by all men from the Lord's time to ours, since many are called James . . . ."[2] The designation "James of Jerusalem" is a modern way of focusing on his important role of leadership within the mother church of the Christian movement.

The Synoptic Gospels and the Family of Jesus

Some Methodological Considerations

THE SYNOPTIC PROBLEM

When Luke begins his gospel he draws attention to the research he undertook in compiling his narrative (Luke 1:1-4). He shows that he made use of a number of sources in writing his narrative although he does not identify them by name: ". . . they were handed on to us by those who from the beginning were eyewitnesses and servants of the word . . ." (Luke 1:2). A literary analysis of the four canonical gospels shows that three of them, Matthew, Mark, and Luke, bear a close resemblance to each other, while the Gospel of John is radically different. This has led scholars to classify the gospels of Matthew, Mark, and Luke as the Synoptic Gospels. The word "synoptic" (derived from two Greek words: *syn* meaning "with" and *optic* from the word *opsis* meaning "seeing" or "sight") can be translated literally as "seeing with the same eyes." These three gospels can be printed in parallel columns that cover most of the same events and are expressed in similar words and expressions. This is surprising, given the fact that Jesus taught in Aramaic and the gospels were all written in Greek.

The close similarities in language, order, and content have led biblical scholars to conclude that the gospels of Matthew, Mark, and Luke must have been dependent on each other and have used the same sources. For the past two centuries New Testament scholars have reached something of a consensus in proposing a solution to this relationship between these

---

[2] Eusebius, *Hist. eccl.* 2:23.4 (Lake, LCL).

three gospels, a solution that has come to be known as the two-document hypothesis.[3] The basis of the relationship between Matthew, Mark, and Luke rests on the conviction that the Gospel of Mark was the first gospel to have been written. The gospels of Matthew and Luke knew the Gospel of Mark and used it as one of their primary sources. In other words, Matthew and Luke rewrote Mark's gospel to bring across their own theological vision and understanding of Jesus for their own communities for whom they were writing.

One example can be given to illustrate the priority of Mark's gospel. Read the opening episodes of the Gospel of Mark (Mark 1:1-13). You will notice that the writer narrates three main episodes: the proclamation of John the Baptist (Mark 1:1-8), the baptism of Jesus (1:9-11), and the temptation of Jesus (1:12-13). If you turn to Matt 3:1–4:11 and Luke 3:1–4:13 you will notice that both Matthew and Luke narrate the same events in exactly the same order. A closer look reveals that the words, phrases, and even quotations from the Old Testament are very similar. While we are looking at it in an English translation that has been made from the original Greek, the similarities still jump out at us from the page. All this points to the conclusion that Mark was the first gospel to have been written and that Matthew and Luke used Mark in the composition of their gospels. The Gospel of Mark is foundational and has a temporal priority over Matthew and Luke.[4]

A further examination reveals that Matthew and Luke have very similar material that is not contained in Mark. This led scholars to postulate that Matthew and Luke were using another source besides the Gospel of Mark. This source has been labeled Q, which is simply an abbreviation for the German word *Quelle* (meaning "source"). In the account of the temptation of Jesus according to the three Synoptic Gospels you can see that while all three gospels mention the temptation, only Matthew and Luke present the actual temptations. This common material in Matthew and Luke is so very close: its structure is the same and it uses the same quotations from the Old Testament. This is an illustration of the source Q. While the Gospel of Mark was a narrative of the ministry and death of Jesus, the source Q contained no narrative. Instead, it presented only the sayings of Jesus.

In a diagrammatic way we can represent the relationship among the three Synoptic Gospels in this way:

---

[3] For a very readable and convincing explanation of the two-document hypothesis see Ivan Havener, *Q: The Sayings of Jesus* (Wilmington: Michael Glazier, 1987).

[4] Ibid. 22–23.

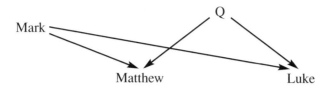

In this study, and especially in examining similar passages from the gospels, I presume this solution to the Synoptic Problem, namely that Mark and Q were two documents Matthew and Luke used in writing their gospels. My methodological approach in the interpretation of the passages involved will demand first of all a thorough understanding of how that passage occurs in the foundational document (Mark or Q) and then how and why Matthew and Luke changed that document or source.

READING THE GOSPELS AS NARRATIVES

Before examining those passages in the gospels that relate to the family of Jesus, we raise the question of the literary nature (or genre) of a gospel. The identification of the overall literary genre of any piece of writing is basic to every form of interpretation. It is valid for all studies of literature and is equally valid for the study of the writings of the New Testament.

The English word "gospel" derives from the Anglo-Saxon word "god-spell," which means "good tidings" or "good news." It is used to translate the Greek word *euangelion.* An examination of the four New Testament writings called gospels reveals that the commonly accepted viewpoint in scholarship has been the one that viewed the canonical gospels as writings that belonged to a literary genre unique to the New Testament itself that conformed to no identifiable genre in the literature of antiquity. In other words, this perspective argued that the early Christians invented this genre themselves. In many ways this viewpoint takes as its basis the opening of the Gospel of Mark: "The beginning of the good news of Jesus Christ, the Son of God" (Mark 1:1). Here "the good news, gospel" *(euangelion)* is judged as identifying the genre of Mark's gospel and the other canonical gospels. This viewpoint is well characterized by Philipp Vielhauer, who argues that the literary genre of the gospels is not dependent on any preceding genre: as such they are unique.[5]

---

[5] See Philipp Vielhauer, *Geschichte der urchristlichen Literatur,* GLB (Berlin and New York: Walter De Gruyter, 1975) 282.

More recently, Helmut Koester[6] has presented a very different perspective and one that to my mind is more faithful to the development of the New Testament documents themselves. In his examination of the origin of the usage of the term "gospel" *(euangelion)* he has shown that the term originally referred to the content of the message of Jesus and not to a genre.[7]

Viewed from this perspective, the meaning of the term *euangelion* in the earliest New Testament writings we possess (namely the writings of Paul) referred to the message of salvation that is encapsulated in the person of Jesus and his preaching. The most detailed description of the Gospel is found in Rom 1:1-6. In this passage Paul refers "the gospel" *(euangelion)* to the content of the message of salvation that he was proclaiming: this message of salvation has its origin in God (it is "the gospel of God") and the essence of its content is the person of Jesus, who was both human ("descended from David according to the flesh") and divine ("God's Son" who was raised from the dead by the Father). The significance for the believer in this Gospel message is that God's grace is communicated to all who believe from the wider Greek and Roman worlds (see also 1 Cor 15:1-8).

Mark and Matthew are the only evangelists to use the noun "gospel." When Mark opens his writing ("The beginning of the good news of Jesus Christ, the Son of God" [Mark 1:1]), he is not referring to the literary genre of his writing, but rather to the content of his message in line with the way in which Paul shows the word being used in the early church. In Mark's understanding the gospel is the message of salvation that Jesus preached. For example, "Now after John was arrested, Jesus came to Galilee, proclaiming the good news of God, and saying, 'The time is fulfilled, and the kingdom of God has come near; repent, and believe in the good news'" (Mark 1:14-15). Mark further shows how Jesus' message of salvation would be carried on by his followers after his death. On one level Mark equates the gospel with the person of Jesus: "For those who want to save their life will lose it, and those who lose their life for my sake, and for the sake of the gospel, will save it" (Mark 8:35). On another level the gospel remains for Mark the message Jesus preached. Speaking about the woman who anointed Jesus at Bethany just before the beginning of his Passion, Jesus says: "Truly I tell you, wherever the good news is proclaimed in the whole world, what she has done will be told in memory of her" (Mark 14:9).

Matthew shows a slight nuance in his use of the noun "gospel." While his usage continues to reflect that of the early church, he always delineates

---

[6] Helmut Koester, *Ancient Christian Gospels: Their History and Development* (Philadelphia: Trinity Press International, 1990) 1–48.

[7] Ibid. 4–5.

the "gospel" through the addition of the qualifier "the gospel of the king-dom": "Jesus went throughout Galilee, teaching in their synagogues and proclaiming the good news of the kingdom and curing every disease and every sickness among the people" (Matt 4:23; see also 9:35; 24:14). This "gospel of the kingdom" was first preached by Jesus, and now it continues to be preached through the followers of Jesus, the church.

From this it emerges that the concept of gospel refers above all to the oral message of salvation that Jesus preached and his followers handed on in their preaching. Evidence shows that it was only toward the end of the second century C.E. that the term "gospel" was identified with a writing.[8] This is illustrated in the work of Justin Martyr (who died in 165 C.E.), who writes: "For the Apostles in the memoirs composed by them, which are also called Gospels, thus handed down what was commanded them . . ." (*1 Apol.* 66:3).[9]

Consequently, we can say that when reference is made to, e.g., the Gospel of Mark, or the Gospel of Matthew, the reference is to the handing on and interpretation of those traditions and sources that ultimately go back to and concern Jesus and his message. In this sense, as Koester has observed, the reference is to the content of the message and not to a literary genre. In order to hand on these traditions related to Jesus of Nazareth, the early Christians made use of those literary genres that were already available to them.

Instead of inventing a genre, Mark turned to his own world and drew upon a genre that was prominent both within the Greco-Roman and Hebrew worlds, namely that of narrative biography, to hand on his interpretation of the traditions and sources about Jesus of Nazareth. For the Greeks and Romans, narrative biography is well attested. The focus in their biographical narratives is chiefly on the character of the person who is described: the reader is called upon to admire and emulate the life of virtue *(aretē)* of the hero.[10] In the world of the Hebrews, narrative biography focused on the office of the person described. It was chiefly in the lives of the prophets that we see the clearest illustrations of this genre of biography developing.[11] Since the writer of the Gospel of Mark was certainly aware of

---

[8] See Koester, *Ancient Christian Gospels,* 26.

[9] Leslie William Barnard, trans., *St. Justin Martyr: The First and Second Apologies,* ACW 56 (New York and Mahwah, NJ: Paulist, 1997) 70–71. See also *1 Apol.* 67:3-4.

[10] As can be seen in the works of Plutarch *(Parallel Lives)* and Suetonius *(Lives of the Caesars).* See *Plutarch's Lives,* I–XI, trans. Bernodotte Perrin, LCL (London: William Heinemann; Cambridge, MA: Harvard University Press, 1959); and *Suetonius,* I–II, trans. J. C. Rolfe, LCL (London: William Heinemann; Cambridge, MA: Harvard University Press, 1951).

[11] See Koester, *Ancient Christian Gospels,* 28–30.

the literature of his own world, both Greco-Roman[12] and Hebrew, it is most likely that they shaped his approach to writing his narrative. The influence of the biographies of the prophets is a credible source of inspiration for the way in which Mark shaped his narrative.[13]

The writer of the Gospel of Mark intends to show that Jesus fulfills the office of Messiah and Son of God, as the opening to the gospel states: "The beginning of the good news of Jesus Christ (Messiah), the Son of God" (1:1). More importantly, Mark wishes to illustrate what type of Messiah Jesus is and how one is to understand him as the Son of God. To do this he relies upon the traditions and sources that were being passed on within the context of the proclamation of the early Christian community.

Against this background of the genre of the Gospel of Mark, one sees that it is not the writer's intention to present a journalistic account of the ministry of Jesus. Instead, he wishes to bring the reader to an awareness of the identity of Jesus and the office he exercises as Messiah and Son of God. Using a narrative biographical approach Mark leads the reader to an understanding of Jesus' identity through the way in which he portrays the characters in the story responding to Jesus. This means that the reader must take the narrative dimension of the Gospel of Mark seriously.[14]

The Gospel of Mark relies on those techniques and characteristics vital to a narrative: characters, setting, plot. As with any narrative, the plot unfolds through conflict that emerges among the characters in the story. To appreciate the message Mark presents, one has to enter into the story world of the narrative of Mark's gospel and remain true to that story.

Living in a world that is informed by a historical consciousness, we often find it difficult to appreciate the significance of entering into the narrative world of the text. We almost always jump into reading the text as though it were a video representation of what actually occurred. Mark, as any narrator does, takes the traditions, sources, and historical events that have come down to him and weaves them into a story of his own making, with his own intentions and purposes. In reading the Gospel of Mark it is important to remain true to the intention that emerges from the narrative. Mark's intention was not to present us with a historical or journalistic account of what happened. Instead, it is his intention to tell a story so that it will have an influ-

---

[12] See Dennis R. MacDonald, *The Homeric Epics and the Gospel of Mark* (New Haven: Yale University Press, 2000).

[13] See Koester, *Ancient Christian Gospels,* 28.

[14] For an excellent introductory understanding of the narrative dimension of the Gospel of Mark see the work of David Rhoads, Joanna Dewey, and Donald Michie, *Mark as Story: An Introduction to the Narrative of a Gospel* (2nd ed. Minneapolis: Fortress, 1999).

ence and impact on the reader of the story. His main intention (the *rhetoric* of the story)[15] is that the reader will respond to the person of Jesus as Son of God and as Messiah. This is what is known as "narrative criticism."[16]

This is not to say that Mark's narrative is "unhistorical." Quite the contrary! While Mark's narrative is based on historical traditions and sources, his intention is not to write history. Instead, the narrator's intention is to tell a story in such a way that it will impact the lives of the readers. The intention is to bring across for the reader the significance of Jesus' office as Messiah and Son of God. The reader must remain true to the world of the narrative in order for the implications of the narrated event to elucidate the office of Jesus as Messiah and Son of God.

Jesus' True Eschatological Family
(Mark 3:19b-21, 31-35; Matt 12:46-50; Luke 8:19-21)

Two things emerge from the previous methodological discussion. First of all, according to the solution to the Synoptic Problem, the Gospel of Mark is the foundational source that the gospels of Matthew and Luke used. The implication for the art of interpretation is that one must understand first of all how Mark presents the picture before one proceeds to examine how Matthew and Luke used that interpretation in composing their own gospels. Second, the understanding of the literary genre of the Gospel of Mark as a biographical narrative provides the framework for reading and interpreting Mark's references to the family of Jesus. Respect must be shown first of all for the story world of the Gospel of Mark before we jump into the historical world.

An examination of the four gospels reveals that they refer to "the brothers (and sisters) of Jesus," identifying their names, but never treating James separately or differently from them. It is amazing how stereotyped are the ideas about "the brothers of Jesus" and James in particular. The majority of scholars unquestioningly consider that James and the "brothers of Jesus" were originally not believers, but in fact were hostile toward Jesus.[17] It is this preconceived idea that we will challenge by approaching the texts with an open mind. There are two important references to the relationship between Jesus and his family in the context of the Synoptic Gospels: the eschatological family of Jesus, and Jesus' visit to Nazareth. We shall consider

---

[15] Ibid. 144.

[16] See Mark Allan Powell, *What Is Narrative Criticism?* (Minneapolis: Fortress, 1990). See also Rhoads, et al., *Mark as Story,* for a description of a "Narrative Method for Interpreting Mark" (6–7).

[17] Pierre-Antoine Bernheim, *James, Brother of Jesus* (London: S.C.M. Press, 1997) 76.

first of all the eschatological family of Jesus (Mark 3:19b-21, 31-35; Matt 12:46-50; Luke 8:19-21).[18]

MARK 3:19b-21, 31-35

This passage occurs in the context of Jesus' early preaching and teaching around the shores of the Sea of Galilee. The narrator sums up Jesus' activity very well: "'Let us go on to the neighboring towns, so that I may proclaim the message there also; for that is what I came out to do.' And he went throughout Galilee, proclaiming the message in their synagogues and casting out demons" (Mark 1:38). As the summary indicates, in addition to his preaching Jesus has performed a number of miracles of healing: the man with an unclean spirit (1:21-28), the healing of Simon's mother-in-law (1:29-31), the cleansing of a leper (1:40-45), the healing of a paralytic (2:1-12), the healing of a man with a withered hand (3:1-6).

Jesus' preaching and healings provoke a twofold reaction. From the side of the Jewish authorities, Jesus' preaching and teaching attract a growing opposition and hostility. The Pharisees react strongly because of the challenge he poses to their traditions, such as fasting (2:18-22), and to their interpretation of the Sabbath rest (2:23-28). On the other hand the ordinary people, the crowds, are attracted to Jesus because of their desire for miracles and healings. Mark dramatizes the response of the crowd in this way: ". . . hearing all that he was doing, they came to him in great numbers from Judea, Jerusalem, Idumea, beyond the Jordan, and the region around Tyre and Sidon" (Mark 3:8-12).

All this is important when we view this passage against the background of the story line of Mark's narrative. As we indicated above, narrative criticism demands that we take seriously the world of the story itself and enter into that world. We argued that the function or purpose of Mark's narration of Jesus' ministry was to illustrate the office of Jesus as Messiah and Son of God. Mark is interested in Jesus' identity and his function for his own people. In effect Mark says in opening his gospel: "I am going to show you who Jesus is: he is the Messiah and the Son of God. I will show you what type of Messiah he is and what his function is."

Turning now to the passage in question, we see how all these elements come together. Both the reaction of the crowd and that of the Pharisees continue. The writer has developed this unit (Mark 3:19b-35) in a stylistic way. The flow of Mark's thought unfolds in this way:

---

[18] For a synoptic chart of the three parallel Synoptic passages see *Appendix A*.

Introduction: Jesus returns "home" (v. 19b)

Part One: Jesus' family goes to restrain him (v. 21)

- They hear about what is happening and wish to restrain Jesus.
- Others are saying that Jesus has gone out of his mind.

Part Two: Jesus' controversy with the scribes (vv. 22-30)

- The scribes make two charges (v. 22)
  - "He has Beelzebul."
  - "By the ruler of the demons he casts out demons."
- Jesus replies to both charges (vv. 23-30)
  - To the second charge: "If a house is divided against itself, that house will not be able to stand" (vv. 23-27).
  - To the first charge: Blasphemy against the Holy Spirit will never be forgiven because they said: "He has an unclean spirit" (vv. 28-30).

Part Three: Jesus' family comes seeking him: Jesus defines his eschatological family (vv. 31-35)[19]

One of Mark's stylistic methods, known as "sandwiching," is clearly evident here: he interrupts an episode to speak about a second episode before returning to the first. Sandwiched in between the narration of Jesus' interaction with his family is the episode of the controversy between Jesus and the scribes who make the double charge that "he has Beelzebul, and by the ruler of the demons he casts out demons" (Mark 3:22). This is again a question of identity. The religious leaders refuse to acknowledge Jesus' authority as Messiah and Son of God and attribute his power to Satan. Jesus tackles the charge head on by showing the illogical nature of this charge. How could Jesus, as an agent of Satan, be casting out demons? "How can Satan cast out Satan?" (Mark 3:23). If Satan is attacking Satan, the kingdom of Satan would never survive. The Jewish leaders continue to fail to recognize Jesus' identity and willfully reject him. The crowds, on the other hand, are eager to find out more about Jesus: that is why they pursue him.

Jesus takes their argument further and shows that if they claim he is possessed by an unclean spirit (v. 30) they are in fact blaspheming against

---

[19] For a similar division see Raymond E. Brown, et al., eds., *Mary in the New Testament* (Philadelphia: Fortress; New York, Ramsey, and Toronto: Paulist, 1978) 54.

the Holy Spirit. Jesus implies that they are attributing the power by which he performs his miracles to Satan rather than to God, to the Holy Spirit.

The meeting between Jesus and his family takes place against this background. The sandwiching technique has the effect of contrasting two reactions toward Jesus: the reaction of Jesus' family to Jesus and the reaction of the crowds and Jewish religious leaders to him. The reader immediately asks: How will Jesus' family react to him? The expectation of the reader is that they would know Jesus' identity and accept him for who he is, the Messiah and Son of God. As a result of "the sandwich" the reader's discovery of the relationship of the family to Jesus is delayed and produces a surprising result.

The Greek of *Part One* (the section that contains the first reference to the family of Jesus [3:19b-21]) has many difficulties associated with it. There are gaps in the narrative that have to be filled in by the reader.

- The first issue involves the reference to "his family." The actual Greek is *hoi par autou,* a general phrase (literally "those among him"), a "marker of a relationship"[20] that can be translated in many ways such as "his friends," "his acquaintances," or "his family."[21] Commentators interpret this in one of two ways:

  ○ As a reference to "his friends," that is, to "his disciples" : This is the way the *RSV* translated it in its first edition and it is the interpretation for which John Painter argues.[22]

  ○ As a reference to "his family" : This is the way the second edition of the *RSV* and the *NRSV* translate it. Brown et al. in *Mary in the New Testament* translate it as "his own."[23] To my mind this is the more logical reading, given the context of the narrative in which Mark is operating with his familiar style of narrating two events by means of his "sandwiching" technique. While 3:21 might at first sight be ambiguous, the clarity is achieved when we reach 3:31, when Jesus' mother and brothers and sisters are described as being

---

[20] See BDAG, *para*, 757.

[21] See Max Zerwick, *Analysis Philologica Novi Testamenti Graeci* (Rome: Pontificii Instituti Biblici, 1966) 84: "*sui, propinqui, familiares* ('his own, neighbors, family')."

[22] John Painter, *Just James: The Brother of Jesus in History and Tradition* (Minneapolis: Fortress, 1999) 21–28; and idem, "Who Was James?" in Bruce Chilton and Jacob Neusner, eds., *The Brother of Jesus: James the Just and His Mission* (Louisville: Westminster John Knox, 2001) 25–29.

[23] Brown et al., *Mary in the New Testament,* 55.

outside the house. If we interpret this in reference to the family of Jesus, the context presents the more natural picture of the family hearing about reports that people were saying that "he has gone out of his mind" (3:21). Out of concern for him, his family comes to restrain him. In this sense Jesus' family is concerned about him and comes to protect him. After the interlude of the controversy between Jesus and the scribes, Jesus is told that his family has arrived and is outside waiting for him (3:31). From the context of its usage I think this is the more natural way to translate this phrase.

- The second issue concerns the family that comes "to take control of Jesus" *(kratēsai).* The Greek verb used here is *krateō,* which means "to take control of someone or something, seize, control."[24] Their purpose is to prevent the crowd from doing harm to Jesus or even Jesus harming himself.

- The reference to Jesus' state of mind *(exestē)* is also problematic. The Greek verb used here is *existēmi,* which means "inability to reason normally, *lose one's mind, be out of one's senses.*"[25] Some commentators are uncomfortable with attributing this to Jesus and consequently identify the crowd as being out of *its* mind. This is a clear example of reinterpreting the text because it does not conform to one's theological perspective.[26] Clearly, the context shows that the reference is to Jesus, not to the crowd: the whole section dealing with the discussion on Beelzebul arises because of the charge that Jesus is the one who is beside himself and the scribes attribute this to Jesus' possession by Satan.

Part Three (3:31-35) returns the focus to Jesus' family after the interlude of the controversy between Jesus and the scribes. From the perspective of form criticism this section (3:31-35) would be the foundation out of which the other parts of this narrative had developed. Scholars refer to this passage as a "biographical apophthegm," namely, a short pithy saying of Jesus that is placed within a narrative context.[27] The saying that is of vital concern is: "Whoever does the will of God is my brother and sister and mother" (Mark 3:35).

---

[24] BDAG, *krateō,* 564.

[25] BDAG, *existēmi,* 350.

[26] See Henry Wansbrough, "Mark III. 21—Was Jesus Out of His Mind?" *NTS* 18 (1971/72) 233–35.

[27] Brown et al., *Mary in the New Testament,* 52.

When Jesus is told that "Your mother and your brothers and sisters are outside, asking for you" (Mark 3:32), there is nothing that implies hostility between Jesus and his family. They were concerned about Jesus and had come to care for him. They have waited patiently for Jesus outside the house because of the large crowd. In the narrative this event provides Jesus with the opportunity to provide a teaching for his hearers. Jesus shows that the important thing in relating to him is not blood relationship, but rather carrying out God's will. As Messiah, Jesus is entrusted with carrying out the will of the Father. In like manner, those who follow Jesus are called upon to carry out the Father's will (3:34-35). Jesus will later demonstrate his all-consuming desire to carry out the Father's will in the Garden of Gethsemane when he prays: "Abba, Father, for you all things are possible; remove this cup from me; yet, not what I want, but what you want" (Mark 14:36). The ties that constitute the new family of Jesus, the "eschatological family,"[28] are those that are forged through doing God's will. This move on the part of Jesus is highly significant in the Gospel of Mark. It shows that Jesus distances himself from the natural bonds that were so vital to first-century C.E. Mediterranean society, where one was identified by one's relationship to a clan, town, or city. This conforms to the countercultural ethos of the movement Jesus is forging. It also conforms to the Q saying in which a disciple responds to Jesus' invitation to follow him: "Lord, first let me go and bury my father." Jesus replies: "Let the dead bury their own dead; but as for you, go and proclaim the kingdom of God" (Luke 9:59-60; Matt 8:21-22). For the Jesus of Mark's gospel the important thing is membership in the new family, the eschatological family, which is forged through obedience to God's will in imitation of the life of Jesus.

Jesus' response does not entail a criticism or hostility on his part to his own human family; neither does it imply the family's opposition toward him. Again the meaning of this passage emerges from the context of Mark's

---

[28] As Painter (*Just James,* 28) and Brown et al. (*Mary in the New Testament,* 58) describe it. The term "eschatological" comes from the two Greek words *eschatos* ("last") and *logos* ("word"). In essence it refers to "a word about the last things." Consequently, it embraces expectations around the end times, referring to the end of history, or the end of the world, or even the end of the present age. The term "eschatological" is used in two ways in reference to Jesus' ministry: By his coming Jesus inaugurates the new eschatological age: the end times begin in his preaching, his teaching, and his ministry. At the same time Jesus' ministry looks forward to a future fulfillment at the end of time. With this in mind the reference to Jesus' "eschatological family" applies to those Jesus has called into relationship with himself through obedience to the Father's will. It is a relationship that begins now with Jesus' inauguration of the eschatological age and will continue into the future in the fulfillment of all eschatological hopes.

narrative. We cannot jump immediately from the world of the text to the historical world and make inferences or judgments regarding the historical attitude of the family of Jesus.[29]

The world of Mark's gospel is divided between the "insiders and the outsiders." In Mark 4:11 Jesus explains to his disciples why he teaches in parables: "To you has been given the secret of the kingdom of God, but for those outside, everything comes in parables." The disciples have been invited to become insiders, members of Jesus' eschatological family, and he initiates them into the meaning of his teaching. In the context of Mark 3:19b-35 the Jewish authorities remained outsiders because of their rejection of Jesus' message. The crowds are also outsiders because they were only interested in Jesus' performance of miracles. In this passage the Markan Jesus challenges his human family to move from being outsiders to becoming insiders. The way they do this is through following God's will.

This lengthy analysis of the role of Jesus' family in this passage of the Gospel of Mark shows no opposition between Jesus and his human family. It demonstrates their concern for Jesus' welfare. It also shows that Jesus challenges them to follow God's will as the prime value in their relationship with him. All this emerges from the framework of Mark's narrative. We are cautioned not to jump immediately from the literary vision of Mark to the historical world of Jesus' family. The only way we can get to that historical world is by viewing all the references to Jesus' family to see how each tradition portrays them. Examining these diverse perspectives together, we may be able to perceive a common core vision. Nothing has been said specifically in this episode about James. None of the "brothers and sisters of Jesus" has been named and nothing has been said specifically about how one is to understand the exact meaning of the term "brothers and sisters."

The Vision of Matthew and Luke on the Eschatological Family

The synoptic chart of the three passages shows quite clearly that Mark is the core passage on which Matthew and Luke have drawn. An examination of the way in which Matthew and Luke have used this episode is a good illustration of source criticism. It is to be noted that neither Matthew nor Luke uses Part One of this episode, namely the reference to the family of Jesus coming to restrain Jesus because they heard he was "out of his mind" (Mark 3:20-21). They probably omitted this Markan vignette because it did not conform to the narrative view of the relationship of Jesus

[29] See Painter, *Just James,* 31.

and his family they had in mind. Instead, they place the episode within another context.

MATTHEW 12:46-50

Matthew's account here clearly follows Mark 3:31-35 with a few noteworthy differences. Mark's account contained three parts: it commenced with a reference to the family looking for Jesus out of concern for him (Mark 3:19b-21) followed by the discussion about Jesus being possessed by Beelzebul or Satan (Mark 3:22-30) and concluded with the discussion about Jesus' true family (Mark 3:31-35). Matthew omits the first part: there is no reference to the family wishing to seek and restrain Jesus.[30] Matthew does present the second part, namely, the discussion about Jesus' possession by Beelzebul. Noteworthy, however, is Matthew's development of the accusation against Jesus: "Whoever speaks a word against the Son of Man will be forgiven, but whoever speaks against the Holy Spirit will not be forgiven, either in this age or in the age to come" (Matt 12:32). Matthew's Jesus makes a twofold accusation. He condemns his own generation (Matt 12:33-42) because it is not willing to see the Spirit working in him: "The people of Nineveh will rise up at the judgment with this generation and condemn it, because they repented at the proclamation of Jonah, and see, something greater than Jonah is here!" (Matt 12:41). Second, Matthew's Jesus sees this generation as the one that is possessed by "unclean spirits" (Matt 12:43-45).

The third part of Mark's episode (Mark 3:31-35) is contained in an almost identical way in Matthew (Matt 12:46-50). The differences are largely editorial corrections Matthew has made. While Mark has the crowd in general telling Jesus that his family is outside looking for him, Matthew makes it far more specific by saying "Someone told him . . ." (Matt 12:47). Further, Mark identified the eschatological family in this way: "And looking at those who sat around him . . ." (Mark 3:34). Matthew, however, is more specific by first of all identifying those around Jesus as "his disciples" (Matt 12:49). This difference is deliberate, as can be seen from the differing attitudes among the evangelists with regard to the disciples. For Mark the disciples struggle in their understanding of Jesus, while for Matthew the disciples are perfect students. They truly grasp Jesus' message and identity. For this reason Matthew singles the disciples out in a way Mark could never do. Matthew identifies them as the ones who do God's will, and he goes on to elaborate, "whoever does the will of my Father in heaven is my brother and sister and mother"

---

[30] See Brown et al., *Mary in the New Testament*, 99.

(Matt 12:50). Matthew remains true to his Jewish heritage by replacing the use of the name "God" with the circumlocution "heaven." We see this as well in the Lord's Prayer that Jesus teaches his disciples. While Luke's version has Jesus addressing the prayer directly to "Father" (Luke 11:2), Matthew's Jesus addresses it in a more transcendent way, "Our Father in heaven" (Matt 6:9).

In rewriting Mark's account, Matthew affirms the disciples. He identifies them as those who belong to Jesus' eschatological family. Nothing is said about the attitude of Jesus' family toward him. To imply an opposition would not do justice to the text. It says more about Jesus' attitude toward the family: for him the important bonds are those that carry out the will of the heavenly Father, not those based on lineage.

LUKE 8:19-21

Luke shows the most redaction in his use of the triple tradition. There is no reference to the first part of Mark's narrative regarding the family of Jesus who come to him because they are concerned about his welfare. Further, Luke has placed this episode in an entirely new context that reflects a very positive approach to Jesus' family. Luke transfers the charge that Jesus is possessed by Beelzebul to a later stage in the narrative (see Luke 11:14-23). The context in Luke's gospel unfolds in this way: prior to this episode (Luke 8:19-21) Luke had narrated the well-known parable of the sower and the seed (Luke 8:4-15). Luke's Jesus explains the seed that had "produced a hundredfold" (Luke 8:8) in this way: "But as for that in the good soil, these are the ones who, when they hear the word, hold it fast in an honest and good heart, and bear fruit with patient endurance" (Luke 8:15). So when a few verses later the Lukan Jesus says "my mother and my brothers are those who hear the word of God and do it" (Luke 8:21), the reader clearly connects back to v. 15 and sees that the family of Jesus is "bearing fruit with patient endurance" (Luke 8:15). The parallel between these two verses (Luke 8:15 and 8:21) is extremely important.

In redacting the passage from Mark's gospel and making it conform to his well-known stylistic features Luke has compressed the narrative succinctly and thereby has greatly reduced the opposition between Jesus and his family. This corresponds to the very positive approach he adopts to the family, especially the mother of Jesus, throughout the gospel, but particularly in the Infancy narratives (chs. 1–2).[31] In Mark's account Jesus calls to his mother and brothers, whereas in Luke they are the ones who approach

---

[31] Ibid. 170, n. 38.

him. However, they cannot reach him because of the large crowd. When Luke's Jesus replies to his family, he does so in a positive way that makes no distinction between his eschatological family and his natural family. In fact, the Lukan Jesus' reaction implies that the natural family is part of his eschatological family "who hear the word of God and do it" (Luke 8:21).

This study has shown how one episode from the triple tradition has been retold in different ways by Matthew and Luke. In none of the accounts is there opposition in the interface between the family and Jesus. The focus is on obedience to the Father's will rather than on family ties. In Matthew and Luke the positive relationship between Jesus and his family is much stronger than in Mark's gospel. This is probably due also to the fact that both Matthew and Luke open their gospels with a reference to the infancy of Jesus. A much more positive and appreciative understanding of the role of Mary, the mother of Jesus, occurs in the Gospel of Luke, which presents her relationship with her son throughout the rest of the gospel.

Rejection in Jesus' Own Town of Nazareth (Mark 6:1-6; Matt 13:53-58; Luke 4:16-30)

This is the second episode in the Synoptic Gospels dealing with the interface between Jesus and his family. Again, according to the solution to the Synoptic Problem, Mark emerges as the source for Matthew and Luke in their retelling of the story.[32]

MARK 6:1-6

From the perspective of form criticism this passage has been identified as an apophthegm.[33] The proverbial saying that forms the heart of this narrative is "Prophets are not without honor, except in their home town" (Mark 6:4). Quite likely the expansion to include kin, family, and home is a Markan development that makes it fit the context of the dispute with the family.[34]

---

[32] For a synoptic chart of the three parallel synoptic passages see *Appendix B*.

[33] See n. 27 above.

[34] This shorter version of the saying as the more authentic is supported by the way it occurs in the Greek Oxyrhynchus Papyri 1, lines 30-35: "Jesus says, 'A prophet is not welcome in his own homeland, nor does a physician heal those who know him'" (my own translation. For the Greek text see Bentley Layton, ed., *Nag Hammadi Codex II, 2-7*, [Leiden: Brill, 1989] 1:120). The Gospel of Thomas (Saying 31) expresses it this way: "Jesus said: 'No prophet is accepted in his own village; no physician heals those who know him.'" (This translation is from Thomas O. Lambdin, "The Gospel of Thomas," in James M. Robinson, ed., *The Nag Hammadi Library in English* [3rd rev. ed. New York: HarperCollins {1978, 1988} 1990] 130.)

This passage occurs in the context of Jesus' Galilean ministry, where Jesus conducted an impressive work of teaching and healing: for example, he had taught alongside the Sea of Galilee (4:1-33), crossed the sea (4:35-41), on the eastern shore healed the Gerasene demoniac (5:1-20), and finally, on returning to the western shore, restored a young girl to life and healed a hemorrhaging woman (5:21-43). This passage narrates a brief return to Jesus' home town of Nazareth before he sends out the Twelve on a mission that is an extension of his own. This passage illustrates Mark's rhetorical purpose very clearly. Mark's intent is to show Jesus' identity as Messiah and Son of God and how people react to that deepening unveiling. In this instance Jesus' home town shows bewilderment about his identity. They argue that it is impossible for him to do the things people claim he does because they know him only too well. They point especially to Jesus' family, his mother and his sisters and brothers. How could he do the things he is doing? It is not in character with their knowledge of Jesus' family.

As regards Jesus' family, Mark notes that Jesus is a carpenter, the son of Mary. Significantly, he does not name Joseph, the husband of Mary (as Luke 4:22 does). Instead he gives Jesus' identity through his mother. Mark identifies Jesus as a carpenter while Matthew identifies Joseph as the carpenter (Matt 13:55). Whether Jesus was a carpenter or only Joseph was is really unimportant. Mark intends to draw attention to Jesus' lowly origins.[35] Why Mark omits any reference to Joseph in this and other scenes related to Jesus' ministry is puzzling. The normal designation would be "son of Joseph," as Matthew and Luke indicate. The identification of Jesus as the son of his mother is most unusual. Scholars have proposed numerous answers to this puzzle.[36] I think the most satisfactory explanation comes from remaining true to the context of Mark's narrative. The crowd identifies Jesus as the son of Mary because Mary is present among them.[37]

---

[35] See Brown et. al., *Mary in the New Testament*, 61.

[36] Ibid. 61–64.

[37] Some scholars go further and argue that Joseph was already dead at the time of this episode. If Joseph had been alive he would most surely have been identified. The most logical interpretation, then, is that Joseph is already dead at the time of Jesus' public ministry, hence the absence of any reference to him (see Brown et al., *Mary in the New Testament*, 64). However, methodologically this is clearly an invalid inference. It jumps from the literary text to the historical deduction! We can only make such a deduction when two or more independent sources agree in presenting a similar perspective or attestation. This is what is called "the criterion of multiple attestation" (See, for example, John P. Meier, *A Marginal Jew: Rethinking the Historical Jesus*. Vol. One: *The Roots of the Problem and the Person* [New York: Doubleday, 1991] 174–75).

In addition to identifying Jesus as "the son of Mary," Mark calls him "the brother of James and Joses and Judas and Simon . . ." (Mark 6:3). This is the first time the names of Jesus' brothers are given. Mark refers to the names of those who were prominent in the early church and were well known to his readers.[38] This is the only direct mention of James in the Gospel of Mark. Mention is also made of Jesus' sisters, although no names are given to them.

Jesus is astonished at their lack of faith and quotes a proverb: "Prophets are not without honor, except in their hometown, and among their own kin, and in their own house" (Mark 6:4). Jesus' criticism is directed principally against his hometown neighbors, but it also contains a veiled criticism of his own family, for he uses the proverb in reference to them as well. Once again it is Mark's perspective that is being presented here and it is to be understood within the framework of the world of Mark's text. Mark's intention is to show that everyone struggles to gain an understanding of Jesus in interfacing with him during the course of his ministry. Mark does not intend to give a historical description of what actually occurred. While Mark presents a picture of the family of Jesus being somewhat opposed to Jesus, the gospel says nothing of the actual historical situation. Mark is speaking rhetorically, not historically. The picture Mark paints is that Jesus' own hometown looks upon him as an ordinary person, and they are unable to view him in any other way. Mark's rhetoric shows that Jesus is "anything but ordinary."[39]

MATTHEW 13:53-58

This passage in the Gospel of Matthew clearly has Mark as its source. Matthew's account occurs at a later stage in Jesus' ministry than it does in Mark's narrative. Matthew narrates this event after Jesus' third sermon dealing with parables (Matt 13:1-52). As with Mark, Matthew notes that Jesus has returned to his hometown, where he teaches in the synagogue, though Matthew omits noting that it occurs on a Sabbath—possibly Matthew thinks his readers would presume it was the Sabbath. By placing the event later in

---

[38] As noted above, scholars who breach the gulf between the literary text and the historical reality point to the fact that Joseph is not mentioned here because he was no longer alive, while Mary and the brothers of Jesus were important figures in the context of the early church. Painter (*Just James,* 32) notes that such a view "would be consistent with Joseph's being older than Mary, if she were his second wife, as proposed by the Epiphanean view. But there is no evidence to support this view." However, as I have noted, such a way of arguing is methodologically inaccurate.

[39] Painter, *Just James,* 33.

Jesus' ministry, after a long period of instructing his hearers, Matthew heightens the gravity of Jesus' rejection by his hometown.[40] The main differences between Matthew and Mark are clearly due to Matthew's editorial changes. There are three major changes Matthew makes to his source, Mark:

- *Matthew identifies Jesus as "the carpenter's son"* (in place of Mark's "is not this the carpenter?"). In the same context Matthew changes Mark's reference to Jesus as "the son of Mary" to read "Is not his mother called Mary?" These are slight changes in nuance, but they are understandable against the background of Jewish sensitivities. It was characteristic of the world of Judaism to describe a person as a "son of" his father, not his mother. While Mark is not sensitive to this issue, Matthew is. That is why he elaborates by identifying Jesus as the "carpenter's son" and avoids referring to Jesus directly as "the son of Mary" (Matt 13:55).[41] Jesus' identification by means of both mother and father conforms to Matthew's opening presentation of Jesus, where Joseph acknowledges Jesus to be his legal son, while Mary is his mother through the power of the Holy Spirit. In the context of Matthew's narrative the reader would then understand the references to his father and mother here in 13:55.[42]

- *A second change made by Matthew's redaction is in the use of the proverb.* While Mark's proverb could imply that the family of Jesus were opposed to him and had rejected him, Matthew deliberately drops the reference to the family of Jesus, thus avoiding the implication that there was hostility in the interface between Jesus and his family: "Prophets are not without honor except in their own country and in their own house" (Matt 13:57).[43] This is significant, for it shows how Matthew deliberately removes Jesus' family from being identified with those who rejected him. Again this conforms to Matthew's deliberate omission of Mark's earlier reference to Jesus' family who came to restrain him (Mark 3:19b-21). At the same time it also fits into the context of Matthew's narrative, in which Jesus' mother gave birth to him through the power of the Spirit. That would

---

[40] See Brown et al., *Mary in the New Testament*, 99–100.

[41] See Vincent Taylor, *The Gospel According to St. Mark: The Greek Text with Introduction, Notes, and Indexes* (London: Macmillan, 1952) 300, and Painter, *Just James*, 37.

[42] See Brown et al., *Mary in the New Testament,* 100.

[43] Note that Mark's account reads: "Prophets are not without honor, except in their hometown, and among their own kin, and in their own house" (Mark 6:4). The reference to "among their own kin" is omitted by Matthew.

demand that his mother would "honor" him and was not among those who rejected him.[44]

- *Finally, the list of the names of the brothers in Matthew varies slightly from Mark's list.* James remains in the first position, showing his importance within this group. Matthew identifies "James and Joseph and Simon and Judas" (13:55), while Mark has "James and Joses and Judas and Simon" (6:3). Mark is consistent throughout his gospel in giving the name of the second brother as Joses rather than Joseph.[45] Probably this is simply an alternative form of the name.

LUKE 4:16-30

This passage in the Gospel of Luke shows the greatest deviation from Mark's version. There are still sufficient similarities to lead one to accept that Luke is using Mark as his source and is developing the scene through his own unique gift of narration. Of first significance is Luke's reversal of Mark's sequence, where the discussion of the eschatological family precedes that of the rejection of Jesus in his own hometown. In Mark, Jesus' rejection occurred after some time had elapsed during which Jesus had preached the message of the kingdom. As we have noted, Matthew's gospel gives a much more extensive ministry of preaching before narrating this event. Luke, however, transfers this event to the opening stages of Jesus' ministry, occurring immediately after Jesus had returned from his baptism to Galilee. Luke also places the rejection (4:16-30) before the identification of the eschatological family (8:19-21). This change is largely attributable to Luke's ability as a storyteller. He presents the narrative in a much more logical way. Jesus grew up in Nazareth, so Luke begins with an event that will be paradigmatic for the rest of the narrative and foreshadows the outcome of the narrative itself. Thereafter he brings Jesus back to Galilee, where Jesus' ministry will flourish.

In line with his second volume, the Acts of the Apostles, Luke develops Mark's reference to Jesus' preaching in a synagogue on a Sabbath by presenting the contents of the sermon. This is a characteristic feature of Greco-Roman historical or biographical works.[46] Jesus' sermon here is paradigmatic in that it presents a summary of his life and ministry: Jesus brings the Old Testament period to fulfillment, as the quotation from Isa 61:1 indicates. The reaction of the synagogue audience to Jesus is indicative of what

---

[44] See Brown et al., *Mary in the New Testament,* 100–102.
[45] See Matt 27:56 and the next section, "Understanding the Term 'Brother of Jesus.'"
[46] See, for example, the numerous speeches in Josephus' works, as well as those of Plutarch.

ultimately will happen in Jesus' ministry: he will be rejected by his own people and put to death. Because of the rejection by his own people Jesus opens up his message to the world of the Gentiles, where his message is positively received. This provides the foundation for the Gentile mission.

Luke is the only writer in this context to identify Jesus with the question "Is not this Joseph's son?" (Luke 4:22). There is no mention of Jesus' mother, or his brothers and sisters. To this question Jesus replies by quoting a proverb, "Doctor, cure yourself" (Luke 4:23). Luke adds the second proverb referring to Jesus' rejection by his hometown, whereas Mark had the reference to "Prophets are not without honor, except in their hometown, and among their own kin, and in their own house" (Mark 6:4). As was argued when examining Mark's treatment of this proverb,[47] the shorter version of the proverb appears to be the more original. Mark is the one who introduced the references to the prophet's rejection by his own relatives and his own house. This is supported by the existence of another tradition in which the shorter proverb appears.[48] Luke avoids any reference to Jesus' family by simply stating, "Truly I tell you, no prophet is accepted in the prophet's hometown" (Luke 4:24). Either Luke has deliberately redacted the proverb in the Gospel of Mark or he has based himself on the existence of this other source that does not identify any hostility to Jesus' family. Whatever the case, Luke has clearly and deliberately avoided any semblance of hostility to or criticism of Jesus' family. This conforms to the very positive picture Luke presents of Jesus' mother and brothers throughout the gospel as well as in the Acts of the Apostles.[49]

Conclusion

From this analysis of the two references to the family of Jesus in the Synoptic Gospels a few conclusions can be drawn. Only Mark refers to the family of Jesus coming to him because they were concerned about having

---

[47] See above, n. 34.

[48] See the Gospel of Thomas, Saying 31: "No prophet is accepted in his own village." It is interesting to note a further point of similarity with the Gospel of Thomas in that this saying also shows a combination of the two proverbs in Luke into one: The Gospel of Thomas (Saying 31) expresses it in this way: "Jesus said: 'No prophet is accepted in his own village; no physician heals those who know him.'" (The translation is from Lambdin, *The Gospel of Thomas,* 130). While it is possible that the Gospel of Thomas has simply used the Gospel of Luke and combined these two proverbs succinctly together, it is far more likely that the Gospel of Thomas reflects the existence of another tradition that is aware of these two proverbs used in connection with the preaching of Jesus.

[49] See Brown et al., *Mary in the New Testament,* 167.

heard reports that Jesus had lost his mind. In the context of Mark's narrative, as well as in the world of Jesus, such a report that someone was out of his or her mind would naturally lead to the conclusion that the person was possessed by an evil spirit. That explains why Mark's narrative goes on to discuss the charge by the scribes that Jesus is possessed by Beelzebul.

In Jesus' response to his family who are seeking him, only Mark uses this passage in the context of the world of his text to challenge the family of Jesus to do God's will. It fits into Mark's narrative storyline, which is concerned with Jesus' identity. All who encounter Jesus are called to come to an awareness of and response to Jesus as Messiah and Son of God. Matthew and Luke each in his own way distance their accounts from any form of criticism of Jesus' family. While using Mark's gospel as their source, Matthew and Luke distance themselves from Mark's rhetorical presentation and offer a stronger and more favorable picture of the interface between Jesus and his family.

The lack of reference to an opposition between Jesus and his family is also seen in another tradition, namely that of the Gospel of Thomas. Saying 99 contains a reference to the family of Jesus that is closer to that of the Gospel of Luke: "The disciples said to him: 'Your brothers and your mother are standing outside.' He said to them: 'Those here who do the will of my father are my brothers and my mother. It is they who will enter the kingdom of my father.'"[50]

This examination of the Synoptic Gospel traditions related to the family of Jesus shows little evidence for any opposition between the family of Jesus and Jesus himself. While Mark's gospel has been used to argue for such an opposition, our analysis has shown that Mark is concerned with a rhetorical, not a historical presentation. The core vision of the family of Jesus that emerges from the independent traditions of Matthew, Luke, and the Gospel of Thomas all indicate a favorable and positive relationship between Jesus and his family.

Understanding the Term "Brother of Jesus"

Emergence of Opposing Views

The vexing question as to how we are to understand the meaning of this term "brothers of Jesus"[51] needs to be raised here. A brief survey of view-

---

[50] Lambdin, *The Gospel of Thomas,* 136–37.

[51] What is said of the "brothers of Jesus" applies equally to the meaning of the "sisters of Jesus."

points shows that three theories emerged for interpreting the term "brothers of Jesus" in the early church. All three views continue to be upheld today.

THE EPIPHANIAN THEORY

This view understands James and his brothers to be children of Joseph's first marriage. Thus they would be considered legal stepbrothers of Jesus. The Greek word *adelphos* is understood as referring to half-brothers or stepbrothers. This view is named after Epiphanius, the Bishop of Salamis, one of its earliest supporters. The earliest evidence for this interpretation is found in the *Protevangelium of James,* an apocryphal writing from the middle of the second century C.E. This view soon gained prominence because it supported the developing belief in the perpetual virginity of Mary that became important in the early church. This interpretation was upheld by some influential early church leaders, such as Clement of Alexandria, Origen, and Eusebius, and it continues to be upheld today by the Orthodox churches. In more recent times this view has been defended by the British scholar Richard Bauckham.[52] The *Protevangelium of James* deals with Mary's miraculous conception and her childhood. The names of her parents are identified as Anna and Joachim. It tells how she was brought up in the Temple and says that the priests gave Mary into Joseph's care. Joseph was already an old man with children of his own.[53] Epiphanius says Joseph was around eighty when he married Mary, so the question of Mary and Joseph entering into sexual relations is excluded. This view upholds the perpetual virginity of Mary at all stages: in the conception of Jesus, in the act of giving birth, and after the birth of Jesus.

THE HELVIDIAN THEORY

According to this theory James and his brothers were the actual sons of Mary and Joseph, making them Jesus' blood brothers. The word *adelphos* is interpreted as having the same meaning as the word "brother" in English.

---

[52] See Richard Bauckham, *Jude and the Relatives of Jesus in the Early Church* (Edinburgh: T & T Clark, 1990) 5–32.

[53] The *Protevangelium of James* describes it this way: "'Joseph, Joseph,' the high priest said, 'you've been chosen by lot to take the virgin of the Lord into your care and protection.' But Joseph objected: 'I already have sons and I'm an old man; she's only a young woman. I'm afraid that I'll become the butt of jokes among the people of Israel'" (Ronald F. Hock, *The Infancy Gospels of James and Thomas,* The Scholars Bible [Santa Rosa, CA: Polebridge Press, 1995] 49).

Helvidius propagated this view very strongly toward the end of the fourth century. Evidence for this position is found among some early Christian writers such as Tertullian (who died around 225 C.E.). Following the attacks of Jerome (who died around 420 C.E.), this view was regarded as heretical in the church. It was revived with the birth of historical critical studies on the Bible. Today it is the majority view of Protestant biblical scholars. Some Roman Catholic scholars have also supported this view, though it is hard to see how it can be reconciled with official Roman Catholic teaching.[54]

THE HIERONYMIAN THEORY

This viewpoint was presented by the influential church teacher Jerome (354–420 C.E.). In his view the word *adelphos* refers to "cousins" of Jesus. Jerome presented this view to refute the teachings of Helvidius. It is first found in his work against Helvidius entitled *Adversus Helvidium de Mariae Virginitate Perpetua*. While there are different variations on this theory, Jerome understood the brothers of Jesus to be the sons of his mother's sister, Mary of Clopas. He went further and argued that many of the references to James in the New Testament are to the same person. Consequently he identified James the brother of the Lord with James the son of Alphaeus, one of the apostles, thus making James a true apostle. This same James is identified as well with James the Less as opposed to James the son of Zebedee (who by implication is James the Greater!). This view was also championed by Augustine and has remained the traditional view of the Catholic Church.

Examining the New Testament Usage

While little agreement has been reached on the meaning and interpretation of the term *adelphos,* as can be seen from the brief delineation of the above theories, there are some things that point toward a solution to the problem. An examination of the use of *adelphos* ("brother") in Greek literature, as well as especially in the New Testament, shows that this term has a wide variety of meanings and usages in different contexts.[55]

---

[54] Among the recent Catholic supporters of this interpretation is John P. Meier. See his *A Marginal Jew,* 1:316–32.

[55] The clearest and most concise discussion of the meaning and reference of the term *adelphos* in the New Testament as well as in extra-biblical writings appears in Brown et al., *Mary in the New Testament,* 65–72, and Joseph A. Fitzmyer, *The Gospel According to Luke I–IX,* AB 28 (New York: Doubleday, 1981) 723–24. I acknowledge my debt to their insights in what follows.

A first reading of the Greek *adelphos* ("brother[s] of Jesus") in the Gospel of Mark takes it to refer to a blood brother or "son of the same mother."[56] However, the word has a much more varied usage. Among the uses and nuances one notes in Greek and in early Christianity, the following are the most significant:

- Early in the world of Christianity the term *adelphos* took the meaning of a *fellow member of the religion,* "hence generally [used] for those in such spiritual communion."[57] For example, the risen Jesus uses the term *adelphoi* to refer to all who had accepted him: "Then Jesus said to them, 'Do not be afraid; go and tell my brothers *(adelphois)* to go to Galilee; there they will see me'" (Matt 28:10).[58] Paul uses this term frequently to address fellow members of his communities (e.g., 1 Cor 1:10).

- *Kinship in religion:* Paul's usage in Rom 9:3 is instructive: "For I could wish that I myself would be accursed (and therefore separated from Christ) for the sake of my own brothers *(hyper tōn adelphōn),* my kin *(tōn syngenōn mou)* according to the flesh" (my own translation). Here Paul juxtaposes in apposition two words, *adelphoi* and *syngenēs,* where the latter indicates "belonging to the same people group, compatriot, kin,"[59] in other words the people of Judaism. The Greek word *adelphoi* has the meaning, then, of "kinsfolk." It is used frequently in this way in the book of Tobit. See, for example, the discussion between Tobit and the angel Raphael regarding Raphael's ancestry: "So Tobias went in to tell his father Tobit and said to him, 'I have just found a man who is one of our own Israelite kindred *(tōn adelphōn hēmōn).*' He replied, 'Call the man in, my son, so that I may learn about his family and to what

---

[56] Henry George Liddell and Robert Scott *A Greek-English Lexicon,* Revised and Augmented by Henry Stuart Jones and Roderick MacKenzie (9th ed. with Revised Supplement, Oxford: Clarendon Press, 1996) 20. It is interesting to note that *LSJ* adds that a second meaning is "kinsman, tribesman" (p. 20).

[57] BDAG, *adelphos,* 18.

[58] The use of *adelphoi* to refer to those in spiritual communion or those who hold the same religious beliefs is not unique to Christianity. Examples of this same usage are found in the religious Greco-Roman world. For example, Josephus uses the term in reference to the Essene community. He writes: "(T)he individual's possessions join the common stock and all, like brothers *(hōsper adelphois),* enjoy a single patrimony" (*B.J.* 2:122; Josephus, *The Jewish War, Books I–III,* trans. Henry St. John Thackeray, LCL [Cambridge, MA: Harvard University Press; London: William Heinemann, 1956). For further examples see BDAG, *adelphos,* 18.

[59] BDAG, *syngenēs,* 950.

tribe he belongs, and whether he is trustworthy enough to go with you'" (Tob 5:9; see also 5:11-22).

- *Neighbor:* For example, "But I say to you that if you are angry with a brother *(tō adelphō)* you will be liable to judgment . . ." (Matt 5:22).

- *Half-brother:* "For Herod himself had sent men who arrested John, bound him, and put him in prison on account of Herodias, his brother *(tou adelphou autou)* Philip's wife . . ." (Mark 6:17-18). Historically we know that Herod Antipas was the son of Herod the Great and Malthace (a Samaritan), while Herod (Philip) was the son of Herod the Great and Mariamme II.[60] Thus they were half-brothers.

- *Relative:* In the LXX *adelphos* can identify someone who is related in some way, a relative or kinsperson. For example, "Then I bowed my head and worshiped the LORD, and blessed the LORD the God of my master Abraham, who had led me by the right way to obtain the daughter of my master's kinsman *(tou adelphou)* for his son" (Gen 24:48; see also 24:27). "Then he (Jacob) told Rachel that he was her father's kinsman (literally "brother," *adelphos*) . . ." (29:12). Liddell and Scott also indicate this usage as "kinsman; tribesman."[61]

While the normal meaning of the Greek word *adelphos* is "blood brother," given the varied usage we have indicated above, the question remains, "In what sense is Mark using the term?" Does he look on the brothers and sisters of Jesus as blood brothers or in the wider sense as relatives or kinsmen? Is there any way to determine this? Two arguments lend weight to the wider understanding of "relative."

In the first instance the Hebrew word 'āḥ (or the Aramaic 'āḥā), besides indicating "blood brother," also has the wider concept of "kin or relative."[62] According to this perspective Mark betrays a Semitic background. Brown et al. comment: "In this case the Greek would reflect an underlying Hebrew/Aramaic usage; but such an interpretation would be methodologically valid only if there were reason to suspect a Semitic background."[63] There is every reason to support the Hebrew/Aramaic background of the writer of the Gospel of Mark. Stylistically Mark has been

---

[60] See *JBC,* "A History of Israel," art. 75, #129, 140, pp. 693–97.

[61] See *LSJ,* 20.

[62] See Ludwig Koehler and Walter Baumgartner, eds., *"'āḥ," Lexicon in Veteris Testamenti Libros* (Leiden: Brill, 1958) 26

[63] Brown et al., *Mary in the New Testament,* 66.

shown to be thinking in Aramaic but writing in Greek. His frequent use of the Greek coordinating conjunction "and" *(kai)* reflects the Hebrew way of joining sentences through the *waw consecutive* construction ("and") rather than the use of conjunctions and subordinating clauses.[64] Further, Mark is the only gospel that preserves seven Aramaic words, which he then explains by translating them into Greek. This indicates that Mark certainly knows Aramaic, but presumes his readers do not. For example, when Jesus restores the little girl to life he says to her: "*'Talitha cum'* [Aramaic], which means, 'Little girl, get up!' [Greek]" (Mark 5:41).[65] All this makes it distinctly possible that Mark understands the word *adelphos* in the wider sense in which it is interpreted in the Hebrew/Aramaic background.

In the second instance Mark lists the names of "the brothers of Jesus" as "James and Joses and Judas and Simon" (Mark 6:3). A more detailed examination of a reference to two of these brothers in the Passion narrative helps to elucidate their relationship to Jesus. A chart comparing the names of those who were at the foot of the cross is revealing.[66]

Mark 15:40	*Matt 27:56*	*John 19:25*
Mary Magdalene	Mary Magdalene	Mary Magdalene
Mary the mother of James the younger and of Joses	Mary the mother of James and Joseph	Mary the wife of Clopas
Salome	The mother of the sons of Zebedee	His mother's sister
		Jesus' mother
		The Beloved Disciple

[64] A quick glance at the Greek text of Mark 1:12-45 will show how Mark connects all his sentences and clauses with the word *kai* ("and"). For a non-Greek speaker this use of "and" is well demonstrated in the 1952 edition of the *Revised Standard Version's* translation of Mark's gospel (the forerunner to the 1989 *NRSV* edition), which has endeavored to remain as close as possible to the original text. More recent translations have lost this sense because of the attempt to translate the material into "good English." Another feature that jumps out at the reader is the frequent usage of the word "immediately" *(euthys).*

[65] The other six examples of the use of Aramaic words or expressions are "Boanerges (that is, Sons of Thunder)" (3:17); "Corban (that is, an offering to God)" (7:11); "'Eph-phatha,' that is, 'Be opened'" (7:34); "Abba, Father" (14:36); "Golgotha (which means the place of a skull)" (15:22); "'Eloi, Eloi, lema sabachtani?' which means, 'My God, my God, why have you forsaken me?'" (15:34).

[66] I acknowledge my debt to Raymond E. Brown's Table 8, "The Women and Others" in his *The Death of the Messiah: From Gethsemane to the Grave* (New York: Doubleday, 1994) 2:1016.

Note that the above chart is not a typical "synoptic chart" in that the comparison is not being made among the three Synoptic Gospels, Matthew, Mark, and Luke. Instead, the comparison is between the traditions used by Mark, Matthew, and John. No specific reference is made to Luke here because he does not list the names of the disciples. He simply states: "But all his acquaintances, including the women who had followed him from Galilee, stood at a distance, watching these things" (Luke 23:49). In Luke's tradition the remembrance of the names of the women is unimportant; it seems that they were not members of, or at least were unknown to, Luke's community.

In these three lists John is the only one to include the mother of Jesus as well as the Beloved Disciple (neither is mentioned by name). Removing those two names from John's enumeration would also reduce his list to three names of women, which is identical to the tradition found in Mark and Matthew. This would seem to point to the existence of a traditional list of names of disciples that was circulating in the early church and was available to all the traditions of early Christianity. An examination of all three lists produces the following observations:

- Mary Magdalene is the same person in each tradition.

- Mark speaks of "Mary the mother of James the younger and of Joses" while Matthew identifies the woman as "Mary the mother of James and Joseph." It is natural to view this woman as the same person, the mother of James and of Joses/Joseph (the latter being a variation in the name).

- Salome (Mark 15:40) could be seen to be the same person as "the mother of the sons of Zebedee" (Matt 27:56) and "his mother's sister" (John 19:25). All three lists have two of the three names in common. One could presume that the third name was the same person; the writers could be using another way to describe her. For example, since John is the only one to identify the presence of Jesus' mother at the cross it is natural that he would give the identity of this woman as Jesus' mother if that was the case. This identification would also explain why the mother of the sons of Zebedee asked Jesus to allow her sons to sit on thrones to his right and left, namely to share in his power (see Matt 20:20-28; compare Mark 10:35-45, where James and John make the request themselves). She was making an appeal based on family bonds to share in Jesus' power. This was a claim Jesus rejected and was in line with his teaching that his family comprised those who did the Father's will, not those who claimed some form of physical family bond.

• It is also possible to identify Mary the wife of Clopas (John 19:25) with Mary the mother of James the younger and Joses (Mark 15:40; Matt 27:56). This would mean that the Mary who is the mother of James and Joses/Joseph is not the same Mary who is the mother of Jesus.[67]

There are obviously a number of suppositions in the above examination, but the important consideration is undoubtedly whether the Mary who is identified as mother of James/Joses is the same as the mother of Jesus. The most compelling argument is that of Brown et al. mentioned above, who reject this identification. It does not make any sense for Mark and Matthew to identify her as the mother of James and Joses/Joseph without identifying her as the mother of Jesus. To state that Mark or Matthew did not know she was the mother of Jesus is an argument that is clutching at straws!

Two further points arise that are of importance for our study of the person of James:

• Is the James mentioned in the context of the crucifixion the same James who is mentioned in Mark 6:3? It is possible that they are two different persons. However, an examination of the references seems to support identification. For example, Mark 6:3 identifies Jesus as "the brother of James and Joses and Judas and Simon" while Matt 13:55 states, "And are not his brothers James and Joseph and Simon and Judas?" One notes clearly here that the variation between Mark and Matthew lies with the name of Joses/Joseph, the exact same variation that occurs in the crucifixion narrative. Brown et al. caution that "the frequency of such patriarchal names as James *(Iakōbos)* and Joseph in the first century warns us against too easily assuming identity."[68] While this is a wise admonition, support for the identity of the two references must surely come from the way Matthew consistently changes the name of Joses to Joseph, viewing them as the same person. A further argument against the identification of these two lists comes from the fact that in the first list (Mark 6:3; Matt 13:55) the names of four brothers are noted, while in the crucifixion scene only two brothers are named (Mark 15:41; Matt 27:56). This argument is based on the demand for consistency. However, we note that neither Mark nor Matthew is consistent in its continued reference to James and Joses/Joseph in the scenes relating the crucifixion, burial, and

[67] See Brown, et al., *Mary in the New Testament,* 70.
[68] Ibid. 70, n. 132.

resurrection.[69] One notices that both Mark and Matthew vary the references by identifying one or other of the brothers (or even none). It is all a matter of using "a type of shorthand."[70] Given the context of the entire narrative of Mark and Matthew, it seems logical to expect that both Mark and Matthew would presume that the reader would identify their references to "James and Joses/Joseph" as referring to the same persons. The fact that they did not list the further names of "Judas and Simon" in the crucifixion-burial-resurrection scenes means simply that they are both using a form of abbreviation. One would also presume that of the four names, James and Joses/Joseph must have been the more important figures.

• What is the meaning of the phrase "James the younger *(tou mikrou)*?" Later tradition has customarily explained this designation as a deliberate way to distinguish this James from the other James, the son of Zebedee, who is then referred to as "James the Greater." However, in the New Testament James, the son of Zebedee, is never referred to in this way, nor is any other James. Probably the best way to interpret this reference is to see *mikros* as referring to James' size, or height.[71]

Little unanimity among scholars has been reached on the meaning of the term "brother" in reference to James as the "brother of Jesus." This shows that there is ambiguity with regard to this word. In effect the meaning of this term is read in one of two ways: either referring to "blood brothers" of Jesus or in reference to relatives, or kinsmen of Jesus. From my examination of the use of this term throughout the context of the gospels it seems to me that the most responsible reading is to see it as referring in the wider sense to relatives or kinsmen of Jesus without specifying exactly the nature or degree of the relationship. One thing, however, is sure, and that is that this term does not designate a cousin, as Jerome understood this term. Greek has a specific word for cousin *(anepsios)*. If a cousin were intended, the New Testament writers would surely have used the Greek word *anepsios*. See, for example, Col 4:10: "Aristarchus my fellow prisoner greets you, as does Mark the cousin *(anepsios)* of Barnabas."

---

[69] See Brown et al., *Mary in the New Testament,* 70 for an excellent chart that delineates the references to the different brothers.

[70] Ibid. 71.

[71] BDAG (*mikros,* 651) defines the meaning of this term *mikros* in this way: "Pertaining to a relatively limited size, measure or quantity, small, short—of stature."

As a result of the above examination I interpret "James, the brother of Jesus" or "of the Lord" as a relative, clansman, or kinsman of Jesus. His mother was known as Mary, but was a different Mary from Jesus' mother. She was the wife of Clopas, who therefore is the father of James. This understanding does not change the meaning of the passage in which Jesus says that the important relationship with him is the one based on doing the Father's will. Whether one is a blood brother of Jesus or his relative, the meaning remains the same. Family ties to Jesus are not what count. Instead it is the eschatological family that is important, where one carries out God's will. In essence this is the same challenge Jesus issued to the sons of Zebedee, James and John, for wanting to sit on his right and his left in his kingdom (Mark 10:35-45; Matt 20:20-28).

As I have argued elsewhere, this issue of whether "James, the brother of Jesus" is his blood brother or a relative is largely a question that arises from our Western cultural world. It is in fact an illustration of imposing the Western cultural context onto the world of the New Testament and betrays an inability to respect the New Testament world itself. This is what Bruce Malina has called *anachronism* and *ethnocentrism*.[72] Using the analogy of present-day rural African societies[73] can offer a direction for viewing the term "brother" in a wider sense as referring to "a wider family network."

> An analogy drawn from societies in Africa can provide a direction toward a solution. In Africa the extended family is the major social network and members of this wider family are designated by the familial terms "brother and sister." The important thing is not physical generation, but rather being part of a family network. It is clearly a problem or issue that belongs to the world of Western culture and thought. It would not arise in the context of societies in Africa and even less in the world of Mediterranean first-century culture. The issue here in referring to James as "the brother of the Lord" is not to identify physical generation, but rather to show that he belongs to the

---

[72] Bruce J. Malina, *The New Jerusalem in the Revelation of John: The City as Symbol of Life with God* (Collegeville: Liturgical Press, 2000) 5, says: "Applying inappropriate references to interpret an author's statements outside the author's historical period is called *anachronism* (for example: if Jesus traveled in Palestine, he must have had a jeep). Applying inappropriate references to interpret what an author says outside the author's social context is called *ethnocentrism* (for example: Jesus condemned divorce; we have divorce in our society, so Jesus must be condemning our type of divorce)."

[73] The use of cultures such as those of rural Africa as an analogy is a valid approach since their style of life, thought patterns, and cultural practices more closely resemble those of first-century Mediterranean cultures.

same family network as Jesus. For these reasons one should respect the wider context of society of that time and see the term as referring to someone who belongs to a wider family network.[74]

As regards the person of James, nothing distinctive is said about him in these contexts. He is simply identified as part of Jesus' family, and his being mentioned first indicates his importance among the other "brothers." With time a more nuanced understanding of his relationship to Jesus emerged, due to a deeper theological reflection. This development fits into the way the understanding and interpretation of the Scriptures have emerged over time.

Two illustrations from the Hebrew Scriptures will show this developing theological reflection more clearly. The first concerns the identity of the Servant in four poems of the prophet Isaiah that center on the figure of the Servant of the Lord (see especially Isa 52:13–53:12)[75]. When these passages are read in the context of the world of the prophet Isaiah, they have been interpreted as referring to the nation of Israel, or to a king who will emerge shortly onto the scene of Israel's history. Through the lenses of the Christian experience of the death and resurrection of Jesus, the early Christians came to understand the identity of the Suffering Servant as a foreshadowing and prediction of the person of Jesus: "He was oppressed, and he was afflicted, yet he did not open his mouth; like a lamb that is led to the slaughter, and like a sheep that before its shearers is silent . . ." (Isa 53:7). From a theological interpretation of the unity of the Scriptures as part of a developing understanding of God's salvific plan, the meaning of the Suffering Servant emerges fully in the life and death of Jesus.

The same is true with the unfolding of the understanding of the person of Jesus. Examining all the New Testament writings together, we come to a clearer understanding of the humanity and divinity of Jesus. Taking only one document or tradition on its own, one can gain a onesided impression stressing only one or the other dimension. It was only in the course of time that reflection on the evidence of Scripture was able to find language and vocabulary to express this twofold dimension through the philosophical categories of nature and person whereby Jesus is identified as "one person with two natures, divine and human."

---

[74] Patrick J. Hartin, *James,* SP 14 (Collegeville: Liturgical Press, 2003) 17.

[75] The four "Servant Songs" are Isa 42:1-4[5-9]; 49:1-6[7]; 50:4-9[10-11]; 52:13–53:12. The bracketed verses are included by some scholars, but not by others. For a more detailed discussion of the concept of the "Servant of the Lord" see David Noel Freedman, ed., *Eerdmans Dictionary of the Bible* (Grand Rapids: Eerdmans, 2000) 1189–90.

We can apply this theological understanding to the concept of "brother." When this term was used in the Gospel of Mark no question arose regarding the exact designation of this term. It was used in the way in which the world of that time used it: referring to the family of Jesus without any precision. In the gospels of Matthew and Luke further precision was called for since Mary, the mother of Jesus, is identified as a virgin in giving birth to her son Jesus. This then demanded that the relationship between Jesus and his mother not be one of opposition, but rather one of carrying out the will of God, as Luke demonstrates so ably. Consequently, the gospels of Matthew and Luke went out of their way to distance their interpretation from Mark's rhetorical understanding of the family of Jesus and to present it in a positive light. As time goes on, hindsight enabled a deeper and clearer interpretation to emerge. Reflection on the virginity of Mary brought precision to the understanding of the term "brothers" of the Lord. It is a theological question of a development of understanding from imprecision to precision, as is the case with the two examples I have cited above in reference to the Servant songs and to the person and nature of Jesus.[76]

While I continue to use the phrase "James the brother of Jesus," I understand this term in the way in which I have argued above, namely as belonging to a family network. Because James is first in the list of names of "the brothers" of Jesus one can conclude that in Mark's mind James was the oldest and possibly the most important of the relatives of Jesus in the consciousness of the early church. This examination has deliberately avoided discussing the issue of the perpetual virginity of Mary, as this is a question that is not considered by the New Testament writers. However, attention will be given to the aspect of the virginity of Mary with regard to her conception when I examine the infancy narratives of Matthew and Luke.[77]

Matthew and Luke's Nativity Narratives

The gospels of Matthew and Luke expanded their source Mark through the use of sources such as the Sayings Source Q and those that were special

---

[76] This theological understanding is viewed by Christians as occurring under the inspiration of the Spirit, who guides the whole process as the Johannine Jesus said: "But the Advocate, the Holy Spirit, whom the Father will send in my name, will teach you everything, and remind you of all that I have said to you" (John 14:25).

[77] As Fitzmyer, *The Gospel According to Luke I-IX,* 724, says: "(t)here is no indication in the NT itself about Mary as *aei parthenos,* 'ever virgin.' This belief in one form or another can only be traced to the second century A.D." Brown et al., *Mary in the New Testament,* 72, give an interesting summary of agreement between Roman Catholic and Lutheran scholars

to each of their gospels and communities.[78] Matthew and Luke each prefaced their gospel accounts with an infancy narrative. Relying upon very different traditions and theological approaches, they independently present very different pictures of the birth of Jesus. It is not my intention to discuss all the complex issues related to these infancy narratives, but I do wish to examine what can be understood and inferred from these chapters regarding the brothers of Jesus.

Matthew's Nativity Account (Matt 1:18-25)

Matthew presents his account from Joseph's perspective. He opens his narrative with a genealogy that traces Jesus' ancestry through Joseph (1:1-17). Despite this, Matthew does not describe Joseph as the physical agent in the generation of Jesus. Instead, his description shows the irregular nature of Jesus' birth: "Now the birth of Jesus the Messiah took place in this way. When his mother Mary had been engaged to Joseph, but before they lived together, she was found to be with child from the Holy Spirit" (Matt 1:18).

Matthew here reflects typical Jewish marriage traditions that involved two stages. The first was the betrothal, when an exchange of consent occurred before witnesses. The woman continued to live at the home of her parents. At a second stage, the bride moved to the husband's home (see Matt 25:1-13).[79] The presumption was that the bride was a virgin when she moved in with her husband. The relationship between Mary and Joseph was still at the first stage; hence Mary's pregnancy would be considered adultery. However, Matthew tells the reader that this pregnancy occurred through the power of the Holy Spirit. Joseph only comes to understand this later, when an angel comes to him in a dream.

---

on the issue of the biblical evidence for the perpetual virginity of Mary and the brothers of Jesus when they write: "But we did agree on these points:

    (1) The continued virginity of Mary after the birth of Jesus is not a question directly raised by the NT.

    (2) Once it was raised in subsequent church history, it was that question which focused attention on the exact relationship of the "brothers" (and "sisters") to Jesus.

    (3) Once that attention has been focused, it cannot be said that the NT identifies them *without doubt* as blood brothers and sisters and hence as children of Mary.

    (4) The solution favored by scholars will in part depend on the authority they allot to later church insights."

[78] Identified simply as M and L for the special sources of Matthew and Luke respectively.

[79] Marriage customs at the time of Jesus are deduced from later rabbinic sources. See Joachim Jeremias, *Jerusalem in the Time of Jesus: An Investigation into Economic and Social Conditions During the New Testament Period* (Philadelphia: Fortress, 1969) 365–68.

What is of concern for this study is Matthew's final comment: "When Joseph awoke from sleep . . . he took her as his wife, but had no marital relations with her *until she had borne a son;* and he named him Jesus" (Matt 1:24-25). At first sight, reading this English translation generates the presumption that after Jesus was born Mary and Joseph had the normal sexual relations of a married couple.

However, two observations need to be raised against this conclusion. First of all, the focus in this particular context is on the birth of Jesus, and the intention of the writer is to stress that Jesus' conception occurred not in the normal course of human sexual relations but as a result of the intervention of the Holy Spirit. The focus is on events prior to the birth of Jesus. There is no intention of saying anything about what happened after the birth of Jesus. Second, this perspective is supported by the use of the Greek preposition *heōs* ("until"),[80] which has the meaning "up to the time that she had borne a son."[81] This preposition says nothing about any future action. Its concern remains with events leading up to the present. Matthew's intention is not to speak about whether Mary had any more children. The text does not answer the question one way or the other. To argue as Painter does that "given that Matthew later introduces the reference to the mother of Jesus with his brothers and sisters (13:53-58), the reader naturally assumes that they were children born to Mary and Joseph subsequent to the birth of Jesus,"[82] is misreading the text. As I have indicated in this particular context as well as in the context of Matt 13:53-58, one has to understand the text according to the way it was understood in the world of Matthew, and not read back meanings from the twenty-first century into the text. The Greek words *adelphos* and *heōs* bear a special meaning in the context of that world and that text, and it is anachronistic to give them meanings they have in the English language today.

Luke's Nativity Account (Luke 1:26-45)

Luke presents the birth of Jesus through the eyes of Mary, not Joseph. The situation of Mary in Luke is similar to that in the Gospel of Matthew. At the time Mary conceived she was betrothed to Joseph, but was not yet married to him. The angel tells Mary that it will be by the power of God that she will conceive: "The Holy Spirit will come upon you, and the power of the Most High will overshadow you; therefore the child to be

---

[80] See Zerwick, *Analysis Philologica Novi Testamenti Graeci,* 2.
[81] See BDAG, *heōs,* 423: "(b) used as preposition . . . until, up to."
[82] Painter, *Just James,* 35.

born will be holy; he will be called Son of God" (Luke 1:35). Luke also presents the belief in a virginal conception of Jesus occurring through the power of God. However, he says nothing about the future marital relationship between Mary and Joseph in this context.

The Gospel of John and the Family of Jesus (John 2:1-12; 7:3-5; 19:25-27)

There are a few important references to the family of Jesus in the Gospel of John. According to our methodological procedure, these passages must be viewed within the context of John's narrative. Among the many unique features of John among the gospels is the role characters play in its story line. In effect John's characters function by providing examples for the reader of the types of faith-responses that are made to Jesus. Jesus is the central character of the entire gospel. The purpose of John's narrative is to bring the reader to a belief in the person and identity of Jesus. As John himself says in the conclusion to the gospel: "But these are written so that you may come to believe that Jesus is the Messiah, the Son of God, and that through believing you may have life in his name" (John 20:30-31).

When the author of John narrates his story, he does so with the intention of showing how his characters respond in belief to Jesus.[83] John shows that there is no one response of faith in Jesus. Each character illustrates a different level of faith. One could in effect map out each response to Jesus and one would immediately see different levels of faith commitment. John presents a wide trajectory of responses to Jesus, ranging from opposition to a deep personal commitment to Jesus. At one end of the trajectory lies the character of the Jews who are opposed to Jesus; at the other end is the character of the Beloved Disciple who demonstrates a firm personal commitment to Jesus.

As was noted in relation to the Gospel of Mark, this is the world the narrator of the Gospel of John has painted. One cannot simply jump from the world of John to the world of history. John does not intend to paint a historical picture, but rather to use his characters to enable his readers to see their own responses to Jesus reflected in the responses of the characters he paints.[84] Within this framework and perspective we must understand the references John makes to the brothers of Jesus. As with other characters, they also emerge within the framework of John's narrative as a group that exhibits a faith response to Jesus.

---

[83] See R. Alan Culpepper, *Anatomy of the Fourth Gospel: A Study in Literary Design* (Philadelphia: Fortress, 1987) 232.

[84] Ibid. 233.

Jesus and His Family (John 2:12)

John 2:12 ("After this he [Jesus] went down to Capernaum with his mother, his brothers and his disciples; and they remained there a few days") acts as a transitional commentary that connects the previous event of the wedding feast of Cana (John 2:1-11) to the following event of Jesus' cleansing of the Temple in Jerusalem (2:13-25). This is the first reference to "his brothers." In the previous episode of the wedding feast of Cana reference is made to the invitation to Jesus, his mother, and his disciples, but no explicit mention is made of his brothers (see John 2:1-2). Yet, the reference to them at the end of this narrative and the return of Jesus to Capernaum with them implies that they must also have been part of the wedding group.

John's gospel shows some interesting points of similarity to Mark's gospel with its reference to the brothers of Jesus. While scholars adopt different positions on the relationship between the gospels of John and Mark, the generally accepted viewpoint, and the one I endorse, is that they were written independently and base themselves on independent traditions.[85] In both John and Mark we note that reference to the presence of the brothers of Jesus occurs at the beginning of Jesus' public ministry. Mark noted that Jesus' mother and brothers came to the region of Galilee from Nazareth looking for him when they heard reports that "he has gone out of his mind" (Mark 3:19b-21, 31-35). In John they all move from Cana to the region of Galilee, specifically Capernaum. The only other reference to the brothers of Jesus in the public ministry of Jesus occurs in the Synoptic Gospels in reference to Jesus' visit to his hometown of Nazareth (Mark 6:1-6; see also Matt 13:53-58; Luke 4:16-30).

Jesus' Brothers as Unbelievers? (John 7:1-10)

This is the one passage in the entire New Testament that forms a basis for the idea that the brothers of Jesus were opposed and hostile to him during the course of his public ministry. It is further argued that a transformation occurred only after the resurrection. For example, the appearance of Jesus to James (to which Paul testifies in 1 Cor 15:7) is seen by many to be the occasion for James' conversion to belief in the Risen Jesus. What are we to make of such interpretations?

---

[85] See, for example, the discussion in Charles Harold Dodd, *Historical Tradition in the Fourth Gospel* (Cambridge: Cambridge University Press, 1963), and D. Moody Smith, *John Among the Gospels: The Relationship in Twentieth-Century Research* (Minneapolis: Fortress, 1992).

The solution lies in examining this passage within the context of John's gospel. It appears within the framework of different responses to Jesus. Chapter 6 contained the account of the feeding of five thousand (6:1-14). This was followed by a long speech, known as the Bread of Life discourse (6:22-40), in which Jesus draws out the significance of this miracle: "I am the bread of life. Whoever comes to me will never be hungry, and whoever believes in me will never be thirsty" (6:35). A close examination of the rest of this chapter shows how John reveals in an insightful way the different responses to Jesus. *The Jews* reject Jesus: "Is not this Jesus, the son of Joseph, whose father and mother we know? How can he now say, 'I have come down from heaven?'" (6:42; see also 6:52). *Many of Jesus' disciples* withdrew from his company, saying, "This teaching is difficult; who can accept it?" (6:60-66). In contrast, *the Twelve* refuse to leave, but continue to remain with Jesus. *Peter* speaks on their behalf and shows the depth of their belief in Jesus: "Lord, to whom can we go? You have the words of eternal life. We have come to believe and know that you are the Holy One of God" (6:68-69). However, Jesus goes on to show that although the Twelve have accepted him, there is one among his intimate associates who will betray him: "'Did I not choose you, the twelve? Yet one of you is a devil.' He was speaking of Judas son of Simon Iscariot, for he, though one of the twelve, was going to betray him" (6:70-71). The responses to Jesus range from *opposition* (the Jews) and *betrayal* (Judas), through *disbelief* (some disciples), to *belief* (Peter and the Twelve), and ultimately *love* (the Beloved Disciple).

It is interesting to note the parallel way in which the description of the Cana episode (John 2:1-12) and this episode of Jesus' interface with his brothers (John 7:1-10) are narrated. Both episodes involve *the family of Jesus*. Mary told Jesus they had run out of wine, with the implicit expectation that Jesus would respond by performing a miracle (John 2:3). The brothers ask Jesus in John 7:3-4 to go up to Judea for the festival of Booths "so that your disciples may see the works you are doing." *Jesus responds in both instances negatively* by saying that his hour has not yet come (see John 2:4 and 7:6, 8). In both instances, despite the apparent rejection of the request, Jesus responds in his own way and in his own time: he changes water into wine at the marriage feast (John 2:7) and goes up to the festival of Booths as the disciples had asked (John 7:10).

In this context the writer makes reference to the brothers of Jesus in the form of an aside: "For not even his brothers believed in him" (John 7:5). By contrasting the request for a miracle with a lack of belief, John draws attention to his fundamental teaching that miracles do not lead to faith. Jesus expresses this concept many times, but the climax of this teaching occurs at the end of the Book of Signs, where John comments, "Although he had performed so many signs in their presence, they did not believe in him" (John 12:37). Given this understanding, when John comments about the unbelief of the disciples what he has in mind is that their relationship with Jesus rests on miracles or signs. This is not true belief. This does not mean that the brothers are opposed to Jesus, as so many interpretations of this verse state. On the line of the continuum of faith, John shows that the brothers certainly are not at the level of opposition to Jesus at which the Jews are portrayed, nor do they show any form of hostility to Jesus. Rather, they are at the initial stages of faith, where faith is seen to rely on miracles and signs. For John that is not true faith. Failure to understand John's theology of faith leads to a false interpretation of the interface between Jesus and his family. They are not opponents, nor are they hostile to Jesus. Instead, they are very much like the disciples, on the periphery of faith. They are present with Jesus in his ministry, journeying with him, but have not yet reached the level of faith that would emerge through the power of love, as is evident in the life of the Beloved Disciple, culminating in the event at the tomb (John 20:8-9).

The fact that Jesus' family is present with him at this point and goes ahead of him to Jerusalem to celebrate the festival of Booths is an indication in John's traditions that at least they were present with Jesus for more than just a few moments at the beginning of his ministry.

The Crucifixion of Jesus and the Absence of James (John 19:25-27)

Above we compared the different traditions regarding the presence of the women at Jesus' crucifixion and death.[86] What is unique to John's narrative is the presence of Jesus' mother and the Beloved Disciple at the foot of the cross. This scene is central to the theology of John's gospel and must be understood within that context. John brings together two characters at the foot of the cross who are never given personal names, namely his mother (whom Jesus addresses as "Woman" [see also John 2:4]) and the Beloved Disciple (John 19:26-27). This tends to point to the fact that these two characters are meant to be understood not in their historical reference, but rather in their symbolic roles. The role his mother plays is not that of her physical motherhood, but rather her spiritual motherhood with regard to the Beloved Disciple. And the Beloved Disciple is seen in the role of the ideal disciple, the one who not only carries out the will of God, but truly

---

[86] See chart above, p. 29.

experiences love for Jesus. It is a reminder of the scene in the Synoptic Gospels where Jesus says: "Here are my mother and my brothers! Whoever does the will of God is my brother and sister and mother" (Mark 3:34-35). The eschatological family depends on being a true disciple who follows God's will. In the Gospel of John something similar occurs. Jesus gives his physical mother the role of the spiritual mother of the true disciple, and the disciple is the spiritual son of the mother. True discipleship is then viewed in terms of a family relationship. Again, interpreting this scene as though it were a criticism of the brothers of Jesus and seeing Jesus replacing his brothers with the Beloved Disciple reads too much into the scene. The focus here is on true discipleship of love—and the relationship is that of mother and son that replaces the mother and disciple.

The fact that the brothers of Jesus are not mentioned here is to be understood in the same way that one understands the absence of the disciples and the Twelve from this scene. Throughout the gospel, John has endeavored to portray the Beloved Disciple as the true disciple, the one who is the example of the true believer. The disciples and the brothers of Jesus remain at different levels of faith. The absence of any mention of James in particular is not to be seen as having any significance. For the community of John, the Beloved Disciple is the true disciple. He demonstrates a discipleship that is clearly more faithful than that of Peter, and by implication that of James as well.

What Have the Gospels Said about the Character of James?

Only the gospels of Mark and Matthew name the brothers of Jesus: "James and Joses (Joseph) and Simon and Judas" (Mark 6:3; Matt 13:55). Since James is mentioned first in both lists of names, it is legitimate to conclude that he is the most important of Jesus' brothers. This was the customary way of presenting a list, with the most significant name placed first.[87] James does not emerge as an individual character in any of the gospels. He simply forms part of the group of "brothers of Jesus." The following consequences and implications emerge for James as one of the brothers of Jesus:

The interface we have identified between Jesus and James is that of relatives and kinsmen. We cannot specify the relationship any further. He is

---

[87] This is seen from the lists of the names of the twelve apostles, where Peter is always placed first (Matt 10:2-4; Mark 3:16-19; Luke 6:14-16). Even more significant is the way Paul and Barnabas are named in the Acts of the Apostles. At the beginning of the missionary journeys Barnabas is mentioned first. Later on the journey Paul is first, giving the impression that Paul had assumed leadership of the mission (compare Acts 13:2 with 13:13 and 13:42).

associated with Jesus in Galilee. As a kinsman, James also comes from Nazareth. Like Jesus, he was brought up within the religious world of Judaism, honoring its religious traditions and sharing in its cultic life. This conforms to the way the gospel narratives portray James in association with his brothers and Jesus in the synagogue of Nazareth on a Sabbath. They are also present at a wedding celebration in another town of Galilee, Cana.

We have argued for care in not making an automatic identification between the literary presentation and the historical reality. An examination of the independent literary traditions of all four canonical gospels, as well as the Gospel of Thomas, shows that there is little to support a supposed opposition or hostility between Jesus and his family. To see them as either opponents of Jesus or having no association with him during his ministry is a false reading of the evidence. Instead, the traditions show a rhetorical intention that wishes to show how groups (such as the disciples) developed and struggled in coming to an understanding of Jesus' identity. The same must have been the case with James and Jesus' brothers. The independent traditions of the Synoptic Gospels and the Gospel of Thomas (and even the Gospel of John in its own way) agree that James and his brothers are challenged first and foremost to place the carrying out of God's will first in their lives.

CHAPTER TWO

Leader of the Jerusalem Community: James in the Acts of the Apostles and Letters of Paul

> "Would you tell me, please, which way I ought to walk from here?"
> "That depends a good deal on where you want to get to," said the Cat.
> "I don't much care where—" said Alice.
> "Then it doesn't matter which way you walk," said the Cat.
> "—so long as I get somewhere," Alice added as an explanation.
> "Oh, you're sure to do that," said the Cat,
> "if you only walk long enough."[1]

This chapter examines the evidence for the character and role of James within the context of the early Christian community after the death, resurrection, and ascension of Jesus. The sources for James are confined to the Acts of the Apostles (which contains a few references) and the letters of Paul. Fortunately these are two very different types of writings with two very distinct intentions. By remaining true to the literary nature of each writing and its intention we shall be able to use both sources to throw light on each other, and from that combined examination we can construct a reliable picture of the character of James in those early decades of the Christian movement.

It is urgent that we respect the methodological way of proceeding. In most studies that attempt to reconcile Acts with Paul's perspective the tendency has been to accept one as historical in preference to the other. Our attempt here is to remain true to the literary nature and intent of each of the writings and to unearth the rich tapestry that lies hidden beneath the text. In this chapter we will try to allow Acts and the letters of Paul to interface with and illuminate each other. A picture of James of Jerusalem will emerge from this examination.

---

[1] Lewis Carroll, *Alice's Adventures in Wonderland,* Books of Wonder (New York: William Morrow & Co., [1866] 1992) 89–90.

The Literary Genre of the Acts of the Apostles and the Writings of Paul

Our understanding of the history of the early Christian Church depends on the letters of Paul and the Acts of the Apostles. Many problems arise in any attempt to reconcile these two independent sources. The way to resolve many of the issues and apparent contradictions that emerge is to remain true to their rhetorical intent, their way of presentation, and their literary genre.

Paul's Letters

Paul's writings are undoubtedly the foundational documents for the early Christian church. They were the first writings of the New Testament to make their appearance. At the same time, they give us a beautiful entry and insight into the thought of Christians at the beginning of the second half of the first century C.E. and the issues that were of special importance to them. Of the thirteen letters traditionally attributed to Paul, only seven are generally agreed by scholars to have come directly from Paul, namely, Romans, 1 and 2 Corinthians, Galatians, Philippians, 1 Thessalonians, and Philemon. The other six letters—the second letter to the Thessalonians, Ephesians, Colossians, as well as the Pastoral Letters (1 and 2 Timothy and Titus)—are writings whose authenticity is questioned since the thought and teaching belong to a period two to three decades after Paul's death.

In interpreting Paul's letters it is important to bear in mind that their literary genre is that of the letter with a particular rhetorical intent. In a letter it is not Paul's purpose to present a history of early Christianity or to provide us with a systematic treatment of his own theology or the theology of his opponents. Instead, Paul's rhetorical intent is to instruct the young communities he had founded more deeply in the Christian faith and way of life. Had there been no problems, Paul would never have written to them. Most of what Paul says is an attempt to correct serious errors and abuses that had crept into these communities since Paul had founded or visited them a few years earlier. In most instances these writings are Paul's pastoral response to concrete situations and problems and must be interpreted against this background.

The Letter to the Galatians

The letter to the Galatians is probably the most important of Paul's letters for our study of the character of James, and it presents some interesting challenges when we try to correlate its reference to certain events with that of Acts. In interpreting the letter to the Galatians it is important to bear in mind its pastoral and polemical intent.

A reconstruction of the historical background of events that can be inferred from this letter shows Paul writing to Christian communities he had founded in the Roman province of Galatia in Asia Minor, or modern Turkey. Most commentators assign this letter to the period of Paul's third missionary journey, toward the end of the 50s C.E. Although it was written at the same time as the letter to the Romans and deals with the same issue concerning the role of the Jewish Law on the path to salvation, the two letters have a decidedly different tone. The letter to the Romans is irenic, since Paul is introducing himself and his theology to a church he hopes to visit soon. The letter to the Galatians, on the other hand, is polemical and combative, since Paul is defending his views against the attacks of those who have come into the community and are preaching a message different from his own. Paul's opponents, who are Jewish Christians and are referred to as "Judaizers" by scholars, were making inroads into these communities, distorting and undermining Paul's basic understanding of the relationship of the Christian and the Jewish Law. Basic to Paul's whole understanding of his relationship to the person of Jesus Christ was that salvation came through Christ, who had set the believer free from the demands of the Jewish Law. Salvation is not earned through obedience to the stipulations of the Law. Instead, it is granted freely through faith in Jesus Christ. Because Paul is reacting strongly to those who are destroying all he has built, his letter bears a strong polemical tone. While this letter was written in the late 50s and was reacting to events that were occurring then, Paul justified his approach and position by revisiting events that occurred ten years earlier when he visited Jerusalem and reached an accord with the Jerusalem leadership regarding his mission to the Gentiles. What Paul has to say about his relationship with the Jerusalem leadership must be interpreted against that background. It is not Paul's intent to give a historical, objective account of what happened. Instead, he presents a rhetorically and emotionally charged attack against his opponents. This must be kept in mind when trying to coordinate what Paul says here with what is contained in Acts.[2]

The Acts of the Apostles

Before we examine what Acts says about James, it is important to consider its literary genre. As mentioned in the previous chapter, understanding

---

[2] See Pierre-Antoine Bernheim, *James, Brother of Jesus* (London: SCM Press, 1997) 131.

the literary genre of any writing is basic to the historical critical method and is essential for understanding and interpreting this writing.

Acts is the second part of a two volume work that commenced with the Gospel of Luke. To capture this idea of a two-volume work we refer to these writings as Luke-Acts. The writer wished to show how God's salvation, which began in the past through God's revelation to Israel, has now been brought to fulfillment in the ministry, teaching, and saving death of Jesus and is then carried to the ends of the earth by the followers of Jesus. The theme of the Gospel of Luke is captured in the sentence "Today this scripture (in reference to Isa 61:1-2) has been fulfilled in your hearing" (Luke 4:21). The gospel focuses on Jesus, who brought to completion in his person the teaching and hopes of the Hebrew Scriptures. On the other hand, the theme and focus of Acts can be expressed through this sentence: "But you will receive power when the Holy Spirit has come upon you; and you will be my witnesses in Jerusalem, in all Judea and Samaria, and to the ends of the earth" (Acts 1:8).

The purpose of Luke-Acts emerges from a closer analysis of the story-line that unfolds in the two volumes. The Gospel of Luke remained faithful to the basic storyline of his source, the Gospel of Mark. Mark developed the storyline according to a geographical structure.[3] Using this geographical structure, Luke enlarges his horizon to create an account that gives voice to his narrative theme, namely that God's salvation was promised in the past but has now been brought through Jesus' ministry and extended through his followers to the ends of the earth. For Luke, geography remains an essential tool for developing this theme. The city of Jerusalem takes on a symbolic role as the place of God's salvation. Luke opens his narrative at the Temple in Jerusalem with the announcement from the angel that Zechariah's wife Elizabeth is to give birth to a son. Thus the author (Luke) shows how the promises made by God in the past are brought to fulfillment in the birth of Jesus. Luke uses the stylistic feature of hymns to provide the connection with the past: Mary, Zechariah, Elizabeth, and Simeon all draw on the Old Testament to show how God's promises in the past are now unfolding and reaching their fulfillment with the birth of Jesus. God's salvation that comes through Jesus begins in the very center of the religious life of Israel, namely Jerusalem and its Temple.

---

[3] The story of the Gospel of Mark opened in Judea at the Jordan River (1:1-13). Jesus then moved to Galilee, where he conducted a ministry of preaching and healing (1:14–4:34). Extending his ministry around the Sea of Galilee (4:35–8:26), Jesus moves to the northernmost part of the territory to Caesarea Philippi, where Peter confesses Jesus to be the Messiah (8:27–9:1). From there he travels on a journey toward Jerusalem (9:2–10:52), and finally reaches Jerusalem, the place of his death and resurrection (11:1–16:8).

In the rest of the gospel, Luke continues to focus on the centrality of Jerusalem in the realm of salvation. Now God's salvation is communicated to the human race through the person of Jesus in his death and resurrection, which replaces the Temple of Jerusalem as the seat of salvation for humanity. At the center of the gospel Luke develops Jesus' journey to Jerusalem to show Jesus' intent to reach the place where God's plan will reach fulfillment. While the journey to Jerusalem comprises two chapters in the Gospel of Mark (9:2–10:52), it occupies some ten chapters in the Gospel of Luke (9:51–19:27). The gospel concludes in Jerusalem with the death and resurrection of Jesus. Acts opens where the gospel ended, in the city of Jerusalem, with the message of salvation going forth to the ends of the earth according to Jesus' instructions (Acts 1:8). Acts offers a stage-by-stage description of the spread of this message of salvation from Jerusalem, through Judea and Samaria to the rest of Palestine, then throughout Asia Minor and Europe until it finally reaches Rome itself, regarded as "the ends of the earth" (Acts 1:8).

It is noteworthy that Acts concludes with the scene of Paul under house arrest in Rome. The author comments: "He lived there two whole years at his own expense" (Acts 28:30). Nothing is said about what ultimately happened to Paul. Was he released, or was he put to death? The author shows that it is not within his purview to provide a biographical account of Paul's life; his focus is rather on the message of salvation, which the messengers of Jesus are spreading. As with the Gospel of Mark, which ended in an abrupt way in order to involve the reader in the transmission of the story, so Luke-Acts also ends on an open note in which the writer extends a challenge to the reader to continue the work of the apostles in spreading the message of salvation to "the ends of the earth" (1:8).

One aspect that is important for the interpretation of Acts emerges from the above presentation. Despite its name, the Acts of the Apostles is not really an account of the deeds and actions of the apostles. As we saw in describing Paul, the author did not provide any further details about what happened to him. The same is true in the description of the other apostles. The writer opens the narrative by showing the need to replace the person of Judas with another follower of Jesus so that the inner group of the Twelve would be restored to its symbolic value. The disciples do this by choosing Matthias (1:12-26). After this, very little is said of any of the Twelve apart from John and Peter. John is not mentioned again after Acts 4:23. Peter, likewise, after filling center stage in most of the first part of the narrative, leaves Jerusalem in Acts 12:17. Apart from Peter's presence at the Council of Jerusalem (Act 15:14), nothing more is said of him. The same is true of the figure of James, as we will observe. He is present among the brothers in the opening scene of Acts (1:14). When Peter leaves Jerusalem, he informs James that he is leaving (12:17). James is presented as the leader of the community in Jerusalem in Acts 15:13-29. Finally, James suggests that Paul undertake a Nazirite vow (Acts 21:17-26).[4] Thereafter James disappears from the scene. Consequently the Twelve, John, Peter, James, and finally Paul, all vanish from the narrative. They are subservient to the message of salvation that continues to unfold.

Luke had demonstrated his intent in the prologue to his gospel (Luke 1:1-4), which resembles stylistically the way historians of the Greco-Roman world introduced their works.[5] A comparison of Luke's prologue with Flavius Josephus' prologue in his work *Against Apion* shows a number of interesting parallels: both speak about how they went about composing their works, the sources they used, and their desire to express the truth in what they communicate. This demonstrates that Luke consciously conforms his writing to all the tenets of a historical writing of that time. Another significant feature that Luke-Acts holds in common with Greco-Roman historiography is the composition of frequent speeches. These speeches are a literary device through which the writer communicates his message and intention and draws the narrative forward. In these speeches the author puts into the mouths of the characters the way in which he/she perceives the speaker feeling and thinking at that particular time.[6]

Luke says that in composing his gospel it is his intent "to write an orderly account . . . so that you may know the truth concerning the things about which you have been instructed" (1:3-4). For Luke the truth is intimately associated with the religious message that is presented. It is not history in our understanding of the term that Luke is intent on presenting. He uses sources and historical events in the service of his theological message.[7]

---

[4] See Chapter Two n. 52 for an explanation of the Nazirite vow.

[5] See, for example, Josephus' prologue at the beginning of each of the two volumes of *Against Apion* (*C.Ap.* 1:1-3; *C.Ap.* 2:1).

[6] Henry J. Cadbury, "The Speeches in Acts," in Frederick John Foakes Jackson and Kirsopp Lake, eds., *The Beginnings of Christianity, Part 1: The Acts of the Apostles,* Vol. 5, *Additional Notes to the Commentary* (London: Macmillan, 1933) 402–27, and Martin Dibelius, *Studies in the Acts of the Apostles,* ed. Heinrich Greeven, trans. Mary Ling (London: SCM Press, 1956) 138–91, have examined these speeches in detail and shown clearly how they are the work of the author.

[7] Robert C. Tannehill, *The Narrative Unity of Luke-Acts: A Literary Interpretation,* Volume Two: *The Acts of the Apostles* (Philadelphia: Fortress, 1994) 3–4, argues that "we must study Acts in terms of 'narrative rhetoric' . . . because the story is constructed to influence its readers or hearers and because there are particular literary techniques used for this purpose."

While Luke's intent is to present a theological understanding of the growth and spread of the Christian movement, this does not mean that his theological vision excludes a historical awareness and concern. His historical concerns are to be judged according to the tenets of his world. One way in which the historical reliability of Acts may be assessed is through a comparison with the writings of Paul.[8] It is not a matter of considering that Paul is historical over against Acts. Rather, each must be judged according to its own rhetorical intent to discern the historicity behind the narrative or polemic. In the course of this examination of James as leader of the church of Jerusalem we will first examine the text of Acts, then refer to Paul's letters, especially the letter to the Galatians, as a way of gaining deeper insight into the historical reality behind the events described.

With this understanding of literary genre and the intent of Acts and the writings of Paul, we turn to examine what information these writings give us with regard to the character of James.

Jesus' Family as Believers (Acts 1:14)

In Acts, Jesus' family is counted among Jesus' disciples. This picture conforms to the one that emerged from our examination of the gospels, where Jesus' family was not portrayed as hostile to Jesus. In the gospels James was always mentioned first among Jesus' brothers, which led to the presumption that he was the most important family member. Acts develops his important role as leader of the Jerusalem church.

After telling of the ascension of Jesus (Acts 1:6-11), the narrator presents Jesus' followers returning to Jerusalem "to the room upstairs where they were staying" (1:13). He lists the names of the eleven disciples (the Twelve minus Judas the betrayer). In comparing this list of names to the one in the gospel (Luke 6:14-16) we note that the order of the names varies slightly. In Acts the order is "Peter, John, James, and Andrew," while in the gospel the sequence is "Peter, Andrew, James, and John." This change in order arises from the fact that in Acts Peter and John emerge as the most important and influential members of the group of the Twelve. Luke remains true to the tradition of placing the more important names first.

Luke notes that the "eleven" disciples were accompanied by "certain women, including Mary the mother of Jesus, as well as his brothers" (Acts 1:14). Together they spend their time in prayer in preparation for the fulfillment of Jesus' farewell promise of the outpouring of the Spirit (1:8).

---

[8] See Bernheim, *James, Brother of Jesus,* 140.

This picture of the mother of Jesus and his brothers conforms to the way in which they were presented in the gospels, namely as believers. The idea of the brothers undergoing a conversion as a result of an appearance of the risen Jesus is without merit. The worst that could be said is that they struggled to come to a full understanding of Jesus' identity and were unable to make a deep faith commitment to him. There was nothing different in this struggle from the way in which Jesus' disciples also wrestled with their understanding and commitment. Too much has been made of Paul's statement in 1 Cor 15:7 ("Then he appeared to James, then to all the apostles"), which has been interpreted as a reference to the "conversion" of James from unbeliever to believer. That is a very selective reading of the text. Why is the same argument not made of the reference to the apostles in the very next phrase of the same verse?

In the perspective of the writer of Acts, the family believes in Jesus much as the Twelve do. In line with the way Luke has referred to the family of Jesus before, he (unlike Mark and Matthew) does not mention the names of Jesus' brothers. This is why it is something of a surprise when Luke introduces the name of James in Acts 12:17. There has been no preparation for James in the context of the narrative. However, that further adds to the impression that James must have been extraordinarily well known in the early church, so that when he is simply named Luke presumes that readers would automatically understand to whom he is referring.

James as Leader of the Jerusalem Church (Acts 12:17; Gal 1:17-19; 2:7-9)

Acts 12:17

The first reference to James in Acts occurs in the context of Herod Agrippa I's violent attack against the church leadership in Jerusalem (Acts 12:1-4). James, the brother of John (and son of Zebedee) and one of the Twelve, was arrested and put to death (12:2). This event can be dated to 44 C.E. Peter was likewise arrested and put in prison. The author notes how the community of believers prayed fervently to God (12:5). According to the narrative, Peter was miraculously delivered from prison (12:6-11). On his escape Peter went to the house of "Mary, the mother of John whose other name was Mark, where many had gathered and were praying" (12:12). Reference is made for the first time to a John Mark (in distinction to John the Baptist and John the son of Zebedee, the brother of James). This is the narrator's way of preparing the reader for the role of this John Mark, a cousin of Barnabas and companion of Paul and Barnabas during the first part of their first missionary journey.

Because he had escaped from prison, Peter cannot stay in Jerusalem and is forced to flee. He instructs those at the gate of Mary's house, "Tell this to James and to the believers" (12:17). The *NRSV* translation "the believers" reproduces the Greek *adelphois* ("brothers"). This word (singular *adelphos*) could be interpreted in two different ways. It was used previously to refer to the family of Jesus, and we have interpreted it as referring to the kinsmen of Jesus who belonged to the circle of his wider family. The fact that the name of James occurs here together with the reference to the brothers adds further weight to the interpretation that the narrator is referring to Jesus' family. There is a second way in which it can be interpreted (and this is how the translators of the *NRSV* read it). This view sees it referring figuratively to the believers and followers of Jesus as "brothers." This is a further indication of the variety of ways in which the word is understood.[9] If this word *adelphos* is taken as referring to the family of Jesus, it is an indication that they exercise an important role already within the body of believers.

The fact that James is the only named person Peter requests be told about his escape from prison and his decision to leave Jerusalem shows James' importance within the body of believers. Peter's simple instruction has been variously interpreted. It has been read in the sense that Peter on escaping from Jerusalem hands over leadership of the church to James. The difficulty with this interpretation can be seen from subsequent events: Why does Peter not take charge of the Council of Jerusalem in Acts 15 when he is present there? Instead, James is the one who gives expression to the consensus of the church. The problem with this interpretation is that it falls into the realm of *ethnocentrism*,[10] to which attention has been drawn previously.[11]

Such an interpretation uses the present-day monarchical form of episcopacy that has developed over two thousand years to explain the leadership of the early church. Concretely, use of this model portrays Peter as a monarchical bishop who hands over his authority to James, who then becomes his successor as the next bishop of Jerusalem. This is the same fallacy that Eusebius (c. 260–339 C.E., the first church historian and bishop of Caesarea in Palestine) made when he summarized the tradition and sources he had received about James. He referred to James, "the brother of the Lord, to whom

---

[9] John Painter, *Just James: The Brother of Jesus in History and Tradition* (Minneapolis: Fortress, 1999) 43, argues here for the understanding of "brothers" as referring to believers in general. However, I think that given the context of the reference to James the more logical interpretation is to read it in reference to Jesus' kin.

[10] See Bruce J. Malina, *The New Jerusalem in the Revelation of John: The City as Symbol of Life with God* (Collegeville: The Liturgical Press, 2000) 5.

[11] See Chapter One n. 72.

the throne of the bishopric in Jerusalem had been allotted by the Apostles."[12] The very words "throne of the bishopric in Jerusalem" show Eusebius reading back his world of the fourth century into the first century.

The best way to resolve the issue is to be faithful to the development of the early church itself and to the role of the apostles and of Peter that is presented by all the traditions of the New Testament. Without doubt the traditions of the gospels are unanimous in presenting Peter as the leader of the group of the twelve apostles. His name is always mentioned first in the list of the Twelve and he is always presented as the spokesperson of the group (see Mark 8:29). Even in the traditions behind the Gospel of John the same role of leadership is indirectly acknowledged for Peter, even though the narrator portrays an ever-sharpening contrast between Peter and the Beloved Disciple.[13] In the opening of Acts, Peter again always takes the initiative and speaks on behalf of the other twelve apostles. Peter's name is mentioned first in the list of the eleven (Acts 1:13), Peter is the one who asks the disciples to choose a successor to Judas to restore the group to twelve (Acts 1:15-26), and Peter is the one who addresses the crowd after the events of Pentecost (Acts 2:14-36).

Peter is undoubtedly the leader of the group. Since all the traditions at the end of the first century acknowledge this role, they must undoubtedly reflect the reality at that time. At the same time, from the very beginning the Jesus movement was not something static but dynamic and missionary. Jesus was a wandering preacher who moved from village to village. When he chose his twelve disciples Jesus sent them out to continue exactly what he had been doing: preaching and healing (Luke 9:1-6).

Jesus' farewell instructions to his followers at the time of the ascension reiterate this missionary dimension of the Twelve. Two independent traditions (found in the Gospel of Matthew and Acts) testify to this missionary dimension of the Twelve after Jesus has left them: In the Gospel of Matthew Jesus says: "All authority in heaven and on earth has been given to me. Go therefore and make disciples of all nations, baptizing them in the name of the Father and of the Son and of the Holy Spirit . . ." (Matt 28:18-19), and in Acts Jesus says: "You will be my witnesses in Jerusalem, in all Judea and Samaria, and to the ends of the earth" (Acts 1:8).

This all leads to the conclusion that Peter's role was not that of a static residential organizer of a specific church, but rather that of a missionary whose task was, as given him by the risen Jesus, to carry the message of salvation to the ends of the earth.

---

[12] Eusebius, *Hist. eccl.* 2:23, 1-3 [Lake, LCL].

[13] See Raymond E Brown, et al., "Peter in the Gospel of John," in *Peter in the New Testament* (Minneapolis: Augsburg; New York: Paulist, 1973) 147.

We return now to the picture of Acts 12:17. When Peter gives the instruction "tell this to James and to the believers," he is not handing over his leadership to James. He is simply asking his hearers to communicate to James and his brothers that he has escaped from prison and will be leaving to continue his missionary ministry. Acts confirms this when it states a few verses later: "Then Peter went down from Judea to Caesarea and stayed there" (Acts 12:19). The reference to Judea is a deliberate reminder of the risen Jesus instructing his disciples to begin their mission from Jerusalem, then to Judea (Acts 1:8). The narrator shows how Peter is fulfilling that command and remains true to his role as missionary leader.

Galatians 1:17-19 and 2:7-9

James' role as distinct from Peter's is that of residential leader of the Jerusalem church. This is not something he has suddenly inherited from Peter. If we take into account information that we glean from Paul's letters, particularly the letter to the Galatians, Paul shows that James was already exercising such a leadership role in Jerusalem even while Peter was present there. Paul talks about his first visit to Jerusalem three years after his conversion when he says "I did not see any other apostle except James the Lord's brother" (Gal 1:17-19). Paul's first visit to Jerusalem would be dated somewhere around 38 C.E.[14] When Paul goes up to Jerusalem for the first time he presents himself as an apostle equal to "those who were already apostles before me" (Gal 1:17). For Paul the essence of an apostle was having received a call and being sent on a mission by the risen Jesus ("Paul an apostle—sent neither by human commission nor from human authorities, but through Jesus Christ . . ." [Gal 1:1; see also Gal 1:11]).[15] Paul did not present himself as inferior to the Jerusalem leaders, but like them he claims

---

[14] Scholars vary in their attempt to provide a chronology of Paul's life. There are some certain dates from which one can work backward and forward. Among the "established dates" that help in situating certain of Paul's activities are: the death of Herod Agrippa I in 44 C.E., the presence of Gallio the proconsul of Achaia in 50–51 C.E. or 51–52 C.E., and Felix as Procurator of Palestine in 58–60 C.E. Using these pointers as a means to identify some of Paul's activities occurring at the same time one is able to build up a chronology of Paul's life and activity. One would place Paul's conversion around 35 C.E. with his first visit to Jerusalem three years later (around 38 C.E.) and his second visit "after fourteen years" (Gal 2:1; i.e., fourteen years after his conversion, or around 49 C.E.). See John L. McKenzie, "Paul," *Dictionary of the Bible* (London and Dublin: Geoffrey Chapman, 1966) 648–51; and Calvin J. Roetzel, "Paul," in David Noel Freedman, ed., *Eerdmans Dictionary of the Bible* (Grand Rapids: Eerdmans, 2000) 1016–20.

[15] The English word "apostle" is derived from the Greek *apostolos,* which designates "messengers with extraordinary status, especially of God's *messenger, envoy*" (BDAG,

a mission that came to him from the risen Lord. It is to be noted that Paul makes a clear distinction between "the Twelve" and an "apostle." Paul never claims to be one of the Twelve, but he does claim the role of an apostle equal to that of all the other apostles. The Twelve were a historical group who had been with the person of Jesus, as Peter says in Acts: "all the time that the Lord Jesus went in and out among us, beginning from the baptism of John until the day when he was taken up from us" (Acts 1:21-22).[16]

Paul's visit lasted fifteen days. During this time he stayed with Peter, but he also met James, whom Paul identifies as an apostle: "but I did not see any other apostle except James the Lord's brother" (Gal 1:19). In this way Paul acknowledges that James too had received a call and mission from the risen Lord. Later, when writing to the Corinthians, Paul gives testimony to the appearance of the risen Jesus and he specifically mentions James again in connection with the group of apostles: "Then he appeared to James, then to all the apostles" (1 Cor 15:7). In these few verses Paul claims a role for himself as apostle that is equal in status to that of the apostles of Jerusalem. Among these he includes James.

In the second chapter of Galatians, Paul refers to a second visit he made to Jerusalem, this time some fourteen years after his conversion, which would place it around 49 C.E. (Gal 2:1-10). Paul visits Jerusalem together with Barnabas and Titus (2:1) with the purpose of gaining acceptance from the Jerusalem leadership for his missionary activity among the Gentiles. Paul again refers to the missionary dimensions of Peter's role and compares it to his own missionary activities.

Using Paul's account to throw light on these descriptions from Acts helps one to conclude that James was an already recognized leader within the community of Jerusalem before Peter left there. To my mind the clearest way to understand the evidence is to see that, in the developing leadership within the early Christian church, James the brother of the Lord exercised residential leadership of the Jerusalem community (and by implication leadership over the Jewish Christian communities) while Peter remained true to his missionary role as the apostle who has been sent to bring the message of salvation to the ends of the earth. This traditional viewpoint is

---

apostolos, 122). The Greek noun *apostolos* is derived from the verb *apostellein,* which means "to dispatch someone for the achievement of some objective, *send away/out*" (BDAG, *apostellō*, 120).

[16] The relationship between the Twelve and the apostles can be expressed in this way: all the Twelve were also apostles (because they had been sent on a mission by the risen Lord). On the other hand, not all the apostles were among the Twelve (since not all the apostles had been with the historical Jesus from his baptism to his ascension).

supported by the first letter of Peter, which ends with greetings being sent from Rome, referred to symbolically as Babylon (see 1 Pet 5:13). With the arrival of Paul (the missionary to the Gentiles) and Peter (the missionary to the Jews) in Rome, "the ends of the earth," the instructions of Jesus in Acts 1:8 are brought to fulfillment. The community of Rome becomes the center of importance in contrast to Jerusalem, since the leadership of the church at Rome is the one that claims the role of continuing the leadership authority of Peter and Paul and not the church leaders in Jerusalem.

Summary

Acts and Galatians indicate clearly that James exercises the role of organizational leadership in the Jerusalem community. It is a role he has been exercising for some time and continues to exercise until his death some twenty years later (62 C.E.). Peter has not handed over leadership to him; rather, Peter continues to fulfill the role assigned to him by Jesus as leader of the whole Christian community and missionary *par excellence* in bringing the message of Jesus to the ends of the earth.

The Interface of Jesus' Followers with Jews and Gentiles

Before we continue with the examination of the texts of Acts and Paul relating to James, it is important to consider the interface of the followers of Jesus with Jews and Gentiles in order to understand the background to the disputes that gave rise to the so-called Council of Jerusalem in Acts 15 (49 C.E.).

Israel's Purity Rules

In recent times remarkably new and important insights have been brought to bear on the way Israel understood the world through the vision of her faith. Basing themselves on models that have emerged from sociology and social anthropology, and applying these insights and approaches to the biblical world and biblical texts, scholars such as Bruce Malina,[17] Jerome Neyrey,[18] and John Elliott[19] have helped to unlock the understanding

---

[17] See, for example, Bruce J. Malina and Richard L. Rohrbaugh, *Social-Science Commentary on the Synoptic Gospels* (2nd ed. Minneapolis: Fortress, 2003).

[18] See, for example, Jerome H. Neyrey, *Honor and Shame in the Gospel of Matthew* (Louisville: Westminster John Knox, 1998).

[19] See, for example, John H. Elliott, *What is Social-Scientific Criticism?* Guides to Biblical Study (Minneapolis: Fortress, 1993); idem *1 Peter,* AB 37B (New York: Doubleday, 2000).

of the biblical world and its faith in a phenomenally important way. Careful attention to these scholars and the results of their scholarship provides a means to understand James' approach and perspective more fully. Studies arising from this social-scientific perspective have shown the increasing importance that cultic, moral, and social purity laws played in the lives of Jews, especially during the time of the emergence of the Christian movement.[20] The function of purity laws was to establish order and to preserve the right relationship between the Israelite people as a nation or as individuals and their God as well as the members of the community.[21]

Purity rules bring order into the world. They divide the world between those who have access to God and those who do not. They also determine what one must do in order to preserve that access. The purity laws were an essential aspect of the socialization process for the people of Israel. They gave the Israelites their identity. These purity rules said: "This is who we are. We are a people in a special relationship with our God. These rules that we observe are rules that preserve this identity and at the same time they forge a bond among ourselves, giving us an identity that is different from those around us."

In effect these purity laws define "the boundaries within which those who belong to the people of Israel live. These purity laws become social markers defining the identity of all who belong to the same community."[22] This helps us to understand the approach of Jews to Gentiles in the first century. For the Jews their map of the world was defined clearly between themselves (who abided by certain purity laws) and all those outside (who did not abide by these laws). Interaction with Gentiles who did not abide by their rules would consequently make the Jews themselves impure, and numerous rituals were defined for what they would have to do in order to restore their state of purity.

---

[20] The work of Mary Douglas was to lay the basis for research on the importance of purity rules in Israel. See especially her *Purity and Danger: An Analysis of Concepts of Pollution and Taboo* (London: Routledge & Kegan Paul, 1966). See also George W. Buchanan, "The Role of Purity in the Structure of the Essene Sect," *RevQ* 4 (1963) 397–406; John H. Elliott, *The Elect and the Holy: An Exegetical Examination of 1 Peter 2:4-10 and the Phrase basileion hierateuma,* NovTSup 12 (Leiden: Brill, 1966); Jacob Neusner, *The Idea of Purity in Ancient Judaism,* SJLA 1 (Leiden: Brill, 1973); idem, "History and Purity in First-Century Judaism," *HR* 18 (1978) 1–17; and Bruce J. Malina, *The New Testament World: Insights from Cultural Anthropology* (Louisville: Westminster John Knox, 1993) 149–83. See also the recent work of Catherine M. Murphy in which she discusses the issue of purity in relation to John the Baptist (*John the Baptist: Prophet of Purity for a New Age,* Interfaces (Collegeville: Liturgical Press, 2003).

[21] See Malina, *The New Testament World: Insights from Cultural Anthropology,* 174.

[22] Patrick J. Hartin, *James,* SP 14 (Collegeville: Liturgical Press, 2003) 74.

Jewish Attitude toward Gentiles

There was no uniform attitude or approach by the Jews of the first century to the Gentiles or pagans of their time. Jewish views and approaches differed according to their time and location. This diversity in attitudes within the world of first-century Judaism is important for understanding the development of early Christianity. Second Temple Judaism in fact showed a variety of what we would call "Judaisms." Even the New Testament illustrates this perspective in its references to Pharisees, Sadducees, and Herodians interacting with Jesus. Besides these groups mentioned in the New Testament, we also have knowledge of the Dead Sea Scrolls community (the Essenes), the Zealots, the Samaritans, as well as the followers of Jesus and the followers of John the Baptist, all of whom claim to represent the true traditions of Israel.[23]

Central to the nature of Judaism is the importance given to the Hebrew Scriptures, which helps to define the group as belonging to and continuing the traditions of Israel. Certain traditions of early Christianity are also at pains to uphold this characteristic for themselves. These traditions are seen to reflect the essence of adherence to the Hebrew Scriptures and the desire for the community to see itself as remaining in Israel's traditions. Chief of these traditions foundational for early Christianity were those that comprised the Sermon on the Mount and the Letter of James.

Turning to the attitude exemplified by the Jews toward the Gentiles, one notices a variety of approaches.[24] In the Hebrew Scriptures there is, generally speaking, an attitude of understanding toward the pagans and their worship of many gods: "For all the peoples walk, each in the name of its god, but we will walk in the name of the LORD our God forever and ever" (Mic 4:5). The prophets envisaged that at the end of time the nations of the world would stream to Jerusalem, where they would join in the worship of the one God on Mount Sinai (see Isa 2:2-3 and 25:6).

---

[23] Jacob Neusner, "Introduction: What is Judaism?" in Bruce Chilton and Jacob Neusner, eds., *The Brother of Jesus: James the Just and His Mission* (Louisville: Westminster John Knox, 2001) 4, gives an insightful description of four characteristic features that mark the essentials of what is meant when something is characterized as "Judaism" in the first century.

[24] The following studies on the relationship between Jews and Gentiles are noteworthy: Louis Feldman, *Jew and Gentile in the Ancient World: Attitudes and Interactions from Alexander to Justinian* (Princeton: Princeton University Press, 1993); Martin Goodman, *Mission and Conversion: Proselytizing in the Religious History of the Roman Empire* (Oxford: Clarendon Press, 1994); Paul R. Trebilco, *Jewish Communities in Asia Minor* (Cambridge: Cambridge University Press, 1991).

In the first century C.E. there is evidence that there was also a variety of attitudes toward the admission of Gentiles into the communities of Jewish believers. The commonly accepted viewpoint has been the one that considers the Judaism of the time of Jesus as a strongly proselytizing movement. This conclusion is largely supported by the Jesus saying: "Woe to you, scribes and Pharisees, hypocrites! For you cross sea and land to make a single convert, and you make the new convert twice as much a child of hell as yourselves" (Matt 23:15).

However, the view that this was a proselytizing[25] period has largely been discredited by more recent studies.[26] While proselytes were not as actively sought as has been proposed, those identified as "those who feared God" were more readily accepted within the context of a Jewish synagogue community. The interest of Gentiles in forming part of a Jewish synagogue was social and cultural attraction more than purely a religious conversion. The ancient world did not have any analogous institution to that of the synagogue that was the heart of every Jewish community, where bonds were formed and a sense of community developed.

More of a concern to the Jews of the first century C.E. was the issue of eating with Gentiles, which would immediately invoke Israel's purity rules. To share a meal with another was a sacred form of hospitality and intimacy. Because purity laws, as we have seen, defined the boundaries of the community, to share a meal with a Gentile would breach every boundary that was essential for the Jewish identity to survive.[27] The various food regulations identified how to distinguish the world of God from the world of the profane. Those who adhered to the purity laws as regards food were intent on maintaining a clear division between the sacred and the profane. To share a meal with Gentiles for whom food regulations were meaningless

---

[25] A distinction is drawn in the Judaism of the first century C.E. between proselytes and "those who fear God." A proselyte is someone who is in the process of converting to Judaism, while "one who fears God" is someone who is interested in and attracted toward Judaism and its institutions, such as its synagogue, yet has no intention of converting to Judaism. Especially when Paul embarks on his missionary activity the narrator constantly draws attention to the makeup of the synagogues in the Diaspora as embracing "those who fear God *(hoi phoboumenoi ton theon)*" (Acts 13:16). Josephus also acknowledges the presence of this group: "Moreover, they were constantly attracting to their religious ceremonies multitudes of Greeks, and these they had in some measure incorporated with themselves" (*B.J.* 7:45 [Thackeray, LCL]).

[26] See Scot McKnight, *A Light among the Gentiles: Jewish Missionary Activity in the Second Temple Period* (Minneapolis: Fortress, 1991).

[27] See E. P. Sanders, "Jewish Association with Gentiles and Galatians 2:11-14," in Robert T. Fortna and Beverly R. Gaventa, eds., *The Conversation Continues: Studies in Paul and John in Honor of J. Louis Martyn* (Nashville: Abingdon, 1990) 170–88.

simply betrayed the very essence of their map of the world, where Jews endeavored to remain in the realm of the sacred. The Gentiles did not have the same map of the world. This was the problem that caused such heartache for Peter and James.

Early Divisions within the Community of the Followers of Jesus: Hellenists and Hebrews

Acts tends to paper over divisions within the early Christian community. There is no mention of the tension between Paul and Peter that Paul narrates in Gal 2:11-14. It is part of Luke's perspective to show the development of Christianity in an irenic way and to portray the early Christians as living in ideal, harmonious communities (see, for example, Acts 2:44-47). However, Acts does draw attention to the first dispute within the early Christian community and to the proposed solution. The dispute was between Hebrew-speaking and Greek-speaking followers of Jesus.[28] The Greek-speaking believers felt discriminated against in the daily distribution of food. To resolve the conflict the apostles appointed seven men to handle the food distribution to the Hellenists. These seven mark the beginning of the group called *diakonoi* ("deacons") in the early church. Their function, as their name indicates, is "to serve."

After the death of Stephen (one of the seven), the Hellenists felt threatened and most of their members migrated north to Antioch where they embarked on a very successful mission, now open to the Gentiles (Acts 11:19-26). Barnabas, whose name means "son of encouragement" (Acts 4:36-37), was sent by the Jerusalem church to Antioch (Acts 11:22) to oversee events there. This was a tough assignment because Barnabas would be representing the Jerusalem church. One of Barnabas' significant achievements was to go to Tarsus and invite Paul to join the community of Antioch (Acts 11:25-26). A comparison of these details with Paul's own account in the letter to the Galatians shows that Paul has a different memory of the events (see Gal 1:18-24).

The Beginnings of the Mission to the Gentiles (Acts 10:1-48; Gal 1:15-17)

In recounting the spread of the message beyond Jerusalem, Luke narrates three important initial events: the conversion of many Samaritans

---

[28] Acts 6:1-7 refers to them as "the Hebrews" and "the Hellenists" respectively.

(Acts 8:4-25), the baptism of the Ethiopian eunuch (8:26-40), and the con-version of Cornelius (10:1-48). The first two events were the result of the activity of Philip, one of the initial seven deacons. The conversion of the Samaritans and the Ethiopian eunuch are examples of the message of Chris-tianity reaching the perimeters of the world of Judaism. In many ways this is a reflection of the mission of Jesus who declared, "I was sent only to the lost sheep of the house of Israel" (Matt 15:24). In the traditions that lie be-hind the Gospel of Matthew, Jesus' task encompasses the reconstitution of the people of Israel. It is the same mission the letter of James endeavors to emulate.

Having reached the perimeters of the Jewish world with the conversion of Samaritans and the Ethiopian eunuch, the Christian mission first extends to the Gentile world with the conversion of Cornelius, "a centurion of the Italian Cohort" (Acts 10:1). In Luke's narrative Peter is responsible for ex-tending the mission beyond the borders of Israel to the Gentiles (Acts 10:47). While it is difficult to separate the legendary from the historical in this ac-count, what is important to discern is that the outreach to the Gentiles was a momentous event in the world of the followers of Jesus and only the leaders of the early Christian movement could have been the ones to lead it in this direction. Noteworthy in this account is the lack of any concern that Cor-nelius and the other male members of his family be circumcised. They were baptized and received the gift of the Holy Spirit without any conditions being imposed upon them, such as first becoming Jews.[29]

In the narrative of Acts, despite Peter's initial outreach to the Gentiles, it is Paul who becomes the missionary to the Gentiles.[30] Without doubt it was Paul's call that led to the rapid increase of the Christian movement, with vast numbers of Gentiles joining it.

While Acts does not consider the mission to the Gentiles exclusively Paul's right, Paul does interpret his mission in this way in his letter to the Galatians (Gal 2:9). Paul is intent on arguing against his opponents that his mission to the Gentiles came as the result of a revelation from God and that he undertook that mission without the direction of other Christian leaders (Gal 1:15-17).

---

[29] See Bernheim, *James, Brother of Jesus,* 161.

[30] The word "Gentiles" translates the Greek words *ta ethnē,* which refer to "people (or) groups foreign to a specific people (or) group" (BDAG, *ethnos,* 276). The Israelites divided the world into two groups of people: the Jews and everyone else, the latter identified as *goyim* (or *ta ethnē*). When dividing the world into "Jews and Gentiles" one is obviously looking at humanity through the eyes of the Jewish world. Literally it would mean "Jews and all other nations."

Both Acts and the letter to the Galatians agree that Paul's mission to the Gentiles came by means of a special revelation from God. This indeed demonstrates the special and momentous nature of the outreach. Only God could justify such a step. Paul, however, takes the argument further by claiming that he alone is the one to take the message to the Gentiles. While Acts shows evidence that this was not Paul's exclusive right, it does show that Paul devoted his missionary activity to bringing Gentiles into the community of believers.

James and the Council of Jerusalem (Acts 15:1-29; Gal 2:1-10)

The large numbers of Gentiles becoming believers as a result of Paul's missionary activity attracted the attention and concern of the Jerusalem church. This led to the convening of a meeting to resolve this issue. The two accounts we possess (Acts 15:1-29; Gal 2:1-10) are very different, and it is hard to achieve a harmonization of their visions. The relationship between these two texts has been the topic of lively and lengthy scholarly discussions. We will examine the two to gain insight into the resolution of the first major crisis within the context of early Christianity.

Galatians 2:1-10

Paul's letter to the Galatians presents the account of his discussion with the leaders of the Jerusalem Church in the form of a private conversation between himself and the "acknowledged leaders" (Gal 2:2). Luke, on the other hand, describes a clearly defined and structured council. The hand of Luke is clearly visible in this narrative. One would imagine that the gathering was more along the lines of a private meeting such as Paul describes (Gal 2:2). There the leaders of the Jerusalem community (James, Peter, John) meet with Paul, Barnabas, and Titus. It is also imaginable that Paul's accusers were present as well.

The background to the visit probably came from Paul's mission being challenged by "false believers secretly brought in, who slipped in to spy on the freedom we have in Christ Jesus, so that they might enslave us" (Gal 2:4). Paul says his visit to Jerusalem came "in response to a revelation" (Gal 2:2). He clearly wishes to indicate that he sees his mission firmly under God's guidance. Paul refers to the leaders in Jerusalem in a variety of ways: first he calls them "acknowledged leaders" (Gal 2:2); his tone changes slightly when he says: "those who were supposed to be acknowledged leaders (what they actually were make no difference to me; God shows no partiality)" (Gal 2:6); finally Paul identifies them as "James and

Cephas[31] (Peter) and John, who were acknowledged pillars" (Gal 2:9). Paul recognizes the way these leaders are acknowledged in the eyes of the followers of Jesus, particularly those in the Jerusalem community. However, his tone betrays hostility, for he stresses that a person's true status is not what is important in the eyes of humans, but rather how that person is viewed in God's eyes.

The image of "pillars" of the church in reference to James, Peter, and John is in line with the image of a building that is found in many New Testament traditions in reference to the Christian church: for example, Jesus is presented as the cornerstone (Mark 12:10; Matt 21:42; Luke 20:17), while the apostles are referred to as the foundation stones of the new Jerusalem ("And the wall of the city has twelve foundations, and on them are the twelve names of the twelve apostles of the Lamb" [Rev 21:14]). James, Peter, and John are seen as the firm support for the Christian church wherever it might extend.

Paul shows that the issue of circumcision was one of the problems of concern, but it had been resolved: "But even Titus, who was with me, was not compelled to be circumcised, though he was a Greek" (Gal 2:3). The outcome of the meeting was the mutual recognition of two separate missions: one to the Jews, the other to the Gentiles. Again Paul identifies his work as coming from God's grace, which is something the Jerusalem leadership is able to discern (Gal 2:9-10). The resolution of this meeting is presented as having been reached easily. But there does seem to be an underlying difference of perception in the agreement, a difference that will emerge later in a conflict between Paul and Peter (with James in the background) in Antioch (Gal 2:11-14). As Paul states the agreement (Gal 2:9-10), it envisages two missions: one to the circumcised (the Jews), the other to the uncircumcised (the Gentiles). James and Peter understood this to refer to two separate missions that were exclusive: Peter would restrict his mission only to the circumcised, while Paul's mission would be to the uncircumcised. In the mind of James and Peter the implication was clearly that Paul would not be evangelizing among the Jews. Paul, however, did not see it this way. While he saw his mission as embracing the Gentiles, he did not consider that it excluded the Jews. Both Paul's letters and Acts present his missionary activity as embracing Jew and Gentile. These different interpretations of the agreement would lead to further friction between "the pillars" and Paul.

---

[31] The identification of Peter by means of the Aramaic name *Cephas* is noteworthy in this context. The Greek word *Petros* (meaning stone) was understood to be "the Greek equivalent of the Aramaic *kēpā = kēphas*" (BDAG, *Petros*, 809). Paul probably uses the name Cephas here because that is the way in which the Jerusalem community referred to Peter.

Acts 15:1-29

As indicated in our consideration of Paul's account, the basic issue of Gentiles becoming Christians was not really the problem. Their ability to belong to the Christian movement was taken for granted. The Christian leadership probably saw it in a way analogous to the situation of Gentiles becoming Jews. If Gentiles were able to join Judaism, obviously Gentiles could become Christians. It was the further issue that gained center stage: What do these new converts to Christianity have to do and abide by when they become Christians?

The issue really concerned circumcision. In the account in Acts, Paul and Barnabas go up to Jerusalem as a result of certain individuals coming to Antioch and teaching: "Unless you are circumcised according to the custom of Moses, you cannot be saved" (Acts 15:1). A second issue arises as a consequence of the first, namely that if a man is circumcised he has to abide by the stipulations of the Mosaic Law. Those who belong to the party of the Pharisees go on to claim: "It is necessary for them to be circumcised and ordered to keep the law of Moses" (Acts 15:5). Since the church in Antioch had been established by Hellenists, the presence of "certain individuals from Judea" must indicate that "the Hebrews" have come to Antioch to reassert their authority over "the Hellenists."

The speeches in the narrative of Acts are compositions from the hand of Luke; nevertheless, a number of important insights emerge from these speeches. First of all, Peter's speech (Acts 15:7-11) reflects the account of the conversion of Cornelius (Acts 11:5-17). But in the composition of the speech Luke seems to have given expression to the theology of Paul: "and in cleansing their hearts by faith he has made no distinction between them and us" (Acts 15:9). In doing this so consciously, Luke indicates that there is no difference between the positions of Peter and Paul. Both unequivocally supported God's choice of the Gentiles for salvation and affirm that no demands are to be made of them regarding such things as circumcision.

The writer Luke presents a speech by James that situates James in a mediating position between Paul and the Jewish Christians (Acts 15:13-29). His decision is that "those Gentiles who are turning to God . . . (should) abstain only from things polluted by idols and from fornication and from whatever has been strangled and from blood" (Acts 15:19-20).

Four significant aspects emerge from James' speech as Luke has constructed it:

First of all, James sees the restoration of Israel taking place in the Jewish Christian community of Jerusalem. The speech is clearly Luke's construction, but that does not mean it does not authentically capture James' thoughts and perspectives.[32] The quotation of the text of Amos 9:11-12 and its interpretation are certainly in line with the way Jewish leadership in Jerusalem would have thought.[33] Luke presents James' argument as resting not on the Hebrew text, but on the Septuagint Greek of Amos 9:11-12.[34] The point here is that James began his argument by showing how God looked favorably on the Gentiles at the very beginning by choosing out of their midst a people for himself (Israel). The intent was (as Amos 9:11-12 indicates) that other nations would come to seek and acknowledge God. This would happen when God restored the people of Israel ("I will rebuild the dwelling of David that has fallen . . ." [Acts 15:16]) in the eschatological age. Jesus' coming began this restoration of the people of Israel. Consequently, James interprets the turning of the Gentiles to embrace Jesus' message as a fulfillment of Amos' prophecy. James says nothing about the need for circumcision in the Gentiles' acceptance of God and Jesus' message. In using this text from Amos, James indicates that the restoration of the people of Israel has begun in Jesus' ministry. As leader of the Christian Jews in Jerusalem, James envisages his role as continuing the work of his brother, Jesus, in restoring Israel. James does not foresee the establishment of a new religion. Rather he sees the religion of Israel being brought to its fulfillment. Gentile conversion would mean their inclusion within the world and religion of Israel.[35]

Second, James emerges in this passage as the organizational leader of the Jewish Christian community in Jerusalem. He is the one who brings the discussion to a conclusion and a decision. The apostles and elders accept his decision to send a letter to communicate the decision to the churches (Acts 15:22-29). The way Luke narrates the interface between the apostles, elders, and James is interesting. James takes the decision in the Jerusalem

---

[32] See Richard Bauckham, "James and the Jerusalem Church," in idem, ed., *The Book of Acts in its Palestinian Setting,* The Book of Acts in its First Century Setting, vol. 4 (Grand Rapids: Eerdmans, 1995) 415–80.

[33] See Richard Bauckham, "James and the Gentiles (Acts 15,13-21)," in Ben Witherington III, ed., *History, Literature, and Society in the Book of Acts* (Cambridge: Cambridge University Press, 1996) 154–84.

[34] The Hebrew text of Amos 9:11-12 reads as follows: "On that day I will raise up the booth of David that is fallen, and repair its breaches, and raise up its ruins, and rebuild it as in the days of old; in order that they may possess the remnant of Edom and all the nations who are called by my name, says the LORD who does this." One can see that James' argument could not be made from this Masoretic text.

[35] As Scot McKnight ("A Parting within the Way: Jesus and James on Israel and Purity," in Bruce Chilton and Craig A. Evans, eds., *James the Just and Christian Origins* [Leiden, Boston, and Köln: Brill, 1999]) says: "That is, James sees the Judaism he leads to be primarily, if not totally, an expression of a restored Israel and not a separate religion—and this at least fifteen years after the ministry of Jesus."

community and the apostles and elders are those who communicate this decision to the wider church. This again supports the contention that James exercises organizational leadership within Jerusalem while the apostles continue to play their role as missionary leaders for the wider church.

Third, James endorses Peter's role and position: Many scholars have tried to argue that because James is the one to make the decision he has assumed Peter's role in the Christian community. That cannot be inferred from this passage. James refers to Peter's experience to justify the decision he has reached. He does not refer to Paul's position at all. James acknowledges Peter's position, especially if Peter is seen to be the apostle to the circumcised as Paul acknowledges (". . . when they saw that I had been entrusted with the gospel for the uncircumcised, just as Peter had been entrusted with the gospel for the circumcised [for he who worked through Peter making him an apostle to the circumcised also worked through me in sending me to the Gentiles]" [Gal 2:7-8]). Peter's argument is the one to which the party of those demanding circumcision would more likely give attention. This supports the view presented here that Peter continues to enjoy his position of leadership as missionary to the Jews. As we have argued, he did not abrogate his position of leadership to James.

Finally, the Lukan construction of James' speech contains a further implication. Not only are male Gentile Christians excused from being circumcised, all Gentile converts are also freed from the stipulations of the Jewish ritual laws. There are only four provisions they are called upon to uphold. These are known as the Apostolic Decree.

While Luke's presentation of the Council of Jerusalem is much more expansive and theological than Paul's version, there is no real contradiction between the two accounts. They both communicate the fundamental perspective that two missions were operating within the early Christian community: one by Peter to the circumcised, the other by Paul to the uncircumcised. The fundamental issue of whether Gentiles were to be circumcised was resolved by freeing them from this requirement and in the end acknowledging that they did not first have to become Jews when they embraced Jesus as Messiah. How Jewish Christians interacted with Gentile Christians within the whole Christian community was not addressed in this agreement. No doubt James must have considered the relationship similar to the way resident aliens lived in the land of Israel, or even in the way in which "those who feared the Lord" were embraced within the context of the Jewish synagogue of the first century C.E. We will return to consider this below in the dispute that erupted between Paul and Peter in Antioch. Of significance for our study of James is the fact that he clearly is the organizational leader of the Jerusalem community and the Jewish Christian communities connected to this community. Paul's letter to the Galatians helps to bring out more clearly James' importance as one of the "acknowledged pillars" of the Church.

The Apostolic Decree (Acts 15:23-29)

Acts presents James ending his speech by delineating the moral rules Gentile Christians have to obey. These same rules form the basis of the instruction or decree the apostles send out by letter to the churches:

> For it has seemed good to the Holy Spirit and to us to impose on you no further burden than these essentials: that you abstain from what has been sacrificed to idols and from blood and from what is strangled and from fornication. If you keep yourselves from these, you will do well. Farewell. (Acts 15:28-29)[36]

A vast body of literature has sprung up to respond to the many questions this Apostolic Decree poses. Most of these problems arise from the fact that Paul makes no mention of the decree in Galatians 1 and 2. Added to that, Paul mentions a conflict that arose between himself and Peter over eating with Gentile Christians (Gal 2:11-14). Scholars argue that the dispute between Paul and Peter is inconceivable if the Apostolic Decree were in effect because it would have settled the issue of the relationship between Jewish and Gentile Christians.

There are basically three ways in which this Decree is interpreted by scholars:

- In the first instance, because Peter and Paul do not seem to know anything about the Decree in Gal 2:11-14 some scholars view it as a later creation of the writer Luke. They see Luke giving expression to what was the accepted situation when he was writing in the 90s and anachronistically tracing the origin back to the Council of Jerusalem.[37] To my mind it seems strange that so important a decision as

---

[36] Note that there is a slight difference between the stipulations found in the Apostolic Decree (Acts 15:29) and the expression of the stipulations in James' speech (Acts 15:20) that gave rise to this decree. The stipulations are placed in a different sequence, and the phrase in James' speech "to abstain from things polluted by idols" (15:20) has been changed to "you abstain from what has been sacrificed to idols" (15:29). The Apostolic Decree is restated again in Acts 21:25, and it assumes the exact same form and content it has in Acts 15:29.

[37] See Painter, *Just James*, 52.

this would become the policy accepted unconsciously by all Christians and that Luke would be the one to give expression to it. Such a decision needs an official stamp to promulgate it and what Acts presents as the origin of the Apostolic Decree seems to me the more reasonable viewpoint.

• Second, some scholars interpret the intent of this Apostolic Decree as referring to the minimum requirements Gentile Christians would have to abide by so that Jewish Christians could share meals with them.

• A third view sees the Apostolic Decree as historical, but not covering the sharing of meals or "table fellowship." The concern the previous two solutions try to meet is why there would be differences over sharing meals between Jewish and Gentile Christians if the Apostolic Decree had given the green light for that to happen. The solution, then, places its composition at a date after the Council of Jerusalem and also after the Antioch dispute. The composition of the Apostolic Decree is either attributed to Luke or to James.

The fallacy in all the above solutions is that they fail to recognize the actual intent of the Apostolic Decree. They commit the all-too-common methodological fallacy of interpretation whereby if the interpreter does not understand what is said, then somehow the text is perceived as wrong and conjecture is thought to be needed to replace the text. Following this line of thought, since the interpreter cannot reconcile Acts 15:22-29 and Gal 2:11-14, Acts is judged to be unhistorical and conjectures are made as to what could have happened. There is a serious methodological principle at issue here. In any situation when I as the interpreter do not understand a text, I should begin with the presumption that the text is correct and that I am wrong. Starting with this presupposition, when I look at this particular text my question should be: "What exactly do the apostles wish to achieve by this decree?" They are battling with this question: "What are the essential laws one must abide by in order to demonstrate one's identity as a follower of Christ?" All laws and regulations have a social formation purpose. They are there to define the individual and the group in contrast to the rest of society. This is the function of all the purity laws. They are in effect saying: "This is who we are as Jewish or Gentile Christians in distinction to the society around us." Or to put it another way: Gentile Christians are distinguished from other Gentiles on the basis that they uphold these moral requirements. The focus is not on setting rules or regulations for internal relationships between Jewish and Gentile Christians. The concern of the Apostolic Decree, then, lies not with the sharing of table fellowship among

Jewish and Gentile Christians.[38] The scope, rather, is for Jewish and Gentile Christians to define themselves in opposition to the wider society.

The origins of the Apostolic Decree are attributed to two sources. First of all, the commandments given to Noah are known as the Noachide commandments. These commandments are derived from Genesis 1–11 and are seen to represent the regulations all human beings are called upon to abide by prior to God's gift of the Law to the people of Israel through Moses. The Rabbis (in the period of time after the birth of the New Testament) argued that the Law of Moses was what the Jewish people were obligated to uphold, while the Gentiles had to adhere to some universal moral norms (of which these Noachide commandments are the clearest illustration). Many different lists of Noachide commandments have been produced, ranging from seven to thirty. There are three central commandments among them: namely avoidance of fornication, idolatry, and the shedding of blood. One can see how the four regulations of the Apostolic Decree have in common the reference to fornication and idolatry, while the decree goes a little further in emphasizing the importance of not eating blood.

Another source for the Apostolic Decree seems to be Leviticus 17–18. Once again the purity rules in Leviticus are socially significant. These laws give expression to the people's identity as Israelites and separate them as a nation from the wider society. This was the essence of Israel's purity laws. Leviticus 17 and 18 also demand that the Gentiles and resident aliens who are living in the land of Israel must abide by these basic laws.[39] As we have noted, these purity rules in Leviticus have a socializing function. They give expression to the identity of the group and help to separate them from the wider society. Leviticus 17:8-9 expresses this very well: "Anyone of the house of Israel or of the aliens who reside among them who offers a burnt offering or sacrifice, and does not bring it to the entrance of the tent of meeting to sacrifice it to the LORD, *shall be cut off from the people*." In this verse the resident aliens are instructed to do what the Israelite people have to do. Further, the punishment for not abiding by these laws is that "they shall be cut off from the people." That is the clearest statement showing that these purity laws have social formation as their design. They say very clearly: this is who we are. Abiding by these laws gives us our identity. To

---

[38] Markus Bockmuehl, "The Noachide Commandments and New Testament Ethics: With Special Reference to Acts 15 and Pauline Halakhah," *RB* 102 (1995) 72–101, has drawn attention to this intent of the Apostolic Decree very well.

[39] See Terrance Callan, "The Background of the Apostolic Decree (Acts 15:20, 29; 21:25)," *CBQ* 55 (1993) 284–97, who has made an interesting study showing how the four prescriptions of the Apostolic Decree are reflected in Leviticus 17–18.

fail to carry them out means that one separates oneself from the community and consequently is cut off from the community. Since God lived in the land of Israel, the land was sacred. This meant that every individual (whether Israelite or resident alien in the land of Israel) was called upon not to defile the land of Israel. Anyone who does not carry out these purity laws is to be banished from the land. Consequently these laws apply equally to Israelites and to resident aliens.

Whatever the sources for the Apostolic Decree, the intent was the same as with the Noachide Commandments and Leviticus 17–18: to define the identity of the group in distinction to the rest of society. For Leviticus it is a way of saying: we who live in this land sacred to the Lord keep these laws that maintain our relationship with God. For the Apostolic Decree it is again a way of saying: this is who we are as distinct from the wider society. We keep these purity laws and these laws give us identity as followers of Jesus. The concern is with external relationships and not internal relationships. The decree does not envisage the issue of table fellowship because it is not concerned with speaking to the issue of internal relationships within the community between Jewish and Gentile Christians.

In conclusion: It is important not to lose sight of the real achievement and significance of both the Council of Jerusalem and the Apostolic Decree. They were two extraordinary decisions that would have implications for the Jesus movement and change its character intrinsically. In the first instance the Council tackled the question: Who can join the Jesus movement? Ultimately the answer was: Anyone can become a follower of Jesus. The Council accepted Paul's ministry and mission to the Gentiles. This was a major step forward and was ultimately to result in vast numbers of Gentiles embracing the Jesus movement. Paul's letter to the Galatians illustrates this acceptance by the apostolic community very positively (Gal 2:7-9). The Jerusalem leaders' giving Paul the right hand of fellowship was the strongest illustration of support for Paul's mission to the Gentiles.

The second major decision of the Council of Jerusalem arose from tackling the question: What obligations are required of one who becomes a follower of Jesus? The response to this question was to acknowledge that to become a follower one did not first have to become a Jew. Paul's approach (which is also reflected in the account of the acceptance of Cornelius) acknowledged the freedom of male Gentile Christians from the ritual of circumcision. The Apostolic Decree took this reflection further and asserted that Gentile Christians were obligated by those purity regulations that resident aliens had to abide by when they lived among Israelites in the sacred land of Israel. In effect only four precepts were to be upheld out of the myriad Old Testament laws that gave identity to Israel's way of life. These purity laws looked to the socialization process of the early Christian community and gave them their distinctiveness.

As we have argued, it was not the focus of the Council of Jerusalem or of the Apostolic Degree to define regulations with regard to table fellowship. The implications of the Apostolic Decree itself for table fellowship would only be worked out later through a struggle among the leaders of the two Christian missions.

Dispute over Table Fellowship (Gal 2:11-14)

Since the Apostolic Decree did not have the question of table fellowship in mind (as we have argued above), there is every reason to consider that it is historical and preceded the incident recorded in Gal 2:11-14. To interpret Gal 2:11-14 correctly it is important to place it in context within the letter to the Galatians. As noted before, in this letter Paul is intent on defending his authority as an apostle. Although Paul had founded the churches in the territory of Galatia, many of his opponents were stirring things up and undermining his teaching. Paul wrote this letter to defend his authority as an apostle and to correct the misunderstandings that had arisen about how to obtain salvation. Paul's vindication for his apostleship takes the form of an autobiographical account of his conversion and his dealings with the leadership of the Jerusalem church. We have already considered most of these passages, but it is important to retrace Paul's line of thought in presenting his autobiographical defense to attain an understanding of this passage (Gal 2:11-14).

Paul begins the vindication of his apostleship by pointing out that the message he preaches is not one that comes from human beings, but from God: ". . . for I did not receive it from a human source, nor was I taught it, but received it through a revelation of Jesus Christ" (Gal 1:12). Paul goes on in Gal 1:13-17 to show how his conversion brought about a change in his theological vision. Originally he was a staunch Jew, zealous for the traditions of his own faith. But it was God who revealed God's Son to Paul and through this revelation gave him a different understanding of how one attains salvation. After his conversion Paul embraced a new strategy: he went into the solitude of the desert to reflect upon his call and to make sense of the new understanding of the message in the context of God's revelation. Paul notes that he did not go immediately to the leaders of the Christian church.

After three years Paul did go up to Jerusalem to meet with the leadership of the church (Gal 1:18). In Jerusalem Paul says that he met with Cephas and with "James the Lord's brother" (Gal 1:19). Paul is at pains to emphasize that the message he proclaims is not one that originated from human agents, but had arisen from the revelation he received at the time of his conversion. After his visit to the leaders of Jerusalem, Paul mentions briefly his first missionary journey, "I went into the regions of Syria and Cilicia" (Gal 1:21). He gives no details. He simply notes how he remained unknown by sight to the churches in Judea, although they did glorify God because "the one who formerly was persecuting us is now proclaiming the faith he once tried to destroy" (Gal 1:23).

Paul mentions that his second visit to Jerusalem occurred some fourteen years after his conversion (Gal 2:1). This passage (Gal 2:1-10) is Paul's account of the Council of Jerusalem and presents a perspective that reveals more tension in the discussions than the account in Acts had given us to understand. Paul shows that he remains true to the message he had received by way of revelation. The outcome of the discussion was that the Jerusalem leadership, whom Paul names as "James and Cephas and John" (Gal 2:9), acknowledged that God's grace was working through Paul and they "gave to Barnabas and me the right hand of fellowship, agreeing that we should go to the Gentiles and they to the circumcised" (Gal 2:9). Alluding to the main concern of the Council of Jerusalem, Paul says that Titus, who came up with him to Jerusalem "was not compelled to be circumcised, though he was a Greek" (Gal 2:3). This agreement is an acknowledgment of two missions: one to the Gentiles, the other to the Jews, and that Paul's responsibility was with the Gentiles.

This brings us to the passage we are considering about Paul's dispute with Peter (Cephas) (Gal 2:11-14). Paul's account here is the only reference to this incident in the New Testament. The outline of the dispute as detailed by Paul is easy to understand and is quite straightforward. In Antioch, Jewish Christians were sharing meals with Gentile Christians. Peter himself was eating freely with Gentile Christians. A delegation arrived from Jerusalem, showing the authority the Jerusalem community exercised over Antioch since its inception, when the church of Jerusalem had sent Barnabas there to oversee the Christian community (Acts 11:22). This delegation is identified as coming from James. Peter stops sharing meals with the Gentile Christians. Paul condemns Peter for hypocrisy, arguing that since Peter is not observing the Jewish purity and dietary laws it is inconsistent that he expect Gentile Christians to do so.

Paul has situated this account of his dispute with Peter and the followers of James some time after the Council of Jerusalem. The main discussion among scholars, as I have shown in the previous section, has been to harmonize Paul's account with the Apostolic Decree. Rather than resort to conjecture as scholars have done in the past because they are unable to follow Paul's thought sequence here, one should try to make sense of it as it stands in the line of Paul's thought. As indicated above, the Council of Jerusalem and the Apostolic Decree envisaged rules that gave identity to the followers of Jesus as opposed to those outside the community of believers. It said nothing about relationships within the community. The Council of Jerusalem and the Apostolic Decree defined those who had embraced Jesus as Messiah, whether from the world of Judaism or from the world of the Gentiles. Neither the Council of Jerusalem nor the Apostolic Decree had given direct attention to the further question regarding how those who had accepted Jesus as Messiah coming from a Jewish and Gentile background would relate among themselves.

The reaction of the messengers sent by James to Peter shows that James considered that Jewish Christians could not share table fellowship with Gentile Christians. For him this was not a contradiction of the Apostolic Decree. Instead, James was approaching the matter from his world view within Judaism. In theory there was no difficulty in allowing Gentiles to share in a meal that Jews had prepared, since the Jews had control of the preparation of the food to ensure that all was done according to the correct purity regulations. However, it does appear that at the time most Jews were reluctant to share a meal with Gentiles for fear they would transgress their purity regulations. As we have indicated above, the purpose of purity laws was to define who an Israelite was in contrast to the wider world. By sharing meals with Gentiles one would be ignoring those boundaries that were vital for order and for preserving access to God.[40] The major concern for Jews of the first century would be with the question of idolatry. To share a sacred meal with those who worshiped false and pagan gods would be anathema. In the case of Jewish Christians sharing a meal with Gentile Christians this question of idolatry would not arise. Nevertheless, the purity concerns still remain. While it may not be possible to define exactly what concern James and his followers had, it is logical to presume that they still saw themselves as being part of the people of Israel and as such reluctant to share a meal with Gentile Christians. Bernheim describes very succinctly the way in which James could have argued his perspective.[41]

The whole issue concerns what it means to accept Jesus as the Messiah. James still sees the following of Jesus as situated within the world of

---

[40] Scot McKnight, "A Parting within the Way: Jesus and James on Israel and Purity," in Chilton and Evans, eds., *James the Just and Christian Origins,* 83–129, defines purity rules very insightfully in this way: "That is, fundamentally, purity is about order, social conditionedness and national security" (85).

[41] See Bernheim, *James, Brother of Jesus,* 180.

Israel. Jesus' mission was to reconstitute the people of Israel, as the prophets had hoped for centuries. Jews of the time allowed "those who feared the Lord" to become part of the synagogue. James saw those pagans who had accepted Jesus as the Messiah as belonging to the community of the followers of Jesus in an analogous way. What was required of pagan Christians to belong to this new movement was exactly the same as required of any "of those who feared the Lord" who wished to belong to the synagogue. No new religion had been created. Instead it was the flowering forth of the religion of Israel and was a fulfillment of Israel's ancient traditions.

When Paul challenges Peter for giving in to James, it is because Peter has reversed himself on his custom of sharing meals with Gentile Christians. Paul does not appeal to the way he (Paul) interprets the Apostolic Decree and does not initiate a discussion on the Apostolic Decree's interpretation and application to this current situation.[42] Instead, Paul challenges Peter on the way he has reversed his behavior.[43] It is also noticeable that Paul does not challenge the followers of James by laying out his interpretation of the Apostolic Decree. Paul's failure to refer to the Apostolic Decree does not mean that it did not yet exist. Instead, it shows that neither Paul nor James thought the Apostolic Decree applied to this situation. The issue of Jewish Christians sharing table fellowship with Gentile Christians had yet to be raised, and consequently the Apostolic Decree did not refer to it.

This is a highly significant passage and this interpretation helps us to understand James' perspective within the Christian community. As leader of the Jerusalem community James is concerned for Jewish Christians who still consider themselves part of Israel's religious heritage.[44] While James welcomes the fact that many Gentiles have acknowledged a belief in the God of Israel and in Jesus as the Messiah, he still upholds the ritual separation between Jews and Gentiles in table fellowship as demanded by purity considerations. In upholding two missions, one to the Jews and the other to the Gentiles, James is in effect upholding two paths in the acceptance of Jesus as Messiah. This does not mean, however, that these Gentile Christians had become Jews. This is something on which both James and

---

[42] Hans Dieter Betz, *Galatians: A Commentary on Paul's Letter to the Churches in Galatia,* Hermeneia (Philadelphia: Fortress, 1979) 106, and Painter, *Just James,* 70, both support the view that Paul does not refer to the Apostolic Decree because he knows it is open to a number of different interpretations. I think, however, that Paul does not see it applying to the situation. I would go so far as to say that if Paul did think the Apostolic Decree was applicable he would have to agree with James and Peter!

[43] I acknowledge my debt to the insights of Bernheim (*James, Brother of Jesus,* 181) here and in what follows.

[44] See Painter, *Just James,* 70.

Paul would agree. James still saw himself as a Jew, required to live by his Jewish cultural vision of the world and to remain true to those purity laws that gave him his identity as a member of the people of Israel. While accepting the freedom of Gentile Christians from the stipulations of the Jewish Law (apart from the requirements set forth in the Apostolic Decree), James would still see himself and his fellow Jewish Christians[45] as bound by the Jewish purity prescriptions.[46]

For Paul the situation was very different. He saw all believers, whether Jewish Christian or Gentile Christian, as forming the one body of Christ (1 Cor 12:12-31). In this body differences no longer have any weight: "As many of you as were baptized into Christ have clothed yourselves with Christ. There is no longer Jew or Greek, there is no longer slave or free, there is no longer male and female; for all of you are one in Christ Jesus" (Gal 3:27-28).

Some scholars assert that James' perspective won out at Antioch.[47] This accounts for the fact that Paul left Antioch after the confrontation and only returned once to Antioch at the end of his second journey (Acts 18:22-23). While this is a conjecture that is difficult to prove conclusively, it is certainly supported by later events. The letter of James seems to have the church of Antioch in mind as one of the churches it addresses: "To the twelve tribes in the Dispersion. Greetings" (Jas 1:1). Tradition has associated the church of Antioch also with the Gospel of Matthew. Matthew's Sermon on the Mount contains a strong stress on the value of the Law, as can be seen from Jesus' statement regarding his role as the one who has come to fulfill the Law (Matt 5:17-20).

Using traditions available to him, Matthew developed the Sermon found in the Sayings Source Q (Luke 6:20-49), giving it a clear Jewish Christian perspective. When the Jewish war against Rome broke out (66 C.E.), and when later the city of Jerusalem was destroyed (70 C.E.), many of the Jewish Christians found their way to Antioch, bringing with them their traditions related to James and Jewish Christianity. Antioch became the center that continued to preserve those traditions associated with Jewish Christianity.

---

[45] While I use the term "Jewish Christian" throughout this monograph, the expression "Christian Jews" would probably be more appropriate because it places the stress on their fidelity to their roots within Judaism.

[46] Bernheim, *James, Brother of Jesus,* 181.

[47] See Ralph P. Martin, *James,* Word Biblical Commentary (Waco, TX: Word Books, 1988) xxxvi–xxxvii; James D. G. Dunn, "The Incident at Antioch (Gal 2.11-18)," *JSNT* 18 (1983) 3–57; and Patrick J. Hartin, *James and the Q Sayings of Jesus,* JSNTSS 47 (Sheffield: JSOT, 1991) 230.

The Interface between James and Paul after Antioch (Acts 21:17-26; 23:12-22)

Paul's dispute with Peter also had implications for his relationship with Barnabas. Barnabas had introduced Paul to Antioch and had ensured that he was accepted into the mainstream of the Christian community there. Barnabas also made the first missionary journey with Paul. Although it is always referred to as Paul's first missionary journey, Barnabas was initially the leader, setting off to preach the Gospel throughout his native island of Cyprus.[48] From there they traveled to Asia Minor, where they established a number of Christian centers in the towns of Lystra, Derbe, and Iconium (*circa* 46–49 C.E.; see Acts 13:1-14:28).

However, in Galatians Paul also indicates that Barnabas was caught up in the dispute over table fellowship (Gal 2:13). This probably explains why Barnabas and Paul part company at the beginning of the second missionary journey. Acts notes that Paul wanted to take Barnabas with him, but that they had a dispute about taking Barnabas's cousin John Mark because he had deserted them during the course of the first journey (Acts 15:36-41). Acts presents the dispute as being over John Mark, but from the letter to the Galatians it appears that there was much more at stake. Paul and Barnabas separated and Paul took a certain Silas along with him on his second journey (*circa* 49–52 C.E.; Acts 15:36–18:22). Paul initiated this journey in order to revisit the communities of Christians he had founded, particularly in Asia Minor.

Acts 21:17-26 against the Background of Paul's Letters

At the end of his third missionary journey (*circa* 53–58 C.E.; Acts 18:23–21:16), Paul returned to Jerusalem. Throughout his journey he had taken up a collection for the poor in Jerusalem. This was in accord with the agreement of the Apostolic Decree, as Paul acknowledges: "They asked only one thing, that we remember the poor, which was actually what I was eager to do" (Gal 2:10). Concern for the poor was a key concern of the Jerusalem church. It also conforms to one of the major themes in the letter of James, namely to treat the poor with equity and justice. Paul shows that he is concerned about the poor as well, that is why he says he is eager to take up the collection. This was a concrete way of demonstrating unity with the Jewish Christians of Palestine. Bringing this contribution to Jerusalem was

---

[48] As noted before, the name of Barnabas appears in the first place when the community of Antioch sends Paul and Barnabas out. This indicates according to the custom of the time that Barnabas is considered the more influential person.

also Paul's way of acknowledging the role and importance of James: it showed that Christians living in the Diaspora were still united with the mother church in Jerusalem.

This psychological perspective on the collection for the poor of Jerusalem also reflected the custom within the world of Judaism, in which all Jewish males over the age of twenty were expected to make a contribution to the Temple, or pay a temple tax. This included those living outside the land of Palestine in the Diaspora. The temple tax is traced back to Neh 10:32-33. Originally the amount was one-third of a shekel, but this was later raised to one-half shekel, which would be the equivalent of a day's wage.[49] This tax was designed to help pay for the upkeep of the Temple. Reference is made to the temple tax in Matt 17:24-27. Josephus also makes mention of the temple tax: "But no one need wonder that there was so much wealth in our temple, for all the Jews throughout the habitable world, and those who worshipped God, even those from Asia and Europe, had been contributing to it for a very long time."[50]

Following the tradition of Jewish Rabbis of the time, who used to support themselves by means of a trade, Paul supported himself through his own trade as a tentmaker (Acts 18:3). While Paul never asked the churches to support him financially, he still upheld the right for an apostle to be supported by the churches (see 1 Cor 9:1-18).

When Paul returned to Jerusalem (Acts 21:17-26), Luke writes that he and his companions were welcomed by "the brothers" *(hoi adelphoi)* in Jerusalem (Acts 21:17). While this word is generally understood in the widest sense as a reference to the Christian community of Jerusalem as "brothers and sisters," it could also refer to the "family of Jesus," since James is mentioned in this particular context. It is another illustration of how this word *adelphos* has many nuances of meaning.

One of the issues scholars have raised regarding this account is that the text makes no mention of James actually receiving the collection Paul had taken up. This has led some to conclude that James and the Jerusalem community may have rejected the collection from the Gentile churches.[51]

---

[49] See Thomas E. Schmidt, "Taxation, Jewish," *Dictionary of New Testament Background,* eds. Craig A. Evans and Stanley E. Porter (Downers Grove, IL, and Leicester, England: InterVarsity Press, 2000) 1163–66. See also Daniel C. Snell, "Taxes and Taxation," *ABD* 6, ed. David Noel Freedman (New York: Doubleday, 1992) 338–40.

[50] Josephus, *A.J.* 14:110 [Marcus, LCL]. Elsewhere Jospehus gives a detailed account of the collection of the temple money in Mesopotamia (*A.J.* 18:312-314 [Feldman, LCL]).

[51] See, for example, James D. G. Dunn, *Unity and Diversity in the New Testament: An Inquiry into the Character of Earliest Christianity* (Philadelphia: Westminster, 1977) 257.

Once again conjecture has been read into the text. When Paul testifies before Herod Agrippa II he says, "Now after some years I came to bring alms to my nation and to offer sacrifices" (Acts 24:17). This certainly seems to imply that Paul did deliver the collection and that it was accepted.

One of Luke's preconceived perspectives is to avoid or gloss over any conflict within the early Christian community and its leadership. From the very beginning Luke presented a picture of the early community as one harmonious family (see Acts 4:32). James is the only apostle in Jerusalem and Paul meets with him "the next day" (Acts 21:18), which indicates the leadership role James plays within the Jerusalem community. As the narrative continues it shows that James' role is not simply limited to Jerusalem, but that he has a concern and responsibility for all Jewish Christians, who look to him as their leader and protector. Luke narrates what surely would be the essence of the meeting of two leaders of the early church who have concern for two different missions. Paul reports how the message of salvation is being embraced by the Gentiles throughout the Roman world. To this James and others within the Jerusalem community reply: "you see . . . how many thousands of believers there are among the Jews, and they are all zealous for the law" (Acts 21:20). This response shows how James and the Jewish Christians are still holding on to their traditions within Judaism. They still observe the demands of the Jewish Law. This is true to the vision we identified above, when the Council of Jerusalem and the Apostolic Decree were concerned with the requirements for Gentiles to enter the Christian movement. They were not directly concerned about Jewish Christians. James shows that Jewish Christians in their allegiance to Jesus as Messiah still continued to uphold their Jewish traditions and purity laws and were proud to do so.

This passage (Acts 21:17-26) indicates that there are two distinct missions within the early Christian church: to the Jews and to the Gentiles. James and Peter bear responsibility for the mission to the Jews, while Paul is the apostle to the Gentiles. James' oversight of the mission to the Jews was based on the understanding that acceptance of Jesus as Messiah did not abrogate their Jewish traditions and roots: Circumcision was still valued highly, as were the Mosaic Law and all the ritual purity laws and customs. Paul's Gentile mission was free from circumcision and all the purity laws.

The question indirectly addressed to Paul in this passage regards the Jewish Christian mission and the value it upholds in the Mosaic Law and its traditions: "What obligations do you see Jewish Christians have with regard to upholding the stipulations of the Jewish Law?" The answer expected from Paul is that he does endorse Jewish Christianity upholding the traditions of the Mosaic Law. Paul is made aware of a "rumor" that is circulating to the effect that "you teach all the Jews living among the Gentiles to forsake Moses, and that you tell them not to circumcise their children or observe the customs" (Acts 21:21). Luke implies that this "rumor" is false. But certainly from a reading of Paul's letters it appears this is a true statement that does reflect his perspective and teaching: Paul no longer saw any value in the Jewish Law and its purity regulations for salvation. He states this very clearly in his letter to the Galatians, where he speaks about the Law as a teacher leading people to Christ (Gal 3:23-29).

Basic to Paul's theology is his belief that salvation comes through faith in Jesus Christ, while the Jewish Law no longer has a role to play in the path to salvation. The Law had a value leading up to the coming of Christ, but now that Christ has come it has been replaced. In this particular context of serious tensions within the Jerusalem community Paul adopts a pragmatic approach and is willing to participate in a Jewish purity ritual. Paul is not giving credence to any salvific value in the ritual. He is doing it as a way of participating in a Jewish custom that gives identity to Jews and shows that he is not opposed to Jewish rituals as such, as long as no claims are being made that they have a role or importance in the realm of salvation. This pragmatic approach of Paul, to my mind, is not simply an invention of Luke, the author. Paul shows this same pragmatic side in his letters. A reflection on his teaching about eating meat offered to idols (1 Cor 8:1-13) bears this out. Paul clearly does not see any problem for a follower of Jesus eating meat that had been offered to idols for, he says, "we know that 'no idol in the world really exists,' and that 'there is no God but one'" (1 Cor 8:4). However, for the sake of those believers who have a scrupulous conscience Paul says it may be prudent to avoid eating such meat so as not to give them scandal (1 Cor 8:7). One can see Paul approaching the issue of Jewish Christians observing the customs of the Jewish Law and traditions in an analogous way. While he does not acknowledge any value to them in the realm of salvation, for the sake of those who still treasure their Jewish roots and heritage, Paul has no difficulty in taking part in rituals in order to bring harmony into the community.

Paul pays for the expenses of four men who are taking part in a Nazirite vow and joins them in the purification rituals.[52] In this way Paul

---

[52] The Nazirite vow is a special vow that Israelite men or women would make that would consecrate them to God for a specific period of time. The regulations relating to this vow are found in Num 6:1-21. During the period of the vow the Nazirite was obligated to abstain from alcohol, to leave his/her head unshaven, and to avoid all contact with a corpse. At the time of Jesus and Paul, taking such a vow was an individual choice, though originally it may have been viewed as a divine gift: see, e.g., Samson (Judg 13:4-14) and Amos (2:11). At the conclusion of the vow the Nazirite has his or her hair cut and it is burned in the sanctuary.

will demonstrate to his opponents that he has not opposed or rejected Jewish rituals and traditions. Events, however, take a different turn. It was not Jewish Christians, but Jews in general from Asia Minor who recognized Paul and falsely accused him of bringing Gentiles into the Temple where they were not allowed to go.[53]

Paul's Arrest in the Temple (Acts 21:27-36)

This visit to the Temple and Paul's attempt to placate the Jewish Christians misfired. Paul was arrested and ultimately would be sent to Rome as a prisoner. No mention is made of James or anyone in the Jerusalem community coming to Paul's assistance. It was Paul's nephew (the son of his sister) who saved Paul from a plot to assassinate him (Acts 23:16). Not too much must be read into the fact that Luke makes no mention of James or the Jerusalem community coming to help Paul. There are two simple points to be made. First, what could they do? Second, one must remain faithful to the intent and purpose of Luke's narrative. His intention is to show the message of salvation being brought to the ends of the earth in fulfillment of the instruction given in Acts 1:8. Paul's arrest had the positive consequence that the message would now be brought to Rome, and Luke wishes to show how this materializes.

Continued Interface between James, Peter and Paul (1 Cor 9:3-6; 15:3-8)

In 1 Cor 9:3-6 Paul defends his role as an apostle and speaks about an apostle's rights. He again draws attention to certain differences between his approach to mission and the approach of Peter (and James). Paul shows that Peter (Cephas) and those involved in the mission to the Jewish people used to travel with their wives and they all received support from those communities to whom they ministered. Paul (and Barnabas), on the other hand, in their mission to the Gentiles did not travel with their wives and

---

It is unknown what the reasons would be for undertaking a Nazirite vow apart from an act of pious devotion "for those who seek a specially close relationship with God. The Nazirite vow may be an ancient Israelite example of this pattern." (See Leslie J. Hoppe, "Nazirite," *Eerdmans Dictionary of the Bible,* ed. David Noel Freedman [Grand Rapids: Eerdmans, 2000] 951).

[53] Inscriptions on pillars leading beyond the court of Gentiles to the court of women contained statements declaring that any Gentile who proceeded farther would be put to death. Two such inscriptions have been discovered (see McKenzie, *Dictionary of the Bible,* 874).

refused to accept support from the churches they visited and ministered to. They worked to support themselves.

While James is not mentioned directly in this passage, once again "the brothers of the Lord" are placed alongside the apostles. They are referred to as having wives who accompany them during their missionary activity. This does not mean that James was also a traveling missionary: the picture we have unearthed so far does not support this view. James was a resident leader at Jerusalem. However, we can infer from this picture that James was married. It is an obvious statement, but one that lies buried behind the text.

In 1 Cor 15:3-8 James is mentioned by name. He is not identified as "the brother of the Lord," but it is clear that this is the James who is meant. Since he is the most influential James in the Christian communities, any other James would have to be identified more clearly. Paul is using traditional formulae here related to the appearances of the Risen Lord. For Paul, as for these early traditions, the proof that Jesus Christ has risen rests on the fact that Jesus has been seen and experienced as alive by numerous followers.

In enumerating those to whom the risen Lord appeared Paul once again lists Peter, James, and himself. They all owe their missions to appearances of the risen Lord. Paul presents the tradition in a parallel way:

- the risen Jesus appeared to Cephas (Peter) then to the twelve. (Peter is one of the twelve.)

- He appeared to James then to all the apostles (James is one of the apostles.)

There is no contrast between Peter and James. Jesus' appearances to Peter and James are on the same level, as is seen from this parallel presentation. The contrast occurs in v. 8, where Paul introduces himself and speaks of an appearance to him, which is taken to refer to his experience of the risen Lord on his journey to Damascus. It is an appearance "to one untimely born" because it occurs years after the ascension of the risen Jesus. In this sense the appearance is contrasted to that of Peter and James. While it might be an appearance of a different order, it is still the basis for Paul's missionary role as an apostle.

James as Leader Within Jewish Christianity

This survey of the role of James in the Jerusalem community as we have unearthed it from a critical examination of Acts and Paul's reactions to

James in the course of his letters has brought a deeper awareness of the struggles of the early Christian church. While the picture of James in the gospels and even to a certain extent in Acts has been obscured, James does emerge from this examination as an important and leading figure of the early Christian community. He is the effective leader of the Jerusalem church and exercises a role of concern and oversight for the whole of the Jewish Christian mission and those communities that emerged as a consequence of Jews' accepting Jesus as the Messiah of the Hebrew Scriptures. The following aspects of the character of James emerge from this examination:

The picture of James is defined by the fact that he was a Jewish Christian. He understood that the mission of his brother Jesus was the restoration of the people of Israel, and James saw his role as leader of the Jewish Christians in Jerusalem as continuing that mission. As Bruce Chilton says: "In the argument of James as represented here, what the belief of gentiles achieves is not the redefinition of Israel (as in Paul's thought) but the *restoration* of the house of Israel."[54] Since his task was not the rejection of Israel, but its "restoration," James continued to observe the Jewish Torah. The purity rules of Judaism continued to define access to God and relationships with others. James continued what Jesus had started under the choice and guidance of God.

James does not envisage that Jews who had accepted Jesus as the Messiah should abandon the Torah, the purity rules and their traditions. In his interface with Peter, Barnabas, and Paul, James has one aim: the preservation of the social map of the world. The Torah defines who belongs to Israel and the people of God. In the mind of James the restoration of the house of Israel demands that one remain faithful to the Torah. In accepting Gentiles who have professed faith in Jesus as Messiah into the community of Jewish Christians, James envisages their position in much the same way as resident aliens were accepted within the land of Israel. Just as resident aliens were obligated to abide by certain purity laws within the land of Israel, so Gentile Christians were also obligated to abide by certain stipulations in the Christian community.[55]

---

[54] Bruce Chilton and Jacob Neusner, *Judaism in the New Testament: Practices and Beliefs* (London: Routledge, 1995) 106.

[55] Commenting on the use of Leviticus 17–18 in explaining James' attitude, McKnight (*Jesus and James on Israel and Purity,* 109) says: "Consequently, what we have here is an innovative Jewish exegesis of the Torah revealing that for James (and the Jerusalem-based Christian Judaism he represents) the Torah contains the answers to life's complex problems, including specific problems about which laws Gentile resident aliens will have to obey in the eschatological renewal."

James' attitude toward a Gentile mission is one of tolerance and acceptance. James does not see his task as leader of the Jewish Christian Jerusalem community as one of actively seeking out Gentile converts, as Paul's mission does. His concern is with Jewish Christians. If Gentiles wish to be associated with them he tolerates the situation in the way Israel of old tolerated the presence of resident aliens in their midst.[56] James sincerely tried to preserve Christian roots in Judaism and continued Jesus' eschatological vision for the restoration of the people of Israel. However, the attempt to preserve two independent missions within early Christianity was an ideal solution that could not endure indefinitely. The larger numbers of Gentiles embracing Jesus as Messiah would in time overwhelm the much smaller numbers of those Jews who did the same.

James emerges from this study as the most influential person within the community of Jerusalem. Paul acknowledges James' position and defers to him as the leader of the Jewish Christian mission by accepting his advice about entering the Temple area. A study of James is indeed a study of the growth of the early Christian church as seen from the perspective of Jewish Christianity. James was the historical link between "his brother" Jesus and the emerging Christian church. Just as the Jesus of Matthew's gospel saw himself as being sent solely to "the lost sheep of the house of Israel" (Matt 15:24; see also 10:5-6), so James restricted his concern to the people of Israel. While he acknowledged the acceptance of a further mission to the Gentiles and the fact that Gentile converts were to be free from circumcision and the stipulations of the Mosaic Law (apart from those prescriptions in the Apostolic Decree), James did not consider that this decision had any effect on his community and mission to Jewish Christians. For him Jewish Christians were still members of the house of Israel. Belief in and acceptance of Jesus as the Messiah did not change the reality that they were still part of the house of Israel whose traditions and purity regulations still applied. For, after all, the purity rules identified the group in contrast to the world around them. James saw his task as leader of the Jerusalem community and ensured that the fulfillment of the eschatological age that had begun with Jesus would endure through fidelity to the heritage of Judaism.

Acts only mentions James on a few occasions, but where it does his authority and position are clearly acknowledged and upheld: he is undoubtedly an important and influential person within the context of the early Christian church. In comparison with Paul (the major character in the

---

[56] See ibid. 110–11.

second part of Acts and to whom thirteen canonical letters are attributed) the few references to James are striking (and one letter is attributed to him). James' importance arises from two factors: he was both an apostle and a brother of the Lord.[57] As a brother of the Lord, James is always mentioned first in the list of the brothers in the gospels. He is the only brother mentioned to whom the risen Lord had appeared, which singled him out for distinction.

Conflict and dispute did define the interface between James and Paul. This emerged from a study of Paul's own writings. Acts endeavored to smooth over these tensions. Some scholars have interpreted the meager references to James in Acts as a deliberate attempt on the part of Luke to try to write James out of the history of the early Christian church.[58]

Paul's mission to the Gentiles and his vision won out over James' vision of a Jewish Christianity. It is simply a fact of history. It is for this reason that the history of the early Christian church is always seen through Paul's eyes. Had the situation developed differently, the history of early Christianity would also have been written very differently. Nevertheless, from this study we have discovered an important and influential figure in the early Christian community. He had a position, authority and leadership that rivaled those of Paul and Paul himself had to defer to him.[59]

A clearer understanding and awareness of the development of early Christianity emerges. Peter's position and role within the community as leader and missionary to the circumcised come into sharper focus. Paul too emerges as someone touched by God's grace, fully convinced of the revelation he has received, a revelation that gives direction to a totally different mission to the uncircumcised. While James tried to preserve Christianity's roots in the house of Israel, Paul's approach ultimately won the day. The decisions taken in the Council of Jerusalem, the Apostolic Decree, and Paul's conviction of the unity of Jew and Greek in the Body of Christ all contributed to the emergence of two separate religions, Christianity and Judaism, from one common heritage. James tried unsuccessfully to hold onto and preserve that heritage for future generations of Jewish Christians. By

---

[57] See William R. Farmer, "James the Lord's Brother, According to Paul," in Chilton and Evans, eds., *James the Just and Christian Origins* (Leiden, Boston, and Köln: Brill, 1999) 140–42.

[58] See Painter, *Just James*, 56.

[59] See Bernheim, *James, Brother of Jesus*, 147; and also Jacob Jervell, "James: the Defender of Paul," in *Luke and the People of God: A New Look at Luke-Acts* (Minneapolis: Augsburg, 1972) 185–207, who says that "Luke uses him (James) as the principal witness in his defense of Paul" (187).

concentrating on the person and character of James we are able to get a new vision of the early Christian church and to unearth a reality of that world that has been lost and forgotten. James' importance will continue to be illustrated in the fourth chapter, when we examine the way in which the character and role of James were understood in the following two centuries.

CHAPTER THREE

Wisdom Teacher: The Letter of James

"Come, we shall have some fun now!" thought Alice.
"I'm glad they've begun asking riddles—
I believe I can guess that," she added aloud.
"Do you mean that you think you can find out
the answer to it?" said the March Hare.
"Exactly so," said Alice.
"Then you should say what you mean," the March Hare went on.
"I do," Alice hastily replied;
"at least—at least I mean what I say—that's the same thing, you know."
"Not the same thing a bit!" said the Hatter.
"Why, you might just as well say that
'I see what I eat' is the same thing as 'I eat what I see'!"[1]

In our study of the figure of James in the New Testament and his interface with the two worlds of Judaism and paganism, we now turn to the New Testament writing that bears the title "The Letter of James." The aim of this study is not to examine this letter in general, or to examine it for its own sake, but rather to see what the letter can contribute toward the scope of our study relating to the figure of James and his interface with the context of his world.[2] Five things form the basis of this study:

---

[1] Lewis Carroll, *Alice's Adventures in Wonderland*, Books of Wonder (New York: William Morrow & Co. [1866] 1992) 97–98.

[2] There is much that one could say about the letter of James and many approaches that could be adopted. In this discussion I draw largely on the results of my recent commentary (Patrick J. Hartin, *James*, SP 14 [Collegeville: Liturgical Press, 2003]) to illustrate what can be deduced about the figure and thought of James of Jerusalem.

- Methodological considerations in reading the letter of James

- The identity of the James of the letter as the "brother of the Lord"

- James' interface with Judaism

  ○ The Twelve Tribes of the Dispersion

  ○ Purity rules and the Law

  ○ James and the Wisdom heritage

- James' interface with Jesus

- James' interface with Paul's thought: Justification, Faith, and Works

Methodological Consideration: The Literary Genre of the Letter of James

The most important methodological issue in any examination of the letter of James is its literary genre. When discussing the gospels in the New Testament we showed that knowledge of the literary form of the four gospels contributed greatly toward a more careful interpretation of these writings. The same is true of this writing of James. The literary genre of the writing may at first sight appear to be obvious. From all outward appearances it is in the form of a letter. It opens in the traditional manner with reference to the author and the recipients. Throughout the writing the author speaks in the manner of a letter writer who addresses his readers directly (e.g., "If any of you is lacking in wisdom . . ." [Jas 1:5]). While the ending of the writing does not conform to the traditional ending of a letter, as known to us from Paul's letters, there is evidence that in the Jewish and Greco-Roman worlds there were various ways in which a letter could come to a conclusion. The ending of a letter known to us from Paul's writings is not the only possibility: many others did exist.[3]

This writing is more than a simple letter. Martin Dibelius[4] has had the greatest influence on studies on the letter of James over the past century. He classified this writing as *paraenesis*. Dibelius defined *paraenesis* in this

---

[3] See Fred O. Francis, "The Form and Function of the Opening and Closing Paragraphs of James and 1 John," *ZNW* 61 (1970) 110–26; Abraham J. Malherbe, *Moral Exhortation: A Greco-Roman Sourcebook* (Philadelphia: Westminster, 1986) 79–82; and Hartin, *James,* 14–15.

[4] Martin Dibelius, *James: A Commentary on the Epistle of James,* Hermeneia, rev. Heinrich Greeven, trans. Michael A. Williams, ed. Helmut Koester (Philadelphia: Fortress, 1976; English translation of *Der Brief des Jakobus* [11th rev. ed. Göttingen: Vandenhoeck & Ruprecht, 1964]).

way: "By paraenesis we mean a text which strings together admonitions of general ethical content. Paraenetic sayings ordinarily address themselves to a specific (though perhaps fictional) audience, or at least appear in the form of a command or summons."[5]

In more recent times Dibelius' views have undergone careful scrutiny and a clearer perception of the nature of the literary genre of James has begun to emerge. John Gammie's studies on paraenetic literature have been largely responsible for this development.[6] He has shown that paraenetic literature is actually a secondary genre of the primary genre, namely Wisdom literature. Paraenetic literature aims at providing direction for a community, with moral advice for action. He makes a further distinction between paraenesis and protreptic discourse, which he distinguishes by means of three criteria: "(1) presence or absence of precepts and purpose for which they are adduced; (2) extent of sustained demonstration and organization with a view to persuade; and (3) breadth of topics covered and/or sharpness of focus."[7]

In effect protreptic discourse presents an argument that develops a theme through a "demonstration which is stylistically expressed in a clear, logical, and syllogistic manner."[8] Protreptic discourse and *paraenesis* both strive toward the social formation of a community.[9] Writings that by their very nature are either protreptic discourse or simple *paraenesis* have as their goal the formation of their readers through the values, goals, and ethos of the social fabric of that community. Peter L. Berger and Thomas Luckmann have given attention to this process, which they define as "socialization": "the comprehensive and consistent induction of an individual into the objective world of a society or a sector of it."[10]

This helps to explain more clearly the rhetorical function of the letter of James. This letter is identified as a protreptic discourse rather than as *paraenesis.*[11] As distinct from *paraenesis,* a protreptic discourse is focused on a vision that embraces all its moral exhortation and gives it direction.

---

[5] Ibid. 3.

[6] John G. Gammie, "Paraenetic Literature: Toward the Morphology of a Secondary Genre," *Semeia* 50 (1990) 41–77.

[7] Ibid. 54–55.

[8] Patrick J. Hartin, *A Spirituality of Perfection: Faith in Action in the Letter of James* (Collegeville: The Liturgical Press, 1999) 47.

[9] Leo G. Perdue, "The Social Character of Paraenesis and Paraenetic Literature," *Semeia* 50 (1990) 23–27.

[10] Peter L. Berger and Thomas Luckmann, *The Social Construction of Reality: A Treatise in the Sociology of Knowledge* (Garden City, NY: Doubleday, 1966) 120.

[11] See discussion in Hartin, *James,* 11–13.

The letter of James focuses on the vision of a call to "friendship with God" as opposed to "friendship with the world."[12] The rhetorical function of the letter of James is the social formation of its readers as the community of "the twelve tribes in the Dispersion" (Jas 1:1). The letter of James sets out the values, the ethos his readers are to adopt as members of these "twelve tribes." They are called to lead a life of friendship with God that is incompatible with a life of friendship with the world, to keep themselves "unstained by the world" (1:27). This duality is a central theme woven throughout the letter.

James has sent this protreptic discourse out as a letter to "the twelve tribes in the Dispersion." This address helps to further delineate this letter as a "Diaspora Letter." The term "Diaspora" refers to Jews living outside their homeland in Palestine/Israel. Examples of such Diaspora letters are 2 Maccabees 1, the Letter of Jeremiah (or Bar 6:1-73), and Baruch's letter in 2 (Syrian Apocalypse of) Baruch (2 Bar 78:1–87:1). Consequently, the letter of James would be understood as written to Jewish communities living outside Palestine/Israel.[13]

Given the above discussion, the letter of James is to be understood as a Wisdom writing that belongs to the secondary genre of protreptic discourse, concerned with the social formation of its readers. It provides a vision that calls believers to live in friendship with God. It presents the values, the ethos, and the way of life necessary for members of that community. This protreptic discourse is sent out in the form of a Diaspora letter to communities of Jewish Christians living outside Palestine/Israel. Reading the letter of James within this framework and understanding will provide a deeper awareness of both its function and its message.

The Identity of the James of the Letter as the "Brother of the Lord"

In the context of this study our examination of the letter of James has a twofold function. We want to see what the letter has to say about the figure of James, and also how that figure interfaces with his cultural and religious context. We cannot prove that the *actual author* of the letter was James, "the brother of the Lord." However, what we can do is to see whether

---

[12] See Hartin, *James,* 13.

[13] Peter H. Davids explains well the implications of understanding the letter of James as a Diaspora letter. See his "Palestinian Traditions in the Epistle of James," in Bruce Chilton and Craig A. Evans, eds., *James the Just and Christian Origins,* NovTSup 98 (Leiden, Boston, and Köln: Brill, 1999) 41.

the *author implied* from the text conforms to the picture of James that is known from outside the text, the picture that has emerged from our previous study of the other biblical texts.[14]

The opening of the letter identifies its author as "James, a servant of God and of the Lord Jesus Christ" (1:1). The fact that the writer found it unnecessary to identify himself further even though many people bore the name James in the New Testament is proof that he must have been an influential and well-known figure. He presumed his readers would clearly know which James he was, and he felt no need to distinguish himself from anyone else.

From this we can make the following deduction. Prior to 44 C.E. three influential followers of Jesus bore the name of James: James the son of Zebedee, James the son of Alphaeus, and James the brother of the Lord. The writer identifies himself as "a servant of God and the Lord Jesus Christ." In the biblical context "a servant" is someone who carries out God's will in his/her life. Just as a slave is dedicated to doing the will of his or her master, so the biblical slave is dedicated to carrying out God's will. In the Hebrew writings Moses, Abraham, and the prophets are all identified by the title "servant." In the New Testament this term "servant" is used in a variety of ways. It refers to Jesus (Phil 2:7) as well as to Christians (1 Pet 2:16). It is also a title referring to a leadership role within the community ("Paul, a servant of Jesus Christ" [Rom 1:1]). In using this title to refer to himself the writer of this letter is making a twofold connection to these traditions. He identifies himself as exercising a leadership role within the community in line with the leadership roles of Moses, Abraham, the prophets, and even Jesus. It is also a profession of faith that identifies his life as carrying out God's will. In the address of the letter the writer does not identify himself as an apostle, as both Paul and Peter do in the opening of their letters. This leads to the conclusion that the writer was not an apostle, since he makes no reference to his apostleship. This would then exclude the two apostles: James the son of Zebedee and James the son of Alphaeus (Matt 10:2-4; Mark 3:16-19; Luke 6:14-16) as the author of the letter. James, the son of Zebedee, was martyred in 44 C.E. at the hands of Herod Agrippa I. A date

---

[14] By *"implied author"* I understand the author that I as a reader construct from the narrative itself. I must always be aware that this is my construction, and that the picture I construct may be (and probably is) very different from the actual author of the letter. It is impossible for a reader to approach a text without any preconceptions or presuppositions. However, the reader must strive to be conscious of the presuppositions she/he brings to bear upon the text. In reading the letter of James the intent here is to allow the letter to speak for itself. This study endeavors to start with the letter itself (rather than with one's preconceived ideas) and determine the picture of the author that emerges from the letter.

prior to 44 C.E. would be too early for this letter to have appeared. Consequently, the only James that can be identified with this letter is James the brother of the Lord and leader of the Jerusalem church.

Further support for this view comes from a deduction from the text itself regarding the implied author:

- *The implied author presumes that the readers know who he is.* He does not find it necessary to identify himself in a more detailed way to distinguish himself from others with the same name. He certainly must have been an influential person well known within the early Christian communities.

- *The implied author is at home within the world of Judaism.*[15] He is writing to the "twelve tribes in the Dispersion." His thoughts and expressions are drawn from the framework of Judaism. Jewish concepts such as the Law, wisdom, perfection all feature prominently in this writing.

- *The implied author is also at home within the world of Christianity.* His connections to the thought of the Sermon on the Mount show the writer handing on the thought and spirit of Jesus. Further, his definition of religion as "to care for orphans and widows in their distress" (1:27) and his concern for the welfare of the poor and marginalized within society all show an understanding of religion that lies close to the heart of Jesus' teaching.

- *The implied author bears the authority of a teacher:* "Not many of you should become teachers, my brothers and sisters, for you know that we who teach will be judged with greater strictness" (Jas 3:1). Here the implied author identifies himself as a teacher ("we who teach").

The picture of the implied author deduced from this writing is that of an authoritative teacher at home both within the worlds of Judaism and Christianity. This certainly conforms to the picture of James the brother of the Lord and leader of the Jerusalem church that we have unearthed from outside this text in the gospels, Acts, and the writings of Paul. Obviously we cannot prove conclusively that James, the brother of the Lord, did in fact write this letter. What we can say is that James, the brother of the Lord and leader of the Jerusalem church, was the person whom the writer in-

---

[15] See the next section, "The Interface of the Letter of James with Judaism."

tended to project as author of this text. This is the tradition the church continued to hand on over the centuries.

There are two ways in which we can understand the identification between the text of the letter and the person who lay behind the text:

- We can see it as being written in a way that resembles Paul's method of writing. At the end of his letters Paul identifies some scribes who helped him in their composition (see 1 Cor 16:21; Gal 6:11). James could be operating in a similar way. A scribe would help him with the literary composition of the text. This would explain the beauty of the polished Greek that is the concern of those who argue that James of Jerusalem would never have had the education necessary to write this text.

- On the other hand one could see the letter being composed shortly after the death of James. A disciple of James writes in the name of James to those communities that acknowledged James' authority in order to use James' teaching to speak to their situations.

In the second instance the composition of the letter would occur shortly after James' death in Jerusalem. A close associate of James with an excellent ability in Greek writes in James' name to those Jewish Christian communities in the Diaspora who recognized James' leadership and authority. The writer reminds his hearers/readers of James' teaching and vision so that they may remain true to the values and way of life that James handed on in fidelity to Jesus' teaching and so withstand the attractions of the world ("friendship with the world" [4:4]) to which they are being drawn. To my mind this solution gives the best account of all the available evidence. In this second sense James, the brother of the Lord and leader of the church in Jerusalem, is the voice behind this text. While he may not have written the text himself as we understand an author doing today, the writer clearly sees himself faithfully handing on the spirit of James' teaching for communities who acknowledged James' authority. An examination of this text gives us, the readers, an insight into the way James' message and authority were understood within the early Christian church, especially in centers of Jewish Christianity that looked to James as their leader and authority shortly after his death in 62 C.E. and before the destruction of the city of Jerusalem in 70 C.E.

The Interface of the Letter of James with Judaism

Our examination of the figure of James in the New Testament has stressed that he remained rooted in the heritage of Judaism and endeavored to preserve these connections with Judaism. The letter of James demonstrates an identical picture. The thought of the letter shows James rooted in his Jewish heritage. The whole document exudes a Jewish ethos to such an extent that some scholars have conjectured that it was originally a Jewish work that had later been "Christianized" through the insertion of two references to Jesus Christ at Jas 1:1 and 2:1.[16] There are three areas that clearly illustrate the author's interface with his Jewish heritage.

(1) "To The Twelve Tribes in the Dispersion"

As a Diaspora letter, this writing is directed to communities of Jewish Christians whom James addresses as "the twelve tribes," heirs to Israel's promises. Since the time of the destruction of the two kingdoms of Israel (721 B.C.E.) and Judah (587 B.C.E.), the people of the house of Israel had hoped that God would in the future restore their nation as God's people. This restoration was viewed in the sense of bringing the tribes together once again, reconstituting the nation as God's twelve-tribe kingdom. This hope is expressed in a really beautiful way in the Psalms of Solomon (from the mid-first century B.C.E.): "See, Lord, and raise up for them their king, the son of David, to rule over your servant Israel in the time known to you, O God" (*Pss. Sol.* 17:21-28).[17]

In the Gospel of Matthew, Jesus presented his mission in terms that were rooted in this hope of the reconstitution of God's people as the twelve-tribe kingdom. When Jesus sends out the Twelve in the Gospel of Matthew he says: "Go nowhere among the Gentiles, and enter no town of the Samaritans, but go rather to the lost sheep of the house of Israel" (Matt 10:5-6). According to the traditions on which the Gospel of Matthew is based, the ministry of Jesus and his disciples was originally directed toward the people of the house of Israel.[18] Their ministry did not embrace an outreach to the Gentiles. Jesus in the Gospel of Matthew bears this out in the episode where the Canaanite woman requests Jesus' healing for her

---

[16] See Louis Massebieau, "L'Epitre de Jacques est-elle l'Oeuvre d'un Chrétien?" *RHR* 32 (1895) 249–83, and Friedrich Spitta, "Der Brief des Jakobus," *Zur Geschichte und Litteratur des Urchristentums* 2 (Göttingen: Vandenhoeck & Ruprecht, 1896) 1–239.

[17] R. B. Wright, trans., "Psalms of Solomon," in James H. Charlesworth, ed., *The Old Testament Pseudepigrapha*. Vol. 2. *Expansions of the "Old Testament" and Legends, Wisdom and Philosophical Literature, Prayers, Psalms, and Odes, Fragments of Lost Judeo-Hellenistic Works* (London: Darton, Longman and Todd, 1985) 667.

[18] See Stephenson H. Brooks, *Matthew's Community: the Evidence of His Special Sayings Material*, JSNTSup 16 (Sheffield: Sheffield Academic Press, 1987) 49–50.

daughter. Jesus' response is: "I was sent only to the lost sheep of the house of Israel" (Matt 15:24).

James' address is to be understood against this background. Jesus' whole ministry was directed toward the reconstitution of God's twelve-tribe kingdom. His followers were sent out to continue this mission to the house of Israel. By using this address James situates himself clearly in the trajectory of the Jesus tradition, where he shows his fidelity to Jesus' mission and how he is extending it. In writing to Jewish Christians outside Palestine, James reminds them at the outset that they are heirs to God's promises of the past: through their acceptance of Jesus as the Messiah they are the beginning of this reconstituted twelve-tribe kingdom. Later in the letter James reminds them that they are the beginning of this creative action that God is working in their midst: ". . . so that we would become a kind of first fruits of his (God's) creatures" (Jas 1:18).

For James the vision of Jesus is firmly rooted in Israel's traditions and gives faithful expression to them. The letter of James emerges at a time when the separation between the traditions of the house of Israel and the traditions of Christianity had not occurred. This is exactly the situation of the figure of James as it emerged from the rest of the New Testament. He did not see any incompatibility between being a follower of Jesus and being a true adherent of Israel's traditions. Both the letter of James and the figure of James reflect a situation that endeavors to remain true to both traditions before the parting of the ways between the traditions of the house of Israel and of nascent Christianity.[19]

(2) The Letter of James, Purity Rules, and the Torah[20]

Chapter Two of the present work drew attention to the importance of purity rules in the life of Judaism and James' attitude toward the admission of Gentiles into the messianic movement of the followers of Jesus. Purity rules at their heart provided a structure for life that would establish correct relationships between the individual, the community, and God. In essence purity rules establish how an individual or a community has access to God and how they interface with one another. Bruce Malina considers that the

---

[19] See Scot McKnight, who expresses well this interface between the figure of James in Acts and the James of the letter ("A Parting within the Way: Jesus and James on Israel and Purity," in Chilton and Evans, eds., *James the Just and Christian Origins,* 129).

[20] For a more detailed examination of James and his relationship to Israel and the purity rules see Hartin, "Excursus 2: James and the Heritage of Israel," in *James,* 71–75.

concept of righteousness lies at the heart of all purity rules: "This is what righteousness is about. For righteousness means proper interpersonal relationships with all those in one's society, between God and covenanted human beings and between human beings and their fellow beings."[21]

The figure of James in Acts showed that he thought adherence to the purity rules was still essential. In defining what laws Gentile believers in Jesus must still uphold (Acts 15:19-20), James gives this justification: "For in every city, for generations past, Moses has had those who proclaim him, for he has been read aloud every sabbath in the synagogues" (Acts 15:21).[22] The Torah remains the foundation for all that one does; it sets forth one's way of life and gives one identity. The purity laws of the Torah establish the boundaries for interaction with one another and set one apart from those outside. Acts 15:19-20 gave the bare minimal purity rules to which Gentile believers in Jesus were to adhere. But it was presumed that Jewish believers in Jesus still continued to adhere to the fullness of the Torah.

The letter of James gives similar importance to the role of purity rules for its communities. As with James' instructions in Acts, the letter of James also advocates the foundational dimension of the Torah for defining one's relationship with God and one another. In the letter of James "the Torah provides a means of social identification for the members of James' community as the 'twelve tribes in the Dispersion' (1:1)."[23] The Torah sets forth the boundaries that separate James' communities from the wider society.[24] When James describes the Torah he uses a number of adjectives that define its role in the socialization process of the community: the Torah is perfect (Jas 1:25); it is the Torah of freedom (Jas 1:25); it is the royal Torah (Jas 2:8) whose essence is found in the law of love (Jas 2:8).

THE PERFECT TORAH OF FREEDOM (JAMES 1:25)[25]

James owes the concept of the Torah as a perfect gift from God to his heritage in the Hebrew Bible: Psalm 19:7-8 expresses the connection very succinctly. A parallelism is forged between the two verses: "*The law of the*

---

[21] Bruce J. Malina, *The New Testament World: Insights from Cultural Anthropology* (rev. ed. Louisville: Westminster John Knox, 1993) 174.

[22] See McKnight, *Jesus and James on Israel and Purity,* 114.

[23] Hartin, *A Spirituality of Perfection,* 79.

[24] See Robert W. Wall, *Community of the Wise: The Letter of James,* The New Testament in Context (Valley Forge, PA: Trinity Press International, 1997) 87, who describes well the social function of the Torah.

[25] This examination draws on the discussion in Hartin, *A Spirituality of Perfection,* 78–92.

LORD *is perfect . . . the precepts of the* LORD *are right.*" The two adjectives "perfect" and "right" are synonymous. The whole function of purity laws is to establish access to God and to define what one must do in order to remain in right relationship with God and one another. The Torah enables one to lead such a life.

The concept of perfection is central to the letter of James.[26] James' idea of perfection derives from the Hebrew writings and ritual practices of Israel and is more readily understood against the background of the purity laws. Perfection in James entails a total allegiance to God and is expressed in the desire to be in right relations with God. Observance of the Torah (like the observance of all purity laws) leads to a total relationship with the Lord. On the community level the Torah is perfect because it establishes the moral boundaries for all those who belong to this way of life and sets them off from groups or societies outside their community. Obedience to the law establishes the identity of all in their relationships with God and one another.

James goes on to describe the Torah as "the law of freedom." In the process of socialization, the Torah provides directions on how to act. As such the Torah enables believers to act freely as God's society, "the first fruits of God's creatures" (Jas 1:18). The Torah liberates them from the evils of the world and provides the freedom to achieve their true identity as God's people.

This positive assessment of the Torah differs markedly from Paul's attitude. Paul saw the Torah as leading to Christ, but once Christ came the value of the Torah ceased (Gal 3:23-25). For Paul the function of Christ was to set believers free from the Torah (see Rom 6:15-23; 7:6-8:2). James' view is very different. He still upholds a positive role for the Torah as does Jesus in the Sermon on the Mount (Matt 5:17-20). Jesus sees his role as bringing the Torah to fulfillment: "Do not think that I have come to abolish the law or the prophets; I have come not to abolish but to fulfill" (Matt 5:17). James provides an identical attitude to the Torah. He also shows the need for keeping the whole law and not selectively deciding what laws one will obey: "For whoever keeps the whole law but fails in one point has become accountable for all of it" (Jas 2:10). For James and the Jesus of the Sermon on the Mount, the Torah provides the direction and

---

[26] Ibid. 57–92. The adjective "perfect" *(teleios)* appears four times in the first chapter (1:4 [twice]; 1:17; 1:25) and again at 3:2. In addition, James uses the verb "to make perfect, to complete" *(teleioō)* at 2:22 and the verb "to fulfill, to accomplish" *(teleō)* at 2:8. The frequency of terminology for "perfect/perfection" is quite remarkable, given the fact that it is a relatively short letter.

foundation for those who are in relationship with God and one another to form the new society of the "first fruits of God's creatures" (Jas 1:18).

THE ROYAL TORAH (JAMES 2:8)

Defining the Torah as "royal" *(basilikon)* is understandable, given the context of Jas 2:5, which speaks about the kingdom: "Has not God chosen the poor in the world to be rich in faith and to be heirs of the kingdom *(basileias)* that God has promised to those who love him?" As we have indicated, the function of the Torah is to give direction and social identification to those who belong to God's twelve-tribe kingdom. The "royal law" refers to the Torah, which gives expression to the right relationships that should endure between all members of God's twelve-tribe kingdom. For James the Torah still holds true for the reconstituted twelve-tribe kingdom begun by Jesus and carried on now by James.[27]

The central expression of the Torah is found in the love command: "You shall love your neighbor as yourself" (Jas 2:8). This command comes from Lev 19:18c, which occurs in the context of a number of commands that deal essentially with the treatment of one's neighbors, particularly those who are poor. The same is true of James' use of this love command. It occurs in the context of his discussion on the unfair discrimination that is meted out to the poor when preference is shown for the rich (Jas 2:1-7). For Jesus the love command encapsulated the heart of his teaching and instructions on preserving right relationships between God and one another in the embrace of God's kingdom. James continues this same tradition. The love command gives a specific focus to the Torah and to the way of life that identifies those who are members of the twelve-tribe kingdom. The law of love provides the focus, the spirit in which James' community must preserve their relationship and ultimately their identity. [28]

SUMMARY

For the letter of James purity for this twelve-tribe people of God consists in adhering to the Torah. Being in a right relationship with God, as we have defined the purpose of purity rules, comes from obedience to the Torah, which James has defined as perfect, bringing freedom, royal and encapsulated in the law of love of neighbor.[29] Without doubt James' definition of religion rests on

---

[27] See Wall, *Community of the Wise,* 122.

[28] See McKnight, *Jesus and James on Israel and Purity,* 123.

[29] Ibid. 117.

this understanding of the Torah when he says: "Religion that is pure and un-defiled before God, the Father, is this: to care for orphans and widows in their distress, and to keep oneself unstained by the world" (Jas 1:27).

The language of purity is at the forefront of this definition of religion: True religion that is "pure and undefiled" *(kathara kai amiantos)* entails demonstrating love for one's neighbor, graphically illustrated through the biblical images of caring for "the widow and orphan." The purity language continues in the further description of how one relates to the world: "to keep oneself unstained by the world" *(aspilon heauton tērein apo tou kos-mou)*. At the heart of the letter of James is the duality between God and the world. A choice has to be made between the two. This opposition between God and the world reaches its climax in Jas 4:4: "Do you not know that friendship with the world is enmity with God? Therefore whoever wishes to be a friend of the world becomes an enemy of God." In other words, the Torah shows how to remain true to friendship with God and consequently this sets one apart from the world.

(3) James and the Wisdom Heritage[30]

A third illustration of how the letter of James remains rooted in the heritage of the house of Israel comes from its interface with the Wisdom tradition. In discussing the literary genre of the letter of James we argued that this writing belonged to the primary genre of Wisdom literature, while at the same time exhibiting a secondary genre that conformed to what is known as a protreptic discourse. In the Wisdom tradition of the Hebrew writings two features were central. In the first instance Hebrew wisdom rested heavily on the theological understanding that God alone is the truly wise being. All wisdom comes from God as God's gift, and human wisdom merely shares in this divine wisdom. This understanding lies at the heart of James' instructions in his letter. James 3:13-18 contrasts two types of wisdom, divine and human. The true wisdom James defines as "the wisdom from above" (Jas 2:17). The first description he gives of "the wisdom from above" is that it is "pure." Here James uses purity language because it is wisdom that comes from God that provides direction on how to maintain true relationships with God and one another. James does not reflect on the nature or the personification of wisdom as some of the writings from the Wisdom tradition of Israel did (e.g., Prov 8:22-36; Sirach 24; Wis 7:25–8:1).

---

[30] For a more detailed examination of James' connection to the Hebrew Wisdom tradition see Hartin, "Excursus 3: The Wisdom of James (The Gift of Wisdom [James 1:5-8])," in *James*, 75–81.

The way to attain this wisdom from God is through prayer: "If any of you is lacking in wisdom, ask God, who gives to all generously and ungrudgingly, and it will be given you" (Jas 1:5).

The letter of James demonstrates much closer affinities with the second element of the Wisdom tradition, namely the presentation of practical instruction on how to lead a successful life. All wisdom instruction was practical in nature and aimed at providing the hearer/reader with directions on how to lead one's life based on the insights and experiences of a "wise person." The clearest illustration of this wisdom instruction seen as emanating from a wise person appears in the person of Solomon. When offered the choice of any gift at the beginning of his rule he chose the gift of God's wisdom to rule his nation (1 Kgs 3:1-14, 16-28). In the Hebrew tradition Solomon became "the wise person" *par excellence* and all the Wisdom traditions were traced back to him to give them their authority. See, e.g., how the book of Wisdom is identified as "the Wisdom of Solomon." It is a writing coming from Alexandria, Egypt, in the first century B.C.E. At times the writer places his wise instructions in the mouth of King Solomon in order to give them authority as true wisdom teachings (see Wis 7:1-22).

In true Israelite fashion James does not reflect upon wisdom in an abstract way. Wisdom is fundamentally practical, and James provides instruction for his hearers/readers on moral action for the life of the community and the individuals within the community as members of God's twelve-tribe kingdom. James' wisdom instruction in effect says this: If you are to live as members of this community, these are the ways you should act. Living according to these wise instructions preserves the community and the individual in right relationship with God.

Every perfect gift comes down from above (Jas 1:17). Among these gifts the most important is that of wisdom. The real consequence of the gift of divine wisdom for the community and the believer is that "we would become a kind of first fruits of his (God's) creatures" (Jas 1:18). A regeneration, a rebirth occurs in the lives of those who receive God's gift of wisdom. It is "the implanted word that has the power to save your souls" (Jas 1:21).[31] This is an incredible development on the Hebrew understanding of wisdom. For the Israelites the gift of wisdom enables them to perceive how to act wisely, while for James the gift goes even farther: it brings with it a transformation within the lives of those who receive it.

---

[31] See Timothy B. Cargal: "Wisdom is 'generously' given by God to those who ask with 'faith.' It is a 'good and perfect gift,' 'implanted' within them and 'able to save [their] souls' from death" (*Restoring the Diaspora: Discursive Structure and Purpose in the Epistle of James*, SBLDS 144 [Atlanta: Scholars, 1993] 90).

A final dimension of James' use of the Hebrew Wisdom traditions is that he also shows fidelity to the way Jesus interpreted those traditions. Like Jesus, James remains concerned for the poor and marginalized within society (Jas 2:1-7). The wisdom received through Torah, and now from Jesus, regenerates the people as the "first fruits of his (God's) creatures" (Jas 1:18).[32]

These observations add one important dimension to the vision we had assembled of James from the study of the gospels, Acts, and the letters of Paul. The James of the letter is the same as the James of Acts and Paul's letters: he stresses that Jesus' followers must remain rooted in the Torah. The new aspect that has emerged from this consideration of the letter of James is that the letter provides the reason for this stress on the Torah. It is the means by which the community is reconstituted as God's twelve-tribe kingdom. James is writing to this reconstituted community to offer them direction and insight into aspects of their life in relationship with God and one another that they need to develop and stress, particularly a concern for the poor. In this sense, then, James is the New Testament Wisdom teacher who has inherited the Wisdom mantle from Jesus.

James' Interface with Jesus[33]

Throughout this study on the figure of James I have intimated on many occasions James' closeness to the figure of Jesus and his message. In this section I wish briefly to examine this interface with Jesus in a little more depth to illustrate where and how this interface occurs. There are two ways in which I would like to show that the letter of James interfaces with the person of Jesus.

James Speaks in the Voice of Jesus

Some scholars maintain that while the letter of James shows certain similarities with the message of Jesus, these similarities come from the cultural context of early Christianity that adopted a common ethical viewpoint and James is simply reflecting that common ethical background.[34] I have argued

---

[32] See Richard J. Bauckham, *James: Wisdom of James, Disciple of Jesus the Sage* (London and New York: Routledge, 1999) 108, who describes well James' fidelity to the Wisdom heritage of Jesus.

[33] For a detailed examination of the relationship between the letter of James and the Sayings Source Q see Hartin, "Excursus 4: James and the Heritage of Jesus (James' Use of the Jesus Traditions [James 1:9-11])," in *James*, 81–88.

[34] See Sophie Laws, *A Commentary on the Epistle of James*, BNTC (London: Adam & Charles Black, 1980) 18; and Todd C. Penner, *The Epistle of James and Eschatology:*

elsewhere that the interface between James and Jesus' ethical teaching is more than reliance upon a common ethical tradition. Instead, James shows an awareness of the sayings tradition. Most of the connections between the letter of James and the Jesus traditions are with the Sermon on the Mount in the Gospel of Matthew.[35] A good example is that of Jas 5:12 and Matt 5:33-37. A brief glance shows the closeness between the two sayings:

James 5:12	*Matthew 5:33-37*
	Again, you have heard that it was said to those of ancient times, "You shall not swear falsely, but carry out the vows you have made to the Lord."
Above all, my beloved, do not swear, either by heaven	But I say to you, Do not swear at all, either by heaven, for it is the throne of God,
or by earth	or by the earth, for it is his footstool,
or by any other oath,	or by Jerusalem, for it is the city of the great King. And do not swear by your head, for you cannot make one hair white or black.
but let your "Yes" be yes and your "No" be no, so that you may not fall under condemnation.	Let your word be "Yes, Yes" or "No, No"; anything more than this comes from the evil one.

While James does not actually quote any saying of Jesus, he does allude to them throughout the letter. Robert Alter has defined the concept of

---

Re-reading an Ancient Christian Letter, JSNTSup 121 (Sheffield: Sheffield Academic Press, 1996) 254.

[35] See, for example, Joseph B. Mayor, *The Epistle of St. James. The Greek Text with Introduction, Notes and Comments, and Further Studies in the Epistle of St. James* (3rd ed. Grand Rapids: Zondervan, [1913] 1954) lxxxv–lxxxvii; W. D. Davies, *The Setting of the Sermon on the Mount* (Cambridge: Cambridge University Press, 1964) 402–403; Peter H. Davids, *The Epistle of James: A Commentary on the Greek Text,* NIGTC (Grand Rapids: Eerdmans, 1982) 47–48; and John Painter, *Just James: The Brother of Jesus in History and Tradition* (Minneapolis: Fortress, 1999) 261–62.

a literary allusion in this way: a "literary allusion . . . involves the evoca-tion—through a wide spectrum of formal means—in one text of an an-tecedent literary text."[36] Studies that have been made over the past two decades on the Greco-Roman art of rhetoric have shown that many aspects of this ancient art of rhetoric help to shed light on the New Testament. The letters of the New Testament are above all rhetorical documents aimed at persuading the hearers/readers regarding the life they lead. The letter of James, as a protreptic discourse, has as its rhetorical intention the persua-sion of its hearers/readers to embrace the vision of life as "the twelve tribes in the Dispersion." James endeavors to persuade them as to what the life of members of such a community entails.

In a recent work that studied ancient rhetorical handbooks Wesley Wachob has shown that one of the rhetorical features of an argument was to use a text that was known to the audience (without identifying it), weav-ing it into the text to support the argumentation. Wachob states that "the artful activation of an antecedent text was a common ploy in rendering a given proposal more readily acceptable to an audience."[37]

What James has done in his use of the sayings tradition of Jesus lies clearly in this vein. James has taken a Jesus saying and reworked it into his own argumentation in such a way that it would evoke the Jesus saying in the minds of the hearers/readers, but it would be expressed formally in a new way conforming to the context of the argument James is making.

Let us take one illustration from the previous discussion: "You do well if you really fulfill the royal law according to the scripture, 'You shall love your neighbor as yourself'" (Jas 2:8). In a Jewish context this passage is immediately identifiable as coming from Lev 19:18c as the center of the admonitions relating to the treatment of others, particularly the poor within the covenant community. A few verses earlier in the same context and chapter Leviticus says: "You shall not render an unjust judgment; you shall not be partial to the poor or defer to the great; with justice you shall judge your neighbor" (Lev 19:15). James has also quoted Lev 19:18c within the context of an argument in which he challenges his community not to dis-criminate against the poor (Jas 2:1-7). The scripture relating to the love command is the fullest support that can be given for the avoidance of every form of discrimination.

---

[36] Robert Alter, *The Pleasures of Reading: In an Ideological Age* (New York: Simon & Schuster, 1989) 112.

[37] Wesley Hiram Wachob, *The Voice of Jesus in the Social Rhetoric of James*, SNTSMS 106 (Cambridge: Cambridge University Press, 2000) 116.

However, this verse would have said more to Jewish Christian hearers/readers. Undoubtedly they would have been reminded of the ethics of Jesus. The heart of his message was the love command that is found in almost every tradition within the New Testament (Matt 22:34-40; Mark 12:28-34; Luke 10:25-28). Further, James identifies this command as the "royal law" or "the law of the kingdom" *(nomon basilikon).* The language of the kingdom is central to Jesus' preaching. If there is one word that is synonymous with Jesus' preaching it is the term "kingdom," whereby Jesus sets forth his call to bring people into relationship with God and one another. James is intent on persuading his hearers/readers that the love command is the essence of relationships within the twelve-tribe kingdom. But this is not a novel invention of James: it is literally at the heart of Jesus' message and proclamation. In the context of James' hearers/readers this verse would have immediately evoked the central message of Jesus and would have acted in a forceful way to support James' argumentation.

Since James was recasting traditional material in new dress he is ultimately producing what can be called "a new performance"[38] of that material. The letters of the New Testament, and in particular the letter of James, were meant initially to be read aloud. Hence "performance" is a suitable description. The letter is meant to be heard by the hearers, so formal attention to the rhetoric of its communication is essential. The rhetorical culture of the ancient world embraced ancient texts (or sayings in the case of James) and performed them in new ways to persuade their audience.

Vernon Robbins has done important research into this field of the rhetorical culture of the ancient world and has made some remarkable contributions to the understanding of the rhetorical nature of the New Testament documents. He has shown how ancient texts treated sources very differently from the way in which modern academics treat their sources today. The ancient rhetorical culture aimed not simply at copying existing sources, but rather at "actualizing" the source in a new way. Robbins has termed this "recitation composition."[39] This is exactly what James has done in composing his letter. He has drawn on the sayings of Jesus (as well as the Hebrew Bible) in order to persuade his own hearers/readers in new and different contexts. In using the sayings of Jesus he has not quoted them directly, but has performed them in his own way to illustrate his argument. The authority of Jesus is the voice that lies behind his argument, and James

---

[38] See Hartin, *James,* 84.

[39] Vernon K. Robbins, "Writing as Rhetorical Act in Plutarch and the Gospels," in Duane F. Watson, ed., *Persuasive Artistry: Studies in New Testament Rhetoric in Honor of George A. Kennedy* (Sheffield: JSOT Press, 1991) 147.

has endeavored to remain true to that voice. In this sense we can say that James now speaks in the voice of Jesus.

James Inherits the Mantle of Jesus

As we have indicated, the movement Jesus initiated was a "Jewish restoration movement."[40] The letter of James continues this vision of restoring the house of Israel. In using the same language Jesus used to define the scope and direction of his own ministry, James continues Jesus' vision of reconstituting God's people. James' focus lies exclusively with his Jewish heritage and preserving that heritage.

Jesus' message also lies at the very heart and center of James' message. Of particular concern to Jesus were the marginalized within Jewish society. In his preaching and in his healing Jesus reached out to the poor, to women, to children, to the sick—in short, to all those society had relegated in one way or another to inferior and subservient positions. This message Jesus preached by word and action was itself heir to the traditions of the Hebrew Scriptures, especially the prophets. Some of the harshest words of the prophets concerned the ill treatment of the poor at the hands of faithful Israel (e.g., Amos 2:6-7).

A failure to care for the poor amounted to a rejection of Israel's whole history and God's protection of their own nation. Since God had cared for them and championed their cause, the Israelites in their turn should extend that same care and concern to others who are poor as a reminder of their own heritage. The position of "the poor" within society was largely due to their lack of status, honor, and power. Social-scientific studies in recent times have shown that the economic situation of the poor was largely a result of their lack of social status within the society.[41] One can see this particularly with the three groups Israelite society identified as the poor: the widow, the orphan, and the stranger (e.g., Deut 24:17-18). Since the widow, the orphan, and the resident alien (or the stranger) have no one within society to champion their cause, they are without influence and power and hence their economic plight becomes all the more tenuous. God then becomes their champion.

Jesus' message of concern for the poor is to be understood against the background of this prophetic challenge to care for the poor. James inherits

---

[40] See McKnight, *Jesus and James on Israel and Purity,* 102–103.

[41] See Bruce J. Malina, "Wealth and Poverty in the New Testament and Its World," *Int* 41 (1987) 354–67; and Patrick J. Hartin, "Poor," in *Eerdmans Dictionary of the Bible,* ed. David Noel Freedman (Grand Rapids: Eerdmans, 2000) 1070–71.

this same concern for the poor, and it becomes one of the dominant themes throughout his letter. When James defines religion he shows he is in line with the tradition of the prophets and Jesus: "Religion that is pure and undefiled before God, the Father, is this: to care for orphans and widows in their distress" (Jas 1:27). By using the traditional categories of the poor ("the widow and orphan"), James reminds his hearers/readers that God is champion of the poor (Jas 5:1-6).

James turns his attention to the poor on three occasions: Jas 1:9-11; 2:1-7; and 5:1-6. One theme that emerges in James' introduction is a belief that God will bring about a reversal of fortunes among the rich and the poor (1:9-11). Then, at the opening to the body of the letter (Jas 2:1-7), James takes up this theme of the rich and the poor and examines their relationship within the context of the Christian community. He presents a graphic example of discrimination within the community whereby people are treated differently according to their economic status. The rich are welcomed into the assembly with honor while the poor are relegated with shame to the lowliest of places. James challenges the community to reflect on its behavior and to realize that it is to imitate God in the way it is called to honor the poor: "Has not God chosen the poor in the world to be rich in faith and to be heirs of the kingdom that he has promised to those who love him?" (Jas 2:5). Finally, James returns to the theme of rich and poor at the end of the body of the letter (Jas 5:1-6). For James, then, the theme of how one treats the poor is central to his whole vision of what the twelve-tribe kingdom should embrace.

James shows that he continues Jesus' vision through an option for the poor and a challenge to his hearers/readers to avoid every form of discrimination. James' ethical instructions show that he is at home both in the traditions of Israel and in the traditions of Jesus. In fact, James lies closer to both traditions than any other writer of the New Testament. The letter of James is the most Jewish of all the writings of the New Testament in that its focus is above all on Jewish Christians. It argues strongly for remaining true to the Torah that is the defining element of the society of the reconstituted twelve-tribe kingdom. At the same time, it remains true to the vision and traditions emanating from Jesus. Jesus interacted above all with his own people and challenged them with new insights into the countercultural values he proclaimed as the center of his kingdom and the relationship with God and one another. James continues this same emphasis on countercultural values, particularly with the centrality given to upholding the equality of all who are members of this reconstituted people of God. In the spirit of Jesus and the prophets before him, James shows a central concern for the wellbeing of the poor and marginalized within society. James' concern for the poor is something Paul also noted when he spoke about James' endorsement (together with the other apostles) for his (Paul's) ministry to the Gentiles: "They asked only one thing, that we remember the poor, which was actually what I was eager to do" (Gal 2:10). James certainly is the true heir to the ministry and teaching of Jesus. The letter of James shows that James truly inherited Jesus' mantle.

James' Interface with Paul's Thought: Justification, Faith, and Works[42]

This is undoubtedly one of the most discussed topics in the letter of James. Because of a perceived opposition between James and Paul on the teaching of justification by faith alone, Martin Luther initially rejected the letter of James from the canon, calling it "an epistle of straw."[43]

Unfortunately, because the letter of James is most often read through the eyes of Paul it is seldom seen in its integrity. Twelve verses dealing with faith and works (Jas 2:14-26) become the center of consideration.[44] Such a focus ignores everything else in the five chapters of this writing.

We have already examined the interface between James and Paul when considering Acts and the letter to the Galatians. In this brief section I wish to examine what the letter of James indicates, if anything, about an interface with Paul and how to correlate that with the information we have gleaned from the rest of the New Testament.

The central issue concerns the theological vision of Paul and James concerning the relationship between justification, faith, and good works. The real problem emerges from the fact that Paul and James use the same vocabulary, but in different contexts and in the framework of different theological visions (e.g., justification *[dikaiosynē]*, to save *[sōzein]*, faith *[pistis]*, law *[nomos]*, and works *[erga]*). What is the exact relationship between Paul and James? Is James reacting against Paul's theological teaching, or is James writing independently of Paul and not in opposition to him? A solution arises from an examination of the meaning of the terms that are used within the context of their own theological vision.

---

[42] For a more detailed discussion on Paul's and James' understanding of justification and the concept of works in relation to justification see Hartin, "Excursus 7: Faith and Works in James and Paul," in *James,* 163–72.

[43] Martin Luther, Preface to his 1522 translation of the New Testament (*Luther's Works: Word and Sacrament I,* vol. 35, ed. E. T. Brackmann [Philadelphia: Fortress, 1960] 362).

[44] See Luke Timothy Johnson, *The Letter of James,* AB 37A (New York: Doubleday, 1995) 114.

Paul's Approach to the Relationship between Justification, Faith, and Works

Paul's theological vision is summed up well in Gal 2:15-16. For Paul justification comes through *"faith in Jesus Christ."* Jews and Gentiles are one in the community of believers because of the justification they have received "through faith in Jesus Christ" *(dia/ek pisteōs Iēsou Christou)*. Recently Richard Hays has argued for an understanding of this phrase as a *subjective genitive*[45] to be translated as "through Jesus Christ's faithfulness."[46] The significance of this interpretation is that the focus is placed on Jesus' action of faithfulness and obedience to the Father, which culminates in the sacrifice of Jesus on the cross. If Gal 2:15-16 is understood in this way it would stress that justification is attained through the faithfulness of Jesus Christ as demonstrated in the sacrifice of the cross and not through humanity's attempt to attain salvation themselves by obeying the stipulations of the Jewish Law. The contrast is between what Jesus has done in his faithfulness on the cross and humanity's reliance on its own efforts. In essence justification comes from reliance on Jesus and not on humanity's own actions.[47]

For Paul the essence of justification remains with God's action of love, which is manifested in the salvific love of Jesus. This leads him to distance himself forcefully from any interpretations and teachings that replace God's actions in Christ with a reliance on one's own actions in an attempt to earn salvation through obeying the Mosaic Law. This is what Paul terms "works of the Law" (see Rom 3:20, 27; 4:2).

James' Approach to the Relationship between Justification, Faith, and Works

James uses the language of justification quite frequently for this short writing:[48] For James the emphasis in the realm of salvation is on what God is doing. God is reconstituting the new twelve-tribe kingdom from "the

---

[45] The customary way to translate *dia/ek pisteōs Iēsou Christou* has been as an *objective genitive*, namely as "faith in Jesus Christ," where Jesus is the object of the believer's faith.

[46] Richard B. Hays, "Justification," *ABD* vol. 3 (1992) 1129–33; see also his "Have We Found Abraham to be Our Forefather According to the Flesh? A Reconsideration of Rom 4:1," *NovT* 27 (1985) 76–98; and "Christology and Ethics in Galatians: The Law of Christ," *CBQ* 49 (1987) 268–90.

[47] See Hays, *Justification*, 1131.

[48] As I have noted elsewhere (*James*, 165): "The verb *dikaioun* occurs on three occasions (2:21, 24, 25); the noun *dikaiosynē* also appears three times (1:20; 2:23; 3:18) while the adjective *dikaios* occurs twice (5:6, 16) and the noun *adikia* once (3:6)."

first fruits of his (God's) creation" (Jas 1:18). For those who have endured patiently and withstood the test there is "the crown of life that the Lord has promised to those who love him" (Jas 1:12). For James, God is the agent of salvation, while humanity is the receiver. God is the cheerful giver: "If any of you is lacking in wisdom, ask God, who gives to all generously and un-grudgingly, and it will be given you" (Jas 1:5). All good gifts (and that in-cludes salvation and justification) are received from God (Jas 1:17).

James 2:1 uses a phrase similar to one that was common in Paul "the faith of our Lord Jesus Christ" *(tēn pistin tou kyriou hēmōn 'Iēsou Chris-tou)*. I have argued that in the context of the letter of James, as in Paul (see above), this phrase is to be interpreted as a subjective genitive.[49] James is concerned with the believer's imitation of Jesus' life that demonstrates a faithfulness in carrying out the Father's will. The faithfulness of Jesus is demonstrated through his good deeds. In a similar fashion the believer must also demonstrate his/her faithfulness through a life of good works.

James 2:14-26 examines the quality of faith that is demonstrated through good works. This is the section commentators have used to set against Paul's thought. However, if we follow the theological vision and understanding as il-lustrated above we see that James is not attacking Paul. James' main thesis is that faith must be demonstrated by works of love. On its own, faith is useless: "Do you want to be shown, you senseless person, that faith apart from works is barren?" (Jas 2:20). James is as opposed to faith on its own as he is to works on its own. The two must be connected: they flow one into the other. True faith expresses itself in works of love, while works of love deepen one's faith. Faith expressed in works of love shows that faith is truly alive. In speaking of the example of Abraham who offered his son Isaac on the altar, James says: "You see that faith was active along with his works, and faith was brought to completion by the works" (Jas 2:22).

Both James and Paul refer to the example of Abraham being justified by God. Each uses this example in his own way to illustrate his different theological vision. In Gal 3:6-9 Paul refers to the example of Abraham and quotes Gen 15:6 to support his argument. In using this quotation Paul's in-tent is to argue that God justified Abraham on the basis of Abraham's faith in God. This then becomes an example for all on the path to salvation: jus-tification of Jew and Gentile occurs on the basis of faith in God and not by means of any actions or works they might perform.

James uses the example of Abraham in a way that is distinctly differ-ent from that of Paul (2:20-23). A close examination of James' argument

---

[49] See ibid. 117.

shows that he has added the account of Abraham's offering of his son on the altar (Gen 22:1-19) to illustrate Abraham's faith in action. Abraham's faith was alive and active because of his works (the offering of his son on the altar). The difference between James and Paul becomes apparent. While Paul was concerned to show that faith rests on the foundation of God and not on works of the Law, James' concern was to show that faith, to be alive, must demonstrate itself through actions of love: a living faith must express itself in action. Paul's opposition was directed to "works of the law," which he saw negatively as an impossible way of trying to earn salvation. James endorsed "good works" that flowed from faith and demonstrated love. There are two different theological visions operative here. Paul is concerned with the situation of someone *before* coming to faith, leading up to faith. James is concerned with the person *after* she or he has come to faith, expressing faith in action. Augustine saw the relationship between Paul and James in a similar way:

> Therefore the opinions of the two apostles, Paul and James, are not opposed to each other when the one says that [the human person] is justified by faith without works, and the other says that faith without works is useless: because the former (Paul) speaks about works that precede faith, while the latter (James) speaks about those that follow faith; as even Paul shows in many places.[50]

What the letter of James shows is that there was an equally important vision that has been overshadowed by Paul's concerns. James' vision is not one that is on the periphery of the New Testament. Instead, it is just as much at the heart of the New Testament as is Paul's. In the Sermon on the Mount, Matthew's Jesus expresses a relationship between faith and actions that is similar to the teaching of James. Or perhaps one should put it the opposite way: James' vision is a clear illustration of what Matthew's Jesus says in the Sermon on the Mount: "Not everyone who says to me, 'Lord, Lord,' will enter the kingdom of heaven, but only the one who does the will of my Father in heaven" (Matt 7:21). Matthew's Jesus goes on to give a parable of the person who built a house on a rock foundation (Matt 7:24-27) which again illustrates the importance of actions being based on a firm faith foundation.

James' vision of a faith that is alive, demonstrating itself through good works, conforms to Jesus' central message. Once again we note the close-

---

[50] Augustine, *De diversis quaestionibus LXXXIII Liber Unus* 76 [*MPL* 50:89]).

ness of James to Jesus' thought in the Sermon on the Mount. Paul also gives expression to this vision when he challenges his hearers/readers in all his letters to ensure that their lives conform to what they believe: ". . . so that you may lead lives worthy of the Lord, fully pleasing to him, as you bear fruit in every good work and as you grow in the knowledge of God" (Col 1:10).

This examination of the interface between James and Paul has shown that there is no real opposition between their thought. Each has a distinctive theological vision and has remained true to that vision. The issues they deal with are also determined by very distinctive contexts. James is writing within the context of a Jewish Christian environment, while Paul is working within the context of a Christianity engaging with the wider Greco-Roman pagan world.

This reveals the beauty and diversity of early Christianity. James bears witness to another stream within early Christianity that was extremely influential in the first two centuries of the Christian movement and reflects the theology and concerns of a world that endeavors to retain its roots within its Jewish heritage. That James' thought and expression differ from those of Paul does not mean they are opposed to and in conflict with Paul's thought.[51] The value of the letter of James is that it provides us with an insight into another stream of tradition within the world of early Christianity that, as we have argued above, is in close proximity to Jesus' thought and vision.

The Contribution of the Letter of James to Our Understanding of James of Jerusalem

While the letter does not identify the writer clearly as "James, the brother of the Lord," the image we have constructed of the implied author clearly supports this picture. The writer is at home within the worlds of Judaism and early Christianity. He is a well-known authority and teacher within that world who does not need to identify himself beyond the simple: "James, a servant of God and of the Lord Jesus Christ." No other James, beyond "James the brother of the Lord" would be able to identify himself so unequivocally.

In its interface with the world of Judaism the letter of James shows that the writer sees the community to whom he writes as the fulfillment of the messianic hopes of the house of Israel. God is working something new

---

[51] As Johnson (*The Letter of James,* 113) says: "The recognition of diversity does not require a conflict model to make sense of earliest Christianity."

among God's people, bringing to birth a new creation of which the Jewish Christians to whom James writes are "the first fruits of his (God's) creatures" (Jas 1:18).

In interfacing with Jesus, the letter of James shows that James has truly inherited Jesus' mantle. Using tremendous skills drawn from Greco-Roman rhetoric, the letter of James performs the Jesus sayings anew, recasting Jesus' voice into James' own voice. In this way James witnesses to the authority of Jesus that lies behind his arguments.

James continues to stress the heart of Jesus' message. Jesus' preaching focused on the downtrodden, the outcasts of society. All the gospel traditions bear witness to this characteristic feature and concern of Jesus' ministry. James takes up the same concern in his letter. The first theme he examines embraces the poor, and he challenges his hearers/readers to make an option for the poor just as God has done. Just as Jesus' vision embraced countercultural values, so too does James set before his hearers/readers the perspective that God reverses the roles of rich and poor within God's kingdom (Jas 1:9).

The letter of James lies in the trajectory that reaches from the prophets through Jesus, in which God is acknowledged as the champion of the poor. James advocates a true respect for the poor, who have a dignity that comes from being creatures of God. A personal religion without social concern is meaningless for James. Again, James shows he is heir to the world of Jesus and of the first century, which has a strong communitarian conviction as opposed to our Western twenty-first-century world, which celebrates individuality. Above all, James' challenge is to live an authentic faith: to put faith into action. James speaks to the hearer/reader as a member of a community of faith. More can be achieved by working together with a shared vision than by working as individuals.

Just as the message of Jesus aimed at reconstituting the twelve-tribe kingdom of Israel, so James continues this mission. He upholds the position and authority of the Torah as the true expression of God's will for God's people. The Torah is the defining element that sets the boundaries for the society, while adherence to the Torah gives identity to the society of God's reconstituted people. The letter of James in its wisdom and its ethical advice presents the social markers for the members of the communities to whom James writes.

How does this perspective from the letter of James interface with the knowledge we have of James from the rest of the New Testament? While the letter of James does not add new details about James of Jerusalem, it does flesh out for the reader in an authentic and graphic way James' interface with Judaism, Jesus, Paul, and the society of his day. The James of the gospels, Acts, and the letters of Paul emerged as an authoritative leader within the early Christian church who endeavored to hold onto and preserve the roots of the gospel message in the house of Israel. The letter of James illustrates well some aspects of that heritage that James struggled to uphold.

The greatest contribution the letter of James makes to the figure of James and his interface with the leaders and thought of early Christianity lies in its witness to its Jewish heritage. The letter shows a strong and vibrant Jewish Christian tradition that flourished side by side with other traditions in earliest Christianity, such as those of Paul and the Synoptic Gospels that make up almost two-thirds of the entire New Testament. James is the only complete writing within the New Testament that witnesses to another thriving tradition that would later disappear. Just as the Sermon on the Mount captures the essence of Jesus' teaching, so too does the letter of James continue a similar message and teaching. The voice of the Jesus of the Sermon on the Mount and the voice of James are very close in reproducing the authentic concerns of Jesus' teaching.[52]

---

[52] Hartin, *A Spirituality of Perfection,* 164.

CHAPTER FOUR

The Tradition Develops:
James Outside the Canonical Writings

> Ever drifting down the stream—
> Lingering in the golden gleam—
> Life, what is it but a dream?[1]

The preceding examination of the canonical writings has demonstrated the important role that James of Jerusalem played in the context of the early church through his leadership of the Jerusalem church *(ekklēsia)*. In this chapter a study of other Christian writings that emerged over the course of the following three centuries will show that the figure of James of Jerusalem continued to play an important role.

Before we examine James' role within these extra-canonical writings it is important to recognize that the concept of a fixed canon of twenty-seven books making up the New Testament, as we know it today, emerged gradually over time. The Easter Letter of Bishop Athanasius of Alexandria (367 C.E.) is the first listing we have of the twenty-seven books of the New Testament together as the only holy books of Christianity. This shows that it was only by 367 C.E. that a consensus had emerged regarding what books constituted the New Testament canon. Athanasius' letter gave expression to the ever-deepening view within the early church that only these twenty-seven books were to be accepted as canonical.[2]

---

[1] Lewis Carroll, *Through the Looking-Glass and What Alice Found There,* Books of Wonder (New York: William Morrow & Co. [1872] 1993) 224.

[2] See Bruce M. Metzger, *The Canon of the New Testament: Its Origin, Development, and Significance* (Oxford: Clarendon Press, 1987) 312, for a translation of this text of the Easter letter of Bishop Athanasius. See also pp. 210–12 of that book for a discussion of the importance of the letter.

Consensus around this view quickly unified the different branches of the Christian church, namely the Syrian, the Greek, and the Western churches. By the end of the fourth century C.E. agreement had been reached throughout the Christian church on what books comprised the New Testament canon. The production of the canon was not the result, for example, of Bishop Athanasius imposing his view on the rest of Christianity. Instead it grew out of an emerging consensus within the scattered Christian communities of the ancient Christian world. Athanasius simply gave expression to what he saw were the accepted writings at that point. A number of factors gave rise to the ultimate acceptance of these writings alongside those of the Hebrew Bible as the sacred writings of Christianity.

Their usage everywhere in the church's worship: The place where the writings first gained a status as sacred writings was in the context of the liturgy. This was largely due to the influence of the Hebrew Scriptures. The Christian liturgy first used and considered the writings of the Hebrew Bible as sacred and authoritative. Alongside these Hebrew writings, certain writings of the apostles were also used, such as Paul's letters. When Paul wrote a letter to one of his communities, such as to the Corinthians, it would be read in the context of a worship service. With time these writings attained the same authoritative status that the Hebrew writings enjoyed in the Christian community. Certain centers of Christianity tended to give more importance to some writings over others. These centers were responsible for their preservation and authoritative status. For example, the church in Antioch gave special importance to the traditions associated with the Gospel of Matthew. The churches of Asia Minor preserved the writings of Paul and John, while the churches of Syria were centers where the traditions associated with James and the Gospel of Thomas flourished.

Their reflection of the traditional faith of the church: The word canon originally meant "standard" or "authority." The "canon of Scripture" referred to those books in which Christians could see their faith reflected. With time the term canon became identified with "the list of books" that contained that standard of faith. The question asked of a particular writing was whether it reflected the faith that had been handed down from the apostles. This was one reason for the rejection of many Gnostic writings.[3] They were judged not to reflect the apostolic faith that was being expressed throughout the wider Christian world. Despite the antiquity of many of the

---

[3] For an explanation of the terms "Gnostic" and "Gnosticism" see the section later in this chapter entitled "James within the Traditions of Gnosticism."

traditions associated with these writings, the way they were now used within Gnostic circles resulted in their rejection by the universal church.

Their origin from the apostles either directly or indirectly: An apostle's authority was vital for the acceptance of a writing within the context of the Christian communities, because it connected this writing to the faith of the apostles. In the world of early Christianity the concept of the "author" promoted the "authority" of the writing. While a particular apostle might not necessarily have physically written a particular text, nevertheless the apostle's name testified to the authentic faith of the Christian community. Many disciples of famous apostles wrote works with the intention of speaking in their name and spirit. The letters of Paul to the Colossians and Ephesians as well as the "Pastoral Letters" (1 and 2 Timothy and Titus) were all probably written by Paul's followers to correct abuses that had arisen in church centers Paul had founded. They endeavored to remind those communities of what Paul had taught by writing in the manner in which Paul would have written had he been alive. However, problems arose when certain centers misused the name of an apostle (especially the names of James and Thomas) in order to give their writings and thought a particular importance and credibility. This happened particularly in centers heavily influenced by the thought of Gnosticism. Despite this manipulation of the figures of James and Thomas, it still shows the important position they held within certain sections of the early Christian movement.

The above discussion has important implications for our study of James of Jerusalem. When examining the thought as well as the authorities and characters that were influential in the early Christian world, it is not sufficient to limit the examination to the twenty-seven books of the New Testament. Such an approach would be *anachronistic,* for it imposes on those first three centuries the concepts of a fixed canon, something that did not yet exist. Different Christian centers accepted different books as their sacred writings. To remain faithful to that particular world one must acknowledge the importance assigned to certain writings (associated with the names of apostles) that did not make their way into what became the canon of the New Testament. Many writings associated with the name of James belong to this category. While they were significant in certain centers of early Christianity, they were not accepted by other Christian churches and hence were ultimately rejected by the Church universal. Even the New Testament letter of James struggled to gain acceptance into the canon of the New Testament.

A number of writings from these early centuries refer to James of Jerusalem. They show that the person of James continued to exercise an important position and authority within the world of early Christianity. In this chapter we will examine briefly[4] what these writings and traditions have to say about the person of James of Jerusalem and see in what way his character conforms to the picture that has emerged from the New Testament writings.

From a methodological perspective this chapter is a study in tradition history. It will show how a tradition develops and is influenced by the socio-cultural context in which it is used. Such a study helps us to interface with the religious and traditional history of the early Christian church and to see the different tendencies and impulses that were dominating the Christian world of that time. It is not always easy to evaluate the material we have because much of it is of a legendary nature. As with the other great apostles (Peter, Paul, Thomas), certain groups used the figure of James to support their own perspectives. One has to get behind the legends to the substance of the picture of James that emerges from these writings.

Outside the Christian Tradition: The Death of James in Josephus

Before referring to information about James gleaned from Christian writings of the first three centuries C.E., I turn to an important (and surprising) source for information on James from outside the Christian community, namely the writings of the Jewish historian Josephus (37/38–101 C.E.). In the course of his extensive writings Josephus makes reference to three characters central to the Christian movement: John the Baptist, Jesus, and James of Jerusalem. In referring to James, Josephus supports the perspective we illustrated in our study of the New Testament texts that James was an important leader within the early Christian community in Jerusalem.[5] A reading of the full extract of this passage (*A.J.* 20:197-203),[6] shows that Josephus'

---

[4] Such a study would be a monograph in its own right. Here the focus will be on the person of James and what we can glean from these writings about him, his role, character, and authority.

[5] Previously scholars were somewhat skeptical about Josephus' references to John, Jesus, and James, claiming that they were Christian insertions into the text that occurred in the course of the transmission of the text by Christian scribes (see Ferdinand Christian Baur, *Paul the Apostle of Jesus Christ: His Life and Work, His Epistles and His Doctrine. A Contribution to a Critical History of Primitive Christianity,* ed. Eduard Zeller, trans. A. Menzies [London: Williams and Norgate, 1876]) 1:160). The very reason the texts of Josephus have survived is that they were transcribed by Christian scribes. It is therefore possible that Christian scribes could have been responsible for these interpolations into Josephus' text. However, today there is a much more positive assessment of these references as belonging to Josephus' original text, especially with regard to the references to James (see the excellent examination in John P. Meier, *A Marginal Jew: Rethinking the Historical Jesus* [New York: Doubleday, 1991] 1:58–59, 72–73).

[6] Josephus, *A.J.* 20:197-203 [Feldman, LCL].

focus lies on the High Priest, Ananus the younger. Josephus situates James' death during the interval between two Roman procurators, Festus and Albinus. This would date James' death to the year 62 C.E. Josephus himself was present in Jerusalem at that time.[7] Ananus, a Sadducee, took advantage of the absence of a Roman procurator in Jerusalem to convene the Jewish Council, where he charged several people with transgressing the Law and delivered them up to be stoned to death. Among those condemned to death Josephus names "James, the brother of Jesus who was called the Christ, and certain others."[8] Following this action the Pharisees complained to Albinus, and Ananus was subsequently removed by Herod Agrippa II.

The significance of this account is that a Jewish writer, Josephus, supports the historicity of the person of James. He shows that he was known as "the brother of Jesus" and that he was well respected in Jerusalem, in both Christian and Jewish circles. This agrees with the picture of James that emerged from the examination of both Acts and the writings of Paul. Josephus further enables us to date James' death to 62 C.E. Josephus does not say what the offense was, but the action of stoning to death was the Jewish punishment for blasphemy.[9] Not much more can be read into Josephus' account except that the decision was opposed strongly by the Pharisees. Josephus comments that the Sadducees (who were in the majority in the Sanhedrin) were "heartless."

James in the Work and Tradition of Eusebius

Eusebius (c. 260–339 C.E.), Bishop of Caesarea in Palestine, was an important church historian, scholar, and teacher who produced a history of the church that took almost a quarter of a century to write (300–324 C.E.). Caesarea had became an important Christian center of knowledge and scholarship when Origen (184/5–253/4 C.E.) had moved there from Alexandria in Egypt in 231 C.E. A major library had been established in Caesarea that unfortunately no longer exists. In writing his church history

---

[7] Josephus became a Pharisee when he was nineteen: "Being now in my nineteenth year I began to govern my life by the rules of the Pharisees, a sect having points of resemblance to that which the Greeks call the Stoic school" (Josephus, *Vita,* 12-13).

[8] Josephus, *A.J.* 20:200. These "certain others" could simply be other Jews whom Ananus wanted killed. Or they could be Christian believers and in this sense the reference would imply a persecution against Jewish Christians. The reaction of the Pharisees that Josephus notes seems to imply that they were fellow Jews who were held in high regard within the Jewish community of Jerusalem.

[9] See the reaction to Stephen in Acts: "We have heard him speak blasphemous words against Moses and God" (Acts 6:11). This led to the stoning of Stephen (Acts 7:54-60).

Eusebius quotes verbatim sources from this library. Eusebius' treatment of his sources differed markedly from the way his contemporaries operated. In the ancient world it was not the custom to identify sources. Instead, writers would freely incorporate their sources into their own works without any acknowledgment. Contrary to this custom, Eusebius identified his sources and quoted them directly. Many of Eusebius' sources have been lost, and his is the only knowledge we have of those sources. This is the case with two of his sources that refer to James.

In his major work, *The Ecclesiastical History,* Eusebius discusses James' death in great detail and relies on three sources: Hegesippus, Clement of Alexandria, and Josephus. The works of Hegesippus and Clement are only available to us from what Eusebius has to say.

Clement of Alexandria

Clement was an important church writer who defended traditional Christianity in the early third century C.E. against Gnostic influences that were growing within Christianity. Eusebius quotes from Clement's work, *Hypotyposes,* a writing that has not been preserved. We know of its existence from some later quotations from this work, which appears to have been a commentary on the Scriptures.[10]

Eusebius quotes from Clement twice (*Hist. eccl.* 2:1.2-5). In the first instance Clement says that "Peter and James and John after the Ascension of the Saviour did not struggle for glory, because they had previously been given honour by the Saviour, but chose James the Just as bishop of Jerusalem."[11] The term "bishop" *(episkopos)* appears in the New Testament (see, e.g., Phil 1:1) in the sense of an overseer of the church. Without doubt this is the role James was exercising. It would be *anachronistic* to understand it in the way the term was being used in the third century and later. Clement also refers to James as "the Just" *(ton dikaion).* He does not explain the phrase which indicates that he is using it in the sense of a title.[12]

Eusebius quotes Clement again in reference to James' death (*Hist. eccl.* 2:1.4-5). Clement makes two interesting statements. First, he is concerned with the faithful transmission of the tradition and shows how it passes from Jesus to "James, John, and Peter" and from them to the apostles and then to the seventy.[13] It is also significant to see that the name

---

[10] See Ralph P. Martin, *James,* WBC 48 (Waco, TX: Word Books, 1988) liv.
[11] Eusebius, *Hist. eccl.* 2:1.3 [Lake, LCL].
[12] See Martin, *James,* lv.
[13] Eusebius, *Hist. eccl.* 2:1.4 [Lake, LCL].

of James is placed first in the list of the tradition. From Clement's perspective James is an important person in the passing on of the tradition from Jesus to the future church. His presence ensures its fidelity.

As regards James' death, Clement's account is brief and seems to reflect an independent Christian tradition: "Now there were two Jameses, one James the Just, who was thrown down from the pinnacle of the temple and beaten to death with a fuller's club, and the other he who was beheaded."[14] The impression given by Clement is that James' death did not occur swiftly: "he *was beaten* to death" *(plēgeis),* which implies that he endured a long beating. The important point communicated about James is that he was a Christian martyr.

Hegesippus

Hegesippus was an early Christian writer who died c. 180 C.E. According to Eusebius, Hegesippus lived around the time of Irenaeus[15] and "belong[ed] to the generation after the Apostles."[16] In the middle of the second century he set out from Asia Minor for Rome and en route he met many church leaders ("bishops"). He is an important figure for testimony to the traditions of the early Christian church. When he returned home he wrote his *Memoirs* (*Hypomnemata* or *Memoranda*) in five books.[17] This work is no longer extant and is only known to us through Eusebius' quotations in his writings.[18]

Eusebius' quotation of Hegesippus on James' death is extensive.[19] While Hegesippus' account of James' death is detailed, he does not identify his sources as Eusebius had done. It is quite possible that he has used both the work of Josephus that says James was stoned to death and the tradition known to Clement that records that James was clubbed to death. Hegesippus tries to reconcile these two visions by producing a unified narrative. Four things are noteworthy in Hegesippus' account:

---

[14] Eusebius, *Hist. eccl.* 2:1.5 [Lake, LCL].

[15] Eusebius (*Hist. eccl.* 4:21 [Lake, LCL]) comments: "At this time there flourished in the church Hegesippus, whom we know from former narratives, and Dionysius, bishop of the Corinthians . . . and above all, Irenaeus, and their correct opinions on the sound faith of the apostolic tradition have come down to us in writing."

[16] Eusebius, *Hist. eccl.* 2:23.3 [Lake, LCL].

[17] At least Eusebius knows of five books (*Hist. eccl.* 2:23.3).

[18] H. Dressler comments: "The work today is known only through fragments quoted in Eusebius's *Historia Ecclesiastica,* although as late as the 17th century the complete work could be found in several Greek monasteries" ("Hegesippus," *New Catholic Encyclopedia* [Washington: The Catholic University of America, 1967] 6:994).

[19] Eusebius, *Hist. eccl.* 2:23.4-18 [Lake, LCL].

(1) James is called "the Just": Hegesippus says that James "was called the 'Just' by all men from the Lord's time to ours, since many are called James, but he was holy from his mother's womb."[20] This phrase, "the Just," distinguishes this James from others bearing the same name. Not only does Hegesippus use this title to refer to James, but he is also at pains throughout the whole narrative to show that James truly was the righteous one. While Hegesippus is an early witness to the use of this title for James, he was not the first. Both the Gospel of Thomas and the Gospel of the Hebrews used this title prior to Hegesippus. For example: "The disciples said to Jesus, 'We know that you will depart from us. Who is to be our leader?' Jesus said to them, 'Wherever you are, you are to go to James the righteous, for whose sake heaven and earth came into being'" (*Gos. Thom.* 12).[21] This shows that this title for James was in common traditional usage in the early Christian centuries, especially in the Nag Hammadi writings.[22] Nevertheless, this is a new way of referring to James, as it does not appear in the New Testament writings. The letter of James does make reference to "the just one" or "the righteous one": "You have condemned and murdered the righteous one *(ton dikaion),* who does not resist you" (Jas 5:6). This usage in the letter of James may be partly responsible for the application of this term to James, as he was put to death without any resistance.

(2) The religious picture of James: James is painted in pietistic terms that largely reflect the picture of a priestly piety (see Lev 10:9; 21:10-12; Ezek 44:17): "He drank no wine or strong drink, nor did he eat flesh; no razor went upon his head; he did not anoint himself with oil, and he did not go to the baths."[23] However, aspects of this piety do not conform to the world of Judaism of the first century C.E. The avoidance of eating meat, using oil, or bathing did not belong to the ascetical practices that were at home in the world of Judaism at that time. They belong more properly to the time of Hegesippus, and he is *anachronistically* pushing them back to the time of James

---

[20] Eusebius, *Hist. eccl.* 2:23.4 [Lake, LCL].

[21] The translation is from Thomas O. Lambdin, "The Gospel of Thomas," in James M. Robinson, ed., *The Nag Hammadi Library in English* (3rd ed. New York: HarperCollins, 1990) 127.

[22] The Nag Hammadi writings are a number of Coptic works that were discovered at Nag Hammadi in Egypt in 1945. They comprise fourth-century papyrus manuscripts consisting in total of twelve codices containing fifty-two titles. Since there are some duplications among the works, there are in effect some forty-five separate titles. These writings come from a Gnostic sect and hence are witness to the thought and expression of Gnosticism.

[23] Eusebius, *Hist. eccl.* 2:23.5 [Lake, LCL].

for apologetic reasons.[24] Quite likely Hegesippus has in mind the rejection of the Roman baths (the reference to the use of oil and bathing, etc.) in order to distance James from the world of Greece and Rome rather than the Jewish rites of purification.[25] There are further aspects as well that do not connect with the world of early Christian Judaism. For example, "(James was) found kneeling and praying for forgiveness for the people, so that his knees grew hard like a camel's because of his constant worship of God, kneeling and asking forgiveness for the people."[26] The idea of "camel's knees" resulting from long periods of kneeling does not reflect a Jewish form of piety. Another major difficulty lies with the priestly description of James: "He alone was allowed to enter into the sanctuary, for he did not wear wool but linen, and he used to enter alone into the temple."[27] Only the High Priest was allowed into the sanctuary and that occurred once a year on the day of Yom Kippur (the Day of Atonement). The picture of James entering the sanctuary is impossible and shows the author's lack of knowledge of the ritual observances of Judaism. While it is Hegesippus' intention to portray James as a very religious and extremely pious person, he does this in an anachronistic way by taking elements from his own world and transposing them back into the past. The further picture of James as one who is well respected by the Jewish groups in Jerusalem is difficult to evaluate. It is certainly true that James was concerned about retaining Christian roots in the world of Judaism. However, what we have in this account is a fanciful and legendary way of giving expression to James' attempt to preserve these bonds.

(3) The martyrdom of James: The structure of the account of James' death embraces a dialogue, a confession by James, the death of James, and its consequences. *A dialogue:* the scribes and Pharisees are concerned about the number of people who are attracted to confess Jesus as the Messiah because of the respect the people have for James. The scribes and Pharisees ask James to speak to the people to stop this flood of conversions. *A confession:* Instead of saying what the scribes and Pharisees wanted him to say, James publicly acknowledges Jesus as the Son of Man who will come again on the clouds of heaven. *James' death:* This is recorded in terms reminiscent of the death of Jesus and Stephen. He is thrown down

[24] See Martin (*James*, lii): "If, as has been argued . . . Hegesippus wrote to attack specific gnostic theological claims and to condemn unbelieving Jewish sects, he could be presenting the piety and death of James in an apologetic context."

[25] See John Painter, *Just James: the Brother of Jesus in History and Tradition* (Minneapolis: Fortress, 1999) 125.

[26] Eusebius, *Hist. eccl.* 2:23.6 [Lake, LCL].

[27] Ibid.

from the battlement of the temple, then stoned, and finally clubbed to death. It is clearly the death of a martyr. *The consequences:* the Roman General Vespasian begins the siege of the city of Jerusalem. Hegesippus interprets the destruction of Jerusalem as an act of divine retribution for James' death. In point of fact, historically James died in 62 C.E., while the siege of Jerusalem began some six years later around 68 C.E.

(4) The legendary and stylistic nature of this account: The description of James' death is painted in idealistic and legendary terms rather than historical ones. The biblical descriptions of the death of Jesus and Stephen clearly influence the narrative: Jesus and Stephen die asking God to forgive their executioners just as James does. Compare the following descriptions: *The death of Jesus:* "Then Jesus said, 'Father, forgive them; for they do not know what they are doing'" (Luke 23:34). *The death of Stephen:* "While they were stoning Stephen, he prayed, 'Lord Jesus, receive my spirit.' Then he knelt down and cried out in a loud voice, 'Lord, do not hold this sin against them'" (Acts 7:59-60). Finally, *the death of James:* ". . . and they began to stone him since the fall had not killed him, but he turned and knelt saying, 'I beseech thee, O Lord, God and Father, forgive them, for they know not what they do.'"[28] Both James and Stephen die confessing Jesus as the Son of Man coming on the clouds. Stephen says: "Look . . . I see the heavens opened and the Son of Man standing at the right hand of God!" (Acts 7:56). James confesses: "Why do you ask me concerning the Son of Man? He is sitting in heaven on the right hand of the great power, and he will come on the clouds of heaven."[29] The description of James' death is also colored by the Wisdom literature, particularly the description in the book of Wisdom of the death of the righteous one: "Let us lie in wait for the righteous man, because he is inconvenient to us and opposes our actions; he reproaches us for sins against the law . . . . Let us condemn him to a shameful death, for, according to what he says, he will be protected" (2:12-20). Hegesippus has taken some basic historical facts and woven them into a legendary narrative that is deeply influenced by the biblical tradition of the death of the righteous one. That there is a basic historical core behind this account cannot be denied, but the legendary accretions are such that this passage adds little in fact to our knowledge of either the character of James or of his death.[30]

---

[28] Eusebius, *Hist. eccl.* 2:23.16 [Lake, LCL].

[29] Eusebius, *Hist. eccl.* 2:23.13 [Lake, LCL].

[30] See Martin Dibelius, *James: A Commentary on the Epistle of James,* Hermeneia, rev. Heinrich Greeven, trans. Michael A. Williams, ed. Helmut Koester (Philadelphia: Fortress, 1976; English Translation of *Der Brief des Jakobus* [11th rev. ed. Göttingen: Vandenhoeck & Ruprecht, 1964]) 16, for a detailed examination and evaluation of Hegesippus' account.

Eusebius' Own Summaries on James

When Eusebius narrates the martyrdom of James, he introduces Clement and Hegesippus, to which we have referred above, with his own summary of James' death.[31] Eusebius puts together the information he has gleaned from his sources, namely Acts (25:11-12; 27:1), Josephus,[32] Hegesippus,[33] and Clement of Alexandria.[34] Eusebius refers to James as "the brother of the Lord."[35] Normally, when Eusebius himself refers to James he is much more precise, saying he "was one of the alleged brethren of the Savior."[36] Eusebius described James as one who "was by all men believed to be most righteous because of the height which he had reached in a life of philosophy and religion."[37] This shows a stress on the tradition that James is "the Just," while at the same time he appeals to the Greco-Roman world by showing that James' knowledge and ability stand alongside the best of their own philosophy.

Eusebius provides a second summary when he concludes his quotation from Hegesippus[38] and implies that, while Hegesippus and Clement agree with each other, the two traditions were nevertheless independent of each other. On the other hand, most scholars argue that Clement is dependent on Hegesippus.[39] Such a view adopts too monolithic an idea of tradition. James was an important character, as Eusebius acknowledges in this summary: "Thus it seems that James was indeed a remarkable man and famous among all for righteousness."[40] This observation is based on Eusebius' own evaluation from his survey of church history and the view within the church at that time. Without doubt accounts of James' death must have circulated in many centers, and these accounts would be influenced by their specific contexts.

Eusebius' Quotations from Josephus

Following the quotations from Clement and Hegesippus, and his own summary of James' martyrdom, Eusebius adds two quotations he has taken

---

[31] Eusebius, *Hist. eccl.* 2:23.1-3 [Lake, LCL].
[32] Josephus, *A.J.* 20:201-202 [Feldman; LCL].
[33] Eusebius, *Hist. eccl.* 2:23.4-18 [Lake, LCL].
[34] Eusebius, *Hist. eccl.* 2:1.3-5 [Lake, LCL].
[35] Eusebius, *Hist. eccl.* 2:23.1 [Lake, LCL].
[36] Eusebius, *Hist. eccl.* 1.12.5 [Lake, LCL].
[37] Eusebius, *Hist. eccl.* 2:23.2 [Lake, LCL].
[38] Eusebius: *Hist. eccl.* 2:23.19 [Lake, LCL].
[39] See F. Stanley Jones, "The Martyrdom of James in Hegesippus, Clement of Alexandria, and Christian Apocrypha, including Nag Hammadi: A Study of the Textual Relations," *SBLSP* 29 (Atlanta: Scholars, 1990) 328 n.30.
[40] Eusebius: *Hist. eccl.* 2:23.19 [Lake, LCL].

from Josephus. The first is not found in any of our existing texts of Josephus' writings. Eusebius wanted to stress the causal connection between the death of James and the siege of Jerusalem by the Romans: "And these things happened to the Jews to avenge James the Just, who was the brother of Jesus the so-called Christ, for the Jews killed him in spite of his great righteousness."[41] While Eusebius attributes this statement to Josephus, it appears in reality to be a Christian theological interpretation of the events that could quite easily have been taken from Christian tradition rather than from Josephus himself. Once again James is identified simply as "the brother of Jesus," not "the so-called brother of Jesus," which would be typical of Eusebius' own style and supports the view that Eusebius is dependent on source material.

The second quotation in Eusebius[42] is taken directly from Josephus[43] and is in close agreement with our editions of Josephus' text. Although the quotation from Josephus is his earliest chronological source, Eusebius leaves it for the end since he wishes to stress the importance of the Christian tradition. Even though James is put to death by the Jewish High Priest Ananus, Josephus shows that James continued to enjoy significant respect and status within the context of the Jewish world.

Summary

This study of Eusebius' account of James and his martyrdom is remarkable for many reasons. Writing at the beginning of the fourth century C.E., Eusebius has illustrated through the use of sources how the importance of James and the significance of his martyrdom continued to be handed on over the centuries. Our study of the New Testament texts showed that James' role and importance especially within the Jerusalem church lay buried beneath texts that focused more on the roles of Paul and Peter. This study has been able to unearth the significant and influential position and role the historical James did exercise within the framework of the early Christian church. The importance of James continued to be upheld and celebrated in the subsequent centuries.

The tradition we have examined in these selections from Eusebius does two things. First, it does not stress those aspects that arose from Acts and the letters of Paul, namely the figure of James as an apostle or as one who had received a special revelation. Instead, the picture of James as a

---

[41] Eusebius, *Hist. eccl.* 2:23:20 [Lake, LCL].

[42] Eusebius, *Hist. eccl.* 2:23.21-24 [Lake, LCL].

[43] Josephus, *A.J.* 20:197-203 [Feldman, LCL].

Jewish Christian is strengthened and highlighted. In Hegesippus, James emerges as a Nazirite, belonging to the priestly world: he is righteous, a Jewish Christian, well respected even by the scribes and Pharisees. Second, Hegesippus uses James' character to speak to his world afresh: as leader of the Christian community in Jerusalem, James was intent on maintaining the true tradition that came from Jesus. That brought him into conflict with Paul (as the letter to the Galatians shows). Hegesippus uses James' character to play the same role as bearer and upholder of the traditional faith against the attacks of the opponents of his own day. As upholder of the true faith, James is an inspiration to Hegesippus' world threatened by heretical tendencies within the church.

James is also referred to for the first time in these traditions as "bishop" *(episkopos)*. While the New Testament witnesses did not use this term to refer to James, they did present him as an important leader within the early Christian community, especially as leader of the Jerusalem church. As we have indicated, Clement and his tradition used the term "bishop" *(episkopos)* from their own world to designate James' role within the Jerusalem church *(ekklēsia)*. This shows clearly how this tradition developed: a term from a later time was used to give expression to the authority and leadership that James did in fact exercise within the Jerusalem church *(ekklēsia)*.

Finally, Clement made allusion to the fact that "(a)fter the Resurrection the Lord gave the tradition of knowledge to James the Just and John and Peter . . . ."[44] This was to become a feature of further reflection and importance, especially in the tradition of those writings that emerged from Gnostic circles.

James' Interface with the Traditions of Jewish Christianity

What is meant by "Jewish Christianity" has long been the subject of debate by New Testament scholars.[45] It is true that Jesus' early followers were all Jews. However, Acts shows that with the acceptance of many Gentile followers into the fold of Christianity, tensions developed between those who wished to hold onto their Jewish traditions and those like Paul who displayed openness to the wider Greco-Roman world. The essence of what we understand by the term "Jewish Christian" refers to those who sought to continue to express their faith in Jesus as the Messiah in terms of

---

[44] Eusebius, *Hist. eccl.* 2:1.4 [Lake, LCL].
[45] See the discussion in Martin, *James,* xlii–xliii.

their Jewish roots. Stanley Riegel some years back gave an insightful overview of the term "Jewish Christianity" and concluded: "Thus it would apply to Christians who were Jews and expressed themselves in the thought-forms of the Semitic world from which they came."[46]

As time went by, the wider Christian church began to distance itself from these Jewish Christian communities because their thoughts did not agree with the wider church. As Jean Daniélou indicates, they tended to deny Jesus' divinity as the only Son of God.[47] This led to the rejection of many of their writings as canonical. The works we refer to here as Jewish Christian all demonstrate these characteristics: they maintain their Jewish roots, yet they are not accepted as reflecting the faith of the universal Catholic Church.[48]

The Gospel of the Hebrews

We only possess a few fragments of this gospel.[49] The passages that have survived did so largely as a result of quotations made of the gospel by early Christian church leaders in their writings. This gospel probably originated in the early part of the second century in Alexandria, Egypt.[50] Jerome quotes from it in his work *De Viris Illustribus*.[51] This quotation emphasizes the resurrection of Jesus, when the risen Jesus appears to James—the first to be so privileged. As we have noted, Paul singles out the appearance to James (1 Cor 15:7), but he notes that Jesus appeared to Cephas (Peter) before he appeared to James. Jesus then goes on to celebrate the Eucharist with James. This passage further implies that James was present at the Last Supper, where he had sworn that "he would not eat bread from that hour in which he had drunk the cup of the Lord until he should see him risen from among them that sleep."[52] These details are at odds with the picture in the canonical gospels, where James' presence is not noted at the Last Supper.

---

[46] Stanley K. Riegel, "Jewish Christianity: Definitions and Terminology," *NTS* 24 (1977/78) 415.

[47] Jean Daniélou, *The Theology of Jewish Christianity,* trans. and ed. by J. A. Baker (London: Darton, Longman & Todd, 1964) 7–11.

[48] See Albertus Frederik Johannes Klijn, "The Study of Jewish Christianity," *NTS* 20 (1973/74) 419–31.

[49] For the fragmentary evidence of the Gospel of the Hebrews see Wilhelm Schneemelcher, ed., *New Testament Apocrypha: Gospels and Related Writings* (rev. ed. Cambridge, U.K.: James Clarke & Co.; Louisville: Westminster John Knox, 1991) 1:177–78.

[50] Philipp Vielhauer and Georg Strecker, "Jewish-Christian Gospels," in Schneemelcher, *New Testament Apocrypha: Gospels and Related Writings,* 1:176.

[51] Ibid. 1:178 (Jerome, *De Viris Illustribus,* 2).

[52] Ibid.

Following the tradition, James is presented as Jesus' brother. Jesus addresses him as "My brother." No further specifications are made with regard to this relationship. James is also called by the title "the Just." This title, as we observed, was used by the Gospel of Thomas, a writing that made its way to Egypt early on. As Helmut Koester observes, the Gospel of Thomas could be the source both for this title and for some of the sayings they hold in common.[53]

This passage is significant for a study of the traditions related to James of Jerusalem because it shows that details of the canonical gospels have been slightly changed in the course of transmission in order to situate James in a unique position among the disciples as the one who holds the highest authority. James is understood as the first witness to Jesus' resurrection and hence "the most important guarantor of the resurrection, (consequently) it is clear that for the G(ospel of the) H(ebrews) he is the highest authority in the circle of Jesus' acquaintances."[54]

The Pseudo-Clementine Literature

The Pseudo-Clementine literature is a body of romance writings that came to be associated with Clement of Rome. The narrative relates the experiences of Clement as a disciple of Peter, whom he accompanied during his missionary journeys.[55] The term is usually associated with two writings, the *Recognitions* (comprising ten books in Latin) and the *Homilies* (consisting of twenty discourses in Greek). These writings are dated to the fourth century C.E. Much study has been devoted to them, especially the *Recognitions* and the *Homilies,* with the intention of discovering the sources that lay behind them. Something of a consensus has emerged among scholars, who see the sources originating within the Jewish Christian community in Pella (Transjordan) in the second century C.E. because large sections of these writings have a distinctively Jewish Christian character. The figure of James was considered important and was venerated highly in these circles.[56]

Three shorter writings precede the Pseudo-Clementines. They are referred to as the *Kerygmata Petrou* ("the preaching of Peter"): an Epistle of

---

[53] Helmut Koester, *Introduction to the New Testament.* 2 vols. (Philadelphia: Fortress; Berlin and New York: Walter de Gruyter, 1982) 2:224.

[54] Vielhauer and Strecker, "Jewish-Christian Gospels," 173.

[55] See Koester, *Introduction to the New Testament,* 2:205.

[56] See Gerd Lüdemann, "The Successors of pre-70 Jerusalem Christianity," in E. P. Sanders, ed., *Jewish and Christian Self-Definition* (Philadelphia: Fortress, 1980) 1:161–73; and Martin, *James,* xlv–xlvii.

Peter to James, the *Contestatio* (an "attestation" that discusses who is to be trusted with Peter's writings) and an Epistle of Clement to James (that speaks of Peter appointing Clement as bishop just before his death).

The character of Peter dominates these writings and not much is really added to the picture of James.[57] The position and authority of James within the world of Jewish Christianity is illustrated and celebrated once again. In Peter's letter to James and in the *Contestatio,* Peter's preaching and teaching are entrusted to James who appears in the role of the one who preserves and guards the tradition. In Peter's letter, James is referred to as "bishop" primarily of the Jerusalem church: "Peter to James, the lord and bishop of the holy church . . ."[58] (1:1). See also the letter of Clement to James: "Clement to James, the lord and bishop of bishops . . ." (1:1).[59] Previously we examined James' designation as bishop when we discussed Clement of Alexandria's references to James the Just as being chosen by Peter, James, and John as "bishop of Jerusalem."[60] While it is an anachronistic attempt to read back into the world of first-century Christianity the ecclesiastical reality of the second century and later, what the tradition does show is the way James is held in veneration as the authoritative leader entrusted with preserving the true tradition. What the Pseudo-Clementine literature demonstrates is how legendary motifs develop in order to celebrate and glorify the lives of the great heroes of early Christianity.

James Within the Traditions of Gnosticism

Gnosticism is a term with wide reference, and not all scholars agree on its definition. In essence "Gnosticism" refers to a number of religious movements that understood salvation as attainable through some secret *gnōsis* ("knowledge") that was only available to the adherents of that movement. Central to most of the Gnostic perspectives was an opposition between the spiritual and material worlds. The latter, including the body, was seen as evil. As a religious movement within Christianity, Gnosticism interpreted the biblical writings with the aid of Greek philosophy and aspects of mystical reflection. Gnostics believed that created beings bore within themselves a spark of divinity. The transcendent God sent a Re-

---

[57] See Johnson, *The Letter of James,* 105.

[58] Georg Strecker, "The Pseudo-Clementines: Introductory Writings," in Schneemelcher, ed., *New Testament Apocrypha,* 2:493.

[59] Ibid. 496.

[60] See the discussion on Clement of Alexandria above.

deemer whose task it was to communicate a secret knowledge *(gnōsis)* to those belonging to the Gnostic movements. This secret knowledge would bring salvation. This salvation ultimately entailed returning to the transcendent God and escaping from one's body. There was consequently no belief in the resurrection of the body.[61]

Our knowledge of Gnosticism is confined to two sources: manuscripts from the adherents of Gnostic groups and the writings of their opponents who condemned them for heresy. The most significant discoveries of Gnostic writings have been: the Askew Codex, containing four texts, published in 1896; the Bruce Codex with three texts, published in 1891; the Berlin Codex with four texts, published in 1955; and most important, the Nag Hammadi Codices containing forty-five separate titles, discovered in 1945.[62]

In the Christian world from the second through the fourth centuries, Gnosticism flourished in Egypt, Syria, and Asia Minor. Although most of the writings emerged during this period of time, many of them were dependent on earlier traditions going back to the first century C.E.

There are four major Gnostic works that contain references to James: the Gospel of Thomas, the Apocryphon of James, and the First and Second Apocalypses of James. We will examine their references briefly.

The Gospel of Thomas

The Gospel of Thomas was one of the tractates discovered among the Nag Hammadi codices. Although these codices were probably buried around four hundred C.E., they were composed long before that date. While the dating of the Gospel of Thomas has been a subject of heated discussion among scholars, it seems best to see this work as containing traditions that go back to the first century C.E. Probably first composed toward the end of the first century, this text was taken up by Gnostic communities, which adapted it to express their own wisdom and thoughts. It was ultimately rejected by the universal church at the end of the fourth century.

There is one saying (logion) in the Gospel of Thomas that refers to James:

---

[61] For two good brief overviews of Gnosticism and how modern scholars approach it differently from previous generations of scholars see Edwin M. Yamauchi, "Gnosticism," in *Dictionary of New Testament Background,* eds. Craig A. Evans and Stanley E. Porter (Downers Grove, IL and Leicester, England: InterVarsity Press, 2000) 414–18; and Paul Mirecki, "Gnosticism, Gnosis," in *Eerdmans Dictionary of the Bible,* ed. David Noel Freedman (Grand Rapids: Eerdmans, 2000) 508–09.

[62] See Mirecki, "Gnosticism, Gnosis," 509.

> The disciples said to Jesus, "We know that you will depart from us. Who is to be our leader?"
>
> Jesus said to them, "Wherever you are, you are to go to James the righteous, for whose sake heaven and earth came into being" (*GThom.* 12).[63]

This is the first evidence we have for the use of the title "the righteous" in reference to James. James is also understood by the Gospel of Thomas as the leader of the church: the same role James plays within the New Testament traditions. Thomas, on the other hand, is seen to have a special place as the recipient of secret knowledge. Saying 13 identifies Thomas (Didymos Judas Thomas) as the one apostle who receives secret wisdom or knowledge *(gnōsis)*. In highly symbolic language, Jesus speaks to Thomas (in the singular) and tells him that he has "become intoxicated from the bubbling spring which I have measured out" (*GThom* 13). To Thomas alone Jesus reveals his secret knowledge. The opening of the Gospel of Thomas proclaims this role for Thomas.[64] As the one who receives the secret sayings of the Lord Jesus, it is his task to transmit them to others. This perspective situates the Gospel of Thomas within the context of Gnosticism. Helmut Koester makes an important and interesting observation in examining Sayings 12 and 13 together in the same context. He sees the juxtaposition of these two sayings as a way of defining and defending the respective roles and authority of Thomas and James within their communities.[65]

The Apocryphon of James

This work is pseudonymous, claiming to have been written by James. From a detailed examination of the sayings material in this writing, Ron Cameron dates it to the first half of the second century in Egypt.[66] This treatise appears among the Nag Hammadi texts; the version there had been translated from Greek into Coptic. It purports to be a letter from James that in turn introduces a secret writing (or *apocryphon*—hence the title). The *apoc-*

---

[63] Lambdin, "The Gospel of Thomas," 127. All the quotations from the Gospel of Thomas are taken from this translation in *The Nag Hammadi Library in English.*

[64] See the *incipit* (beginning) of the Gospel of Thomas: "These are the secret sayings which the living Jesus spoke and which Didymos Judas Thomas wrote down" (Lambdin, "The Gospel of Thomas," 126).

[65] Koester, *Introduction to the New Testament,* 2:152–53.

[66] Ron Cameron, *Sayings Traditions in the Apocryphon of James,* HTS 34. (Philadelphia: Fortress, 1984) 130, argues for an early independent sayings tradition for the *Apocryphon of James.*

ryphon has Jesus appear to the disciples five hundred fifty days after the resurrection. The risen Jesus takes James and Peter aside and reveals to them his definitive teaching.[67] At the end of the dialogue Jesus ascends to heaven, leaving James and Peter behind (*Ap. Jas.* 15.5-10). James and Peter in turn make known the revelations of Jesus to the disciples. The disciples were displeased about future believers ("about those to be born") and so James writes: "And so, not wishing to give them offense, I sent each one to another place. But I myself went up to Jerusalem, praying that I might obtain a portion among the beloved, who will be made manifest" (*Ap. Jas.* 16.1-10).[68]

An examination of the tradition related to James shows a continuation of his traditional image as well as a stress on some new aspects. While James is not identified as "the brother of the Lord," James of Jerusalem is clearly intended. James and Peter are mentioned together as the important leaders of the church who together hold a special authority. James is always named first and is connected with Jerusalem as its leader. Consequently, he is the one who sends the disciples out to other places to preach the message while he remains behind in Jerusalem.

On two occasions the stress in this writing is on James as a recipient of secret revelation (*Ap. Jas.* 8.30-36; and 13.35–14.1). While some characteristic features of Gnosticism may be absent from this writing, this picture of James as a recipient and transmitter of a special revelation places this work within the context of the Gnostic writings. James' position and authority emerge from his action of sending out the other disciples to different lands while he himself remained in Jerusalem (*Ap. Jas.* 16.5-11).

First and Second Apocalypses of James

Two tractates within the Nag Hammadi codices bear the name "the Apocalypse of James." Scholars have named them the First and Second Apocalypses of James respectively in order to distinguish them.

THE (FIRST) APOCALYPSE OF JAMES (V,3)

Scholars argue that this writing emerged from Jewish Christian traditions in Syria.[69] It is in fact a "revelation dialogue" between Jesus and his

---

[67] *Ap. Jas.* 1.2.30-35.

[68] All quotations from the *Apocryphon of James* are taken from: "The Apocryphon of James [I,2]," trans. Francis E. Williams, in Robinson, *The Nag Hammadi Library,* 30–37.

[69] See William R. Schoedel, "The (First) Apocalypse of James (V,3)" in Robinson, *The Nag Hammadi Library,* 262–68. All quotations are from this translation.

brother James. While James is called the brother of the Lord, he is identified in this way only in a spiritual, not a physical sense: "I have given you a sign of these things, James, my brother. For not without reason have I called you my brother, although you are not my brother materially" (*1 Apoc. Jas.* 24.13-16).

James addresses Jesus as "Rabbi," while the narrator of the tractate refers to Jesus as "the Lord." Two revelations to James occur in this writing. The first takes place before the arrest of the Lord (*1 Apoc. Jas.* 25.7-10). The second occurs after James has heard of the Lord's sufferings (*1 Apoc. Jas.* 30.15). On the occasion of the second revelation Jesus identifies James in this way: "The just is his servant. Therefore your name is 'James the Just.' You see how you will become sober when you see me" (*1 Apoc. Jas.* 31.30–32.9).

In the context of the developing tradition this reference to James as "the Just" is significant. Previously, especially in Hegesippus, James is referred to as the Just one from his birth. It is also a title the scribes and Pharisees used in reference to James. However, in *1 Apoc. Jas.* this title is conferred on James by the Lord only after Jesus' suffering. As the Just one James is also called "his servant." That reminds one of the letter of James, which identifies James with this specific title: "James, a servant of God and of the Lord Jesus Christ . . ." (Jas 1:1). The tractate ends with a foreshadowing of James' death: "We have no part in this blood, for a just man will perish through injustice" (*1 Apoc. Jas.* 43.14-20). The Lord had warned James that he would share in his suffering: "James, thus you will undergo these sufferings" (*1 Apoc. Jas.* 32.15).

The traditional image of James continues with his identification as the Just One and as brother of Jesus. Both terms are defined more precisely than in previous traditions. In the Gnostic tradition the picture of James stresses that he is a recipient of a special revelation from the Lord. While James and Peter were clearly distinguished from the rest of the apostles, in *1 Apoc. Jas.* James is not only distinguished from them, he is superior to them. This superiority is attributable to his role as the recipient of special knowledge *(gnōsis)*.

William R. Schoedel insightfully discusses the question of why the figure of James should assume such importance and popularity within the world of Gnosticism, especially seeing that James was a Jewish Christian.[70] He argues insightfully that the Gnostics needed a hero whose authority would support their teachings. James is an obvious choice, since he

---

[70] Ibid. 261.

was not one of the Twelve: he was outside that group and so they could appeal to him as the representative of a form of Christianity that was different from the traditions of Peter and yet had an authenticity and reliability that stemmed from the remarkable revelation God communicated to James. "Our apocalypse, in short, was attempting to present an alternative to the apostolic authority claimed for the teaching of a steadily advancing catholic form of Christianity."[71]

THE (SECOND) APOCALYPSE OF JAMES (V,4)

Although the title identifies this writing as an apocalypse, the contents show it is rather a "revelatory discourse" in which James hands on a revelation he had received from the risen Jesus.[72] Continuing the tradition, James is identified as the brother of the Lord. His relationship to Jesus is presented in a somewhat confusing way that is different from the other traditions: "He said to me, 'Hail my brother; my brother, hail.' . . . (my) mother said to me, 'Do not be frightened my son, because he said "My brother" to you (sg.). For you (pl.) were nourished with this same milk. Because of this he calls me "My mother." For he is not a stranger to us. He is your [step-brother]'" (*2 Apoc. Jas.* 50.14-20).

Jesus goes on to declare to James: "Your father is not my father. But my father has become a father to [you]" (*2 Apoc. Jas.* 51.20). This tractate contains another description of James' martyrdom, but it is more developed than that of Hegesippus. This is preceded by a discourse of James that contains revelations of the Lord. What is striking about this writing is the combination of disparate elements. While the description of James' death is close to that of the traditional source, there does not seem to be any literary dependence.[73] At the same time, James' revelatory discourse clearly places it within the ambient of Gnostic writings.[74]

The language of Gnosticism is evident in the discourse. James declares that he received his revelation from the Pleroma: "I am he who received revelation from the Pleroma [of] Imperishability" (*2 Apoc. Jas.* 46.6). James goes on to acknowledge that "Now again am I rich in knowledge [and] I have a unique [understanding], which was produced only from above . . ."

---

[71] Ibid.

[72] See Charles W. Hedrick, trans., "The (Second) Apocalypse of James (V,4)," in Robinson, *The Nag Hammadi Library,* 270–76.

[73] See Roy Bowen Ward, "James of Jerusalem in the First Two Centuries," *ANRW* II, 26.1 (Berlin and New York: Walter De Gruyter, 1992) 810.

[74] See Johnson, *The Letter of James,* 102.

(*2 Apoc. Jas.* 47.7). The picture of James as a recipient of revelation reaches its culmination in *2 Apoc. Jas.* 55.15–56.13 insofar as the risen Jesus describes James in terms that suggest "that James is intended to perform the function of gnostic redeemer":[75] "You are an illuminator and a redeemer of those who are mine, and now of those who are yours. You shall reveal (to them); you shall bring good among them all" (*2 Apoc. Jas.* 55.15).

A further insight that arises from this position as Gnostic redeemer is that James' role and position within the Gnostic communities rivals that of Peter (and the other apostles) within the Christian community:[76]

> . . . [but I] wish to reveal through you and the [Spirit of Power], in order that he might reveal [to those] who are yours. And those who wish to enter, and who seek to walk in the way that is before the door, open the good door through you. And they follow you; they enter [and you] escort them inside, and give a reward to each one who is ready for it. (*2 Apoc. Jas.* 55.4-14)

This is somewhat analogous to the position of Peter, to whom Jesus gave the keys of the kingdom (Matt 16:18-19). This contrast between James and Peter illustrates how the Gnostic tradition claims for James a role that contends with that of Peter within the wider church. James' role gives the Gnostic tradition the assurance of their access to the secret revelation of Jesus and to a pathway to salvation that James is able to open up for them.

Summary

The tradition of the Nag Hammadi writings shows James as an important Gnostic teacher (even redeemer in *2 Apoc. Jas.*) who has received secret revelations from the risen Lord. He communicates these revelations to the members of his community through these writings. One can clearly see a deepening understanding of this role from the more sober presentation in the *Gos. Thom.* to the Gnostic Redeemer of *2 Apoc. Jas.* The position and authority of James within the Gnostic communities is greater than that of Peter and the other apostles.

The importance of the character of James is found within all major streams of early Christianity, as is evident from the numerous references to him in extra-biblical literature. James' position was first acknowledged

---

[75] Hedrick, "Second Apocalypse," 269.
[76] Ibid., 269–70.

within the world of Jewish Christianity and was then taken up by other groups or centers where the image of James lent importance and significance to their own understanding and emphases within Christianity.[77] In the context of Gnosticism James' image developed from one who held a position of authority to one who was the bearer of a secret tradition. The starting point for reflection on James as a recipient of revelation must undoubtedly be 1 Cor 15:7, where specific mention is made of the risen Jesus' appearance to James. James' leadership, as well as his knowledge and the revelation he communicates, does not come via the other apostles. It is independent of them, since James received it directly from the Lord. In comparison to Peter and the other apostles, James is the recipient of revelation that stands out and is unique in that he is the brother of the Lord.

Protevangelium of James

Brief attention must be paid to one further writing, namely the *Protevangelium of James*. It is extremely difficult to situate this writing within the trajectories about James we have traced in this chapter. For this reason I shall treat it briefly here. Its importance is twofold. First of all, it identifies clearly the relationship of James to Jesus as that of stepbrothers, not blood brothers. The second aspect of this writing is a corollary of the first: it gives clear expression to the perpetual virginity of Mary. As we have noted in examining the birth narratives in Matthew and Luke, the texts stress that Jesus' birth resulted from the intervention of the Holy Spirit. The stress on Mary's virginity was the way the biblical writers gave expression to this belief. However, references in the canonical gospels to the virginity of Mary do not consider the further issue of whether Mary remained a virgin after Jesus' birth. The *Protevangelium of James* bears witness to the fact that by the mid-second century C.E. the belief that Mary remained a virgin was widespread in the early Christian church. The *Protevangelium of James* was an extremely popular writing in the early Christian world, being translated into almost every language of that time (including Syriac, Ethiopic, Georgian, Sahidic, Slavonic, Armenian, and Latin).[78] The earliest text we possess dates back to the third century (Bodmer Papyrus 5).[79] This manuscript shows that it has already undergone many changes, proving it must have been composed some time before the mid-second century C.E.

---

[77] See Painter, *Just James,* 170.

[78] See Painter, *Just James,* 198.

[79] Papyrus Bodmer 5 gives the title of this work as "Birth of Mary: Revelation of James." This title shows that the focus of the narrative is on Mary and not Jesus.

As mentioned, this work was very popular, both in the Eastern and Western Churches. Many of the elements of popular tradition derive from this writing, such as the names of Mary's parents, "Anna and Joachim" (*Prot. Jas.* 1–2). Some scenes were very popular in Christian art, such as the one in which Joseph's son (James?) leads the she-ass on which the pregnant Mary rides, with Joseph bringing up the rear (17.2).

Joseph is presented in the narrative of the *Protevangelium of James* as a widower with sons when he married Mary: "(But) Joseph answered him: 'I (already) have sons and am old, but she is a girl'" (*Prot. Jas.* 9.2).[80] While the sons are not named, it is clearly implied that James was a step-brother to Jesus and not a blood brother. The writer reminds the reader that Joseph has sons when Joseph goes to enroll following the decree of Caesar Augustus (*Prot. Jas.* 17.1).

Salome and the midwife test Mary once she has given birth and dis-cover that she is still a virgin (*Prot. Jas.* 19.3–20.1). Finally, the writing con-cludes with an identification of the author: "Now, I, James, who wrote this history, when a tumult arose in Jerusalem on the death of Herod, withdrew into the wilderness until the tumult in Jerusalem ceased" (*Prot. Jas.* 25.1).

This account defines James as Jesus' stepbrother. James is presented as a witness to the birth of Jesus during the rule of Herod the Great prior to 4 B.C.E. This would imply that James would have been more than seventy years old at his death in 62 C.E. This is a clear indication that the writer is using the figure of James as an authority to bear witness to belief in the perpetual virginity of Mary. The narrative was written for "the glorification of Mary."[81]

Summary

This chapter has traced the way James was understood and portrayed in very different traditions over the course of three centuries and shows how widespread was the tradition regarding the person of James. Attention was devoted to three major trajectories in which the figure of James was important: the traditions of Eusebius and the trajectories of Jewish Chris-tianity and Gnosticism. The role of James in these writings is highly sig-nificant when compared to the New Testament, which tended to exclude James from the picture.

---

[80] The translation of the text of the *Protevangelium of James* is taken from Schneemelcher, *New Testament Apocrypha,* 1:426–39.

[81] Ibid. 425.

The New Testament picture of James as the authority of the church of Jerusalem was consistently remembered over those centuries. Other dimensions of the character of James were embellished, aspects that conformed to the needs and perspectives of those churches where James was celebrated as a hero. The study shows how the tradition itself is absorbed and defined by the context and sociocultural situation in which it is handed on.

Future centuries looked on James not just as an authoritative leader, but also as a recipient of revelation from the risen Jesus. This was a development far from the picture of James that emerged from the letter of James. The roots for this view of James lay in Paul's first letter to the Corinthians, where James is identified by name as one to whom the risen Jesus had appeared (1 Cor 15:7). This resurrection appearance became the foundation for those beliefs that presented James as the recipient of special revelation. Especially in the tradition of Gnosticism, James was the one to whom Jesus communicated a secret knowledge that placed him over Peter and the other apostles. The Gnostics claimed James for their own in order to defend their traditions against those of the wider Christian church. Even though James was a Christian Jew, the Gnostics claimed him as their own hero. They embraced James to justify their traditions and to distance themselves from the wider church that claimed Peter and Paul for its authorities. This appearance becomes the basis for James becoming a bearer of Gnostic revelation (in the Apocryphon of James) and a Gnostic Redeemer (The [Second] Apocalypse of James).

The world of Jewish Christianity also claimed James as its authoritative leader. In terms of theology James was identified as the "Just One" whose piety was renowned. He was blameless, and his martyrdom gave courage and hope to all who suffered, especially those who experienced persecution. His death, as we have seen, is the one feature that received the most attention in the tradition. As a Christian martyr, he died a death resembling those of Jesus and Stephen. The fact that his death is also mentioned in the writings of Josephus is testimony to the authority he enjoyed even outside the Christian community.

Reflecting on the passage from Clement of Alexandria that was examined above, Schoedel insightfully notes that this passage identifies three stages in the development of the tradition about James: "[T]here were three main (no doubt overlapping) stages in the development of the image of James: (1) as James the Just, a symbol of Jewish-Christian values; (2) as the recipient of postresurrection revelation in a Gnosticizing milieu; and (3) as a colleague of the apostles of the Lord in a catholicizing milieu."[82]

---

[82] Schoedel, "The (First) Apocalypse of James (V,3)," 261.

This study has tended to support Schoedel's contention that the image of James embraced three stages (sometimes overlapping) in the developing tradition of the first centuries. However, rather than seeing this appropriation and endorsement of the character of James as taking place in subsequent developments over the course of the centuries, it is best to see it as occurring simultaneously in different and very diverse centers. In fact, in all the major trajectories of early Christianity the character of James held an important sway: within the world of *Jewish Christianity* James was venerated as the leader *par excellence* who championed Jewish-Christian values; within the world of *Gnosticism,* James was presented as the recipient of a postresurrection revelation from the Risen Lord; finally, within the world of *orthodox Christianity* James was an apostle working together with the other apostles.

CHAPTER FIVE

The Legacy of James of Jerusalem

> The disciples said to Jesus,
> "We know that you will depart from us.
> Who is to be our leader?"
> Jesus said to them, "Wherever you are,
> you are to go to James the righteous,
> for whose sake heaven and earth came into being."[1]

We have followed the character of James of Jerusalem through a trajectory spanning the writings of the New Testament and those emerging in the subsequent three centuries of early Christianity. The focus has been on James' interface with his own world of Judaism and early Christianity and with the characters that made up that world. This examination has revealed James to be a significant figure within the context of Christianity's birth and growth. In examining the texts themselves, we have shown how the methodologies of interpretation such as narrative criticism, source criticism, and the social-scientific methodology operate in practice. This study endeavored to illustrate the importance of remaining faithful to the methodology itself. Failure to do so results in some false and incredible deductions deriving from the texts.

In this final chapter I wish to highlight the legacy of James of Jerusalem by presenting a synthesis of the memory of James left behind by the various writings within the trajectory. At the same time it is my wish to delineate the vision James of Jerusalem had for early Christianity. Despite

---

[1] Thomas O. Lambdin, trans., "The Gospel of Thomas," Saying 12, in James M. Robinson, ed., *The Nag Hammadi Library in English* (3rd ed. New York: HarperCollins, 1990) 127.

the fact that James' vision faded and ultimately lost out to Paul's, James of Jerusalem still holds an importance and significance for today.

The Memory of James

The Memory of James Within the New Testament

The examination of the New Testament sources for the figure of James of Jerusalem showed that he struggled with the central issues of self-definition, identity, and diversity in interface with the world around him and the other central characters within the early Christian movement, especially Paul and Peter. In investigating the evidence provided by the methodological investigation we are surprised to find that the picture of James is very different from the one that is traditionally presented.

JAMES AND JESUS

Later interpreters presented a picture of James and his brothers as being unbelievers in the beginning. Following an appearance of the Risen Jesus (1 Cor 15:7), James became a believer in Jesus. His emergence onto the stage of Christianity was late and paralleled Paul's own journey from unbeliever to believer following a conversion experience. This picture conforms to a common view that attempts to downplay James' role and influence within the world of early Christianity. In fact, it arises from unconscious presuppositions that are brought to bear upon the text. While it is impossible and also unnecessary to read a text without any presuppositions, it is essential that one approach a text with a conscious awareness of the presuppositions that one brings to the text. The unconscious presupposition that operates in any encounter with the person of James is that he was a secondary character compared with Peter and Paul.

Our careful examination of the New Testament sources has revealed a very different picture of James of Jerusalem. When referring to his eschatological family in the Synoptic Gospels as those who carry out his Father's will, Jesus does not intend a criticism of his own human family or kindred. Jesus is concerned about the bonds that empower one to carry out the will of the heavenly Father, not the bonds that are based on lineage. As indicated before, Mark's gospel is concerned with Jesus' identity and the response engendered in all who encounter him. Just as Mark's gospel portrays the disciples struggling to understand Jesus' identity, so too does Jesus' family. This is part of Mark's rhetoric in bringing the reader to an awareness of who Jesus is and calling them to respond to Jesus as Messiah and Son of God. Mark's gospel is a rhetorical presentation of the reality.

In a similar vein, the Gospel of John is concerned about the faith response to Jesus. John's gospel presents individuals and groups in interface with Jesus to highlight these faith responses. Given this context, John's statement that "not even his brothers believed in him" (John 7:5) is not to be understood as an indication of hostility between Jesus and his family. Rather, it is a commentary on the quality of their faith. For John a faith that rests solely on signs is an incomplete faith. This is the type of faith on which Jesus' family relied. They wanted Jesus to go up to Jerusalem to perform signs for others to see. John uses Jesus' family as a foil to argue that signs do not lead to faith. True faith in Jesus is based on a relationship of love, as the figure of the Beloved Disciple illustrates.

When the gospel narratives are subjected to a close reading, a picture emerges of Jesus' family interacting with Jesus during the course of his ministry. Very much like the disciples, Jesus' family strives to come to a deeper appreciation of Jesus' identity and mission. To present a picture of the family as hostile to Jesus, or even as unbelievers, reveals a false understanding of the rhetorical function of each of the Gospels. While we cannot immediately jump the divide between the narrative world and the historical reality, we can deduce a common picture from all the gospels of Jesus' family interacting with him in some manner during the course of his ministry.

While James does not emerge as an independent figure within the gospel traditions, he is part of Jesus' family circle. Like Jesus, James is from Nazareth. He grows up within the cultic and religious world of Judaism of the first century C.E. absorbing his Jewish heritage. He is challenged by his brother Jesus to place foremost in his life the following of God's will, which in the Jewish context implies the Torah.

LEADER OF THE JERUSALEM COMMUNITY

Paul's letter to the Galatians implies that James was an important figure within the Jerusalem community from the very beginning. When Paul goes up to Jerusalem after his conversion he meets with Peter and then notes specifically that he called on James (Gal 1:19). Paul singles out "James and Cephas and John" (Gal 2:9) as the three pillars of the Jerusalem community. Noteworthy is the order in which Paul lists them: James is mentioned first, which demonstrates his prime position within the Jerusalem community.

When we read Acts and Galatians together, we see that James was a leader within the Jerusalem community from the beginning. It was not a role he inherited when Peter left Jerusalem (Acts 12:12-19). Rather, he was already exercising that role together with Peter and John from the beginning. The clearest way to understand the evidence is to see James exercising a residential leadership within the Jerusalem community. This leadership role also embraced caring for other Jewish Christian communities in the Diaspora since many had been founded from the Jerusalem community itself. The establishment of the Christian community at Antioch is a clear illustration of the authority Jerusalem (and by implication James) exercised over that community (Acts 11:22).

The roles of Peter, James, and Paul within the early Christian community are clearly defined. As the residential leader of the Jerusalem community James had responsibility also for those Jewish Christian communities in the Diaspora. Peter, as an apostle, was entrusted with bringing the message of salvation to the ends of the earth. The sources show that Peter's main concern and area of concentration was to bring that message to people from the world of Israel, while Paul's task was that of the apostle to the nations (Gal 2:7-8).

The Antioch incident (Gal 2:11-14) witnesses to the leadership role James continued to exercise over the Jewish Christian communities. Paul shows how Peter and Barnabas responded to James' concern about sharing table fellowship with non-Jewish Christians. Not only did Peter and Barnabas follow James' direction, but all the Jewish Christians listened to James as well. Paul was the odd one out (Gal 2:13-14).

As leader of the Jewish Christian communities and in particular the Jerusalem community, James was predominantly concerned with the self-definition and identity of Jesus' followers. Like his brother Jesus, James saw his task as preserving his Jewish heritage. He did this by working for the restoration of the people of Israel following the direction set by Jesus' ministry. James did not envision the followers of Jesus belonging to a new religion; they were the true heirs of God's promises made to Israel. In Jesus' life and ministry these promises had begun to be realized. This messianic movement belonged fully within the world of Israel's faith and heritage. James sought to remain true to this vision.

As leader of the Jewish Christian communities in Jerusalem and the Diaspora, James approached every issue from the framework of his Jewish heritage. The decision of the Council of Jerusalem and the Apostolic Decree illustrate this approach very well. Circumcision was not required of the Gentile men who followed Jesus, and no ritual or cultic laws were required of Gentile believers beyond the stipulations that belonged to all Gentiles, namely the Noachide commandments and Leviticus 17–18. These stipulations were important for James, as they were a way of demonstrating an identity: for the followers of Jesus these were the laws that gave them an identity in distinction to the society around them. These stipulations enabled them to define the boundaries.

While the issue of sharing table fellowship did not specifically arise in the context of the discussion of Acts 15, James' approach logically followed from that of his own tradition, namely the prohibition of Jews sharing meals with Gentiles. James would see this continuing within the world of Jesus' followers. Since Gentile Christians had been freed from the requirement of circumcision, Jewish Christians would have difficulty sharing meals with them, for they would still be eating with the uncircumcised, which was tantamount to betraying their very heritage. Bernheim notes the serious implications this approach had: "By refusing to share a table with them, the Jewish Christians were showing that they did not think them complete Christians."[2] Just as in the world of Judaism pagans were allowed to associate with the synagogue in varying degrees as proselytes and "God-fearers," so followers of Jesus from the pagan world were seen to belong to their communities, provided they followed certain stipulations. If the men were not circumcised, it would be logically impossible for Jewish Christians to share table fellowship with them, as that would be a betrayal of their very identity, something which the purity rules were intent upon preserving.

James' ethnic and religious background as a Jewish Christian defined his whole perspective. James saw his role as remaining faithful to the directions set by Jesus in striving for the restoration of God's twelve-tribe kingdom. Fidelity to Torah was the center for retaining access to God and for defining boundaries in interface with others. The struggle with Peter, Barnabas, and Paul related to James' concern with preserving the centuries-old Jewish social map of the world. In relation to Paul's outreach to the Gentile world, James' attitude was more one of tolerance than active support. In effect James' approach was to confine himself to the world of Jewish Christians. If Gentiles wished to associate with the Christian movement, James had no objection. He viewed their relationship with Jewish Christians as analogous to the relationship that existed between Jews and resident aliens within the world of Palestine. Conflict and dispute defined the interface between James and Paul, as James endeavored to remain firm in his adherence to the concept of Christianity as a reconstitution of God's twelve-tribe kingdom (Jas 1:1).

The Memory of James Beyond the New Testament Picture

Besides continuing the New Testament view of James as the "brother of Jesus" and leader of the Jerusalem community, the writings beyond the

---

[2] Pierre-Antoine Bernheim, *James, Brother of Jesus* (London: SCM Press, 1997) 181.

New Testament reflect more on the significance of these aspects. At the same time they add two entirely new features to this picture, that of Christian martyr and Gnostic revealer.

CHRISTIAN MARTYR

One of the most valuable accounts of James' death comes not from within the Christian world, but from outside, from the Jewish historian, Josephus. He hands on an authentic tradition related to James' death and shows how respected James was within the worlds of both Judaism and Christianity. Josephus notes that even the Pharisees were against the stoning of James.

The writings of Eusebius showed how the traditions continued to reflect upon James' death. As an illustration he appeals to the works of Hegesippus and Clement of Alexandria. The quotation from Hegesippus shows that a new title has been applied to James, namely "the Just." This title grows in popularity and becomes a traditional term for identifying James, especially in the Nag Hammadi writings (for example, *GThom.* 12).

In his detailed description of James' death Hegesippus shows how legendary elements have grown around the person of James. The fact that Hegesippus himself may have constructed this account on the basis of traditional material illustrates the important role James continued to play in the imagination and world of the first four centuries. I agree with Johnson's assessment: "It is doubtful whether either Eusebian account adds anything reliable to our historical knowledge concerning the death of James, even though Eusebius himself claims that Hegesippus' account is 'in agreement' with that of Clement."[3] However, it is also important to see how these accounts functioned within the world of early Christianity. They did not have a historical consciousness that forms the horizon within which we view and judge everything. What was significant was the important role of James within the imagination of that early Christian world. The legendary motifs witness to this. As a martyr, James was understood to be in line with the first great martyrs, Jesus and Stephen. Just as the Acts of the Apostles described Stephen's death in terms that were reminiscent of Jesus' death and were clearly intended to show that Stephen's death emulated that of Jesus (Acts 7:54–8:1), so too the tradition rests on the foundational descriptions of the deaths of Jesus and Stephen in describing James as a faithful follower whose death reflected and emulated their deaths.

---

[3] Luke Timothy Johnson, *The Letter of James,* AB 37A (New York: Doubleday, 1995) 100.

Taking the traditions of Josephus together with those of Hegesippus, Clement, and Eusebius himself, one concludes that there is a basic historical core that testifies to the fact that James did indeed die the death of a Christian martyr. His death was provoked by growing hostility within Jerusalem between the Jewish followers of Jesus and those who interpreted their traditions differently.

These accounts also show that subsequent traditions reflected more clearly on what lay buried beneath the surface of the New Testament writings. The importance of James' adherence to the Jewish roots of Christianity continued to be celebrated in subsequent centuries.

GNOSTIC REVEALER

In one of the quotations from Clement that Eusebius quotes, Clement states: "After the Resurrection the Lord gave the tradition of knowledge to James the Just and John and Peter . . . ."[4] Noteworthy is the position of James, mentioned first in this list. This attribution of special knowledge that is revealed to James became an important point of reflection for the circles of Gnosticism. The starting point for this tradition probably lies in Paul's reference to James as one of the foundational witnesses to the resurrection of Jesus in 1 Cor 15:7, "Then he appeared to James, then to all the apostles."

The Apocryphon of James focuses on this picture of James as the receiver of divine revelation. Not only is James a recipient of special knowledge, he also has the responsibility of transmitting this knowledge to others. His acknowledged authority is seen when he sends out the other apostles on their missions while he remains behind to oversee the Jerusalem community. This focus on James' authority as well as the special revelation he received from the Risen Lord was pivotal in the world of Gnosticism. The Gnostics turned to James as one who could give authority to their own traditions. As we have shown, James was outside the group of the Twelve and was representative of a tradition different from that of Peter and Paul. The Gnostics highlighted this difference and claimed that they were heirs to the special revelation James had received. The culmination of this approach emerges clearly in the (Second) Apocalypse of James (55.4-20).

Within the world of Gnosticism, James is presented as a rival to Peter. In comparison to Peter and the other apostles, James holds a special position as one who is the brother of the Lord and whose knowledge does not derive from the other apostles but has come via a special revelation.

---

[4] Eusebius, *Hist. eccl.* 2:1.4 [Lake, LCL].

AUTHORITATIVE LEADER

Within the context of another tradition, that of Jewish Christianity, the character of James continued to be greatly venerated. Certainly the world of the New Testament situated James within those traditions that were intent on preserving the Jewish origins and heritage of Jesus' followers. Over time those Jewish Christian communities tended to promote viewpoints that were out of harmony with the wider Christian communities, such as a denial of the divinity of Jesus as the only Son of God. James was the one they turned to in support of their perspectives. Since James was painted as the first disciple to witness an appearance of the risen Lord, his authority was presented as surpassing that of the other apostles. James has been entrusted with preserving the true traditions they argued were to be found within the world of these Jewish Christian communities.

Summary

The character of James began as a champion for the orthodoxy of Christianity. As leader of the Jerusalem community, James' task was to preserve the roots of the Jesus movement in its Jewish heritage. The New Testament world accepted and respected James' leadership. However, as time went on the character of the Jesus movement changed. With the acceptance of vast numbers of Gentiles into the Jesus movement it became a people whose origin was rooted in the Gentile world. This new dimension of Christianity turned to the traditions of Peter and Paul for direction and authority, while the position of James receded into the background. Within the trajectories of Jewish Christianity and Gnosticism the figure of James became important as a champion of an alternative tradition. Finally, the character of James would be rehabilitated within the world of orthodox Christianity as an apostle among other apostles. This clearly explains the reason for the late acceptance of the letter of James as a canonical writing: because James was the acknowledged authority within the worlds of Jewish Christianity and Gnostic Christianity any writing bearing his name would be treated with suspicion. However, as the church in the fourth century sought a more unified Christianity and an agreement on the canon of the New Testament, the letter of James would gain acceptance as witness to an important legacy and heritage. In a sense James was rehabilitated into the world of orthodox Christianity.

James and His Interface with His World

In the past century Walter Bauer produced a significant work that was to force scholars to rethink the development of Christianity in the course of the first three centuries.[5] The book was originally published in Germany in 1934, but it was only with its reprint in German in 1964 and translation into English in 1971 that the impact of his views began to be appreciated. Bauer's thesis was that the growth of Christianity did not occur in a monolithic and harmonious way as the Acts of the Apostles tended to present the picture. Instead Bauer envisioned the growth evolving around a number of independent Christian geographical centers that appropriated the Christian traditions in their own ways. While I do not endorse all Bauer's perspectives, many aspects of his vision are supported by our examination, especially where James is seen to exercise an important role within certain centers of early Christianity. The focus on the character of James within the worlds of Jewish Christianity and Gnosticism shows how those two worlds appropriated James' heritage in order to support their own distinctive views and perspectives.

James was indeed a "giant" in the context of early Christianity. His authority was unique. He had a special relationship to Jesus and was the leader of the mother church in Jerusalem. James represented a flourishing branch and tradition of early Christianity that had subsequently died out within the early church. James' vision was to hold onto Christianity's roots within the world of Judaism. He attempted to remain true to the two poles of Judaism and the message of Jesus. The letter of James is a wonderful testimony to his ability to marry both traditions with a focus on the Law, the sayings of Jesus, and an express concern for the poor.

In trying to accommodate Paul's vision of a mission to the Gentiles, James still remained true to his Jewish heritage. He saw Gentile Christians associating with Jewish Christians in the same way Jews associated with Gentiles in the context of the synagogue. While upholding their freedom from the circumcision ritual, they still had to abide by the Noachide commandments that dealt with the interaction of Jews and Gentiles.

James realized most clearly what was at issue for *Jewish Christians* in his conflict with Paul. Paul in turn realized what was at issue *for the world at large*. For each the focus of attention was different.[6] The earliest traditions of Christianity were intent on retaining the bonds with their roots within the house of Israel. The character of James bears witness to this, as does the letter of James. This is probably one of the strongest arguments in

---

[5] Walter Bauer, *Rechtgläubigkeit und Ketzerei im ältesten Christentum,* BHT 10 (Tübingen: J.C.B. Mohr [Paul Siebeck], 1934); English translation *Orthodoxy and Heresy in Earliest Christianity,* trans. R. A. Kraft and G. Krodel (Philadelphia: Fortress, 1971).

[6] See John Painter, *Just James: The Brother of Jesus in History and Tradition* (Minneapolis: Fortress, 1999) 275.

favor of assigning an early date to the letter of James because of its firm roots within its Jewish heritage. The letter of James is intent on defining the boundaries within Judaism that separate those members who acknowledge Jesus to be the long-awaited Messiah from those belonging to the rest of Judaism. As Robert W. Wall defines the relationship:

> Earliest Christianity's relationship with Judaism remained important in its every effort for religious and societal legitimacy; believers understood themselves to be faithful Jews and members of a Jewish congregation. The contested issues were parochial and *intra muros:* first-generation believers argued that they belonged to "messianic" Judaism—the "true" eschatological Israel of God—while "official" Judaism constituted the "rest of Israel." Only in this rather limited sense can some New Testament writings be thought of as marking boundaries between Christianity and Judaism.[7]

James' evaluation proved to be insightful and prophetic. With large numbers of believers entering the Jesus movement from the world of the Gentiles, Paul's vision soon gained supremacy and more and more the world of Jewish Christianity began to shrink. Beginning within the world of the house of Israel, the Christian movement became predominantly Gentile Christian. James' vision lost out to Paul's. As time went by, Jewish Christians felt alienated from the larger numbers of Gentile Christians. At the same time they were excluded from their fellow Jews. The movement that tried to remain true to the traditions and vision of James ultimately became a sect within the confines of the Christian movement. Their inability to accept openness to the Gentile world would spell their ultimate doom. James' vision and hope ultimately died. Historical reasons were as much responsible for that demise as were theological reasons. In 70 C.E. and then again in 135 C.E. Jerusalem was destroyed by the Romans. This brought an end to the Jewish Christian church in Jerusalem. Eusebius gives an impressive account of this Jewish Christian church in Jerusalem and its dissolution.[8]

With the end of Jewish Christian leaders in Jerusalem the importance of Jerusalem also began to diminish. The focus was on the mission to the Gentiles, and the heritage of the mission to the Jews became insignificant. Without doubt this led to the marginalization of Jewish Christianity within

---

[7] Robert W. Wall, *Community of the Wise: The Letter of James,* The New Testament in Context (Valley Forge, PA: Trinity Press International, 1997) 291.

[8] Eusebius, *Hist. eccl.* 4:5-6 [Lake, LCL].

the framework of the Christian movement. The roots within Judaism were either forgotten or ignored: a Gentile Christian church had taken root.

Besides the historical reasons for the decline of the importance of Jewish Christianity and by implication James' place within the wider world of the second and third centuries C.E., there were also a number of theological reasons that led to their decline and marginalization. The main concern lay with understanding the role of the Torah in the lives of the followers of Jesus. For Paul the Torah had a preparatory function in that it prepared the way for Jesus. Paul describes this function beautifully in his use of the image of the *paidagōgos*:[9] "Therefore the law was our disciplinarian *(paidagōgos)* until Christ came, so that we might be justified by faith. But now that faith has come, we are no longer subject to a disciplinarian *(paidagōgos),* for in Christ Jesus you are all children of God through faith" (Gal 3:24-26). For Paul the Torah was a guide that led toward Christ. It was the Christ event that replaced the Torah in the world of salvation. Salvation came through the death and resurrection of Jesus. For Paul the death and resurrection of Jesus capture the heart of his teaching. Paul is concerned with reflection on the theological understanding and significance of the Christ event, since everything else proceeds from it. One's very way of life is a response to belief in Jesus. James, on the other hand, is concerned with the type of life one leads, which must conform to God's will as expressed in the Torah. For James the Torah continues to remain operative, as it is the eternal expression of God's moral will for God's people. Since James is intent on upholding the continuity between the followers of Jesus and their Jewish heritage, his letter shows that he is not intent, as Paul is, on defining the significance of the Christ event. His mention of Jesus' name on only two occasions in the letter bears this out. It is not that Jesus is unimportant for James. On the contrary, we have seen how James deliberately situates himself within the trajectory Jesus has initiated, and James remains true to that heritage. But the focus for James is on ethics and on the way of life one leads. Both James and Paul agree on the need for a theological underpinning of one's ethics. For Paul it is the salvific death of Jesus, while for James it is God's manifest will in the Torah that gives direction to the way one leads one's life (ethics).

---

[9] BDAG explains the term *paidagōgos* in this way: "Originally 'boy-leader,' the man, usually a slave (Plut., Mor. 4ab), whose duty it was to conduct a boy or youth (Plut., Mor. 439f) to and from school and to superintend his conduct generally; he was not a 'teacher' . . . . In our literature one who has responsibility for someone who needs guidance, a guardian, leader, guide" (748).

Within the world of Jewish Christianity an overemphasis on ethics without a theological underpinning ultimately led to its rejection as heresy. One such sect within the ambient of Jewish Christianity was a group called the *Ebionites*. They were a group of ascetics who had established themselves in Syria and Transjordan. They strongly opposed Paul's teachings because they interpreted them as rejecting any concern for ethical action. The Ebionites, on the other hand, degenerated into a form of legalism, where concern rested solely on the fulfillment of the stipulations of the law. They led lives of very strict poverty. What the Ebionites, however, do show is how the positions of Paul and James can both be pushed to the extremes where Paul would be seen to uphold the theological without a concern for the ethical, and James, on the other hand, would be seen to stress the ethical to the exclusion of the theological. Such an interpretation distorts the perspectives of both Paul and James, as we have endeavored to show throughout this study.

An interesting insight regarding the future impact of Jewish Christianity is that of Hans-Joachim Schoeps, who argued that Islam inherited the mantle of Jewish Christianity.[10] One noteworthy feature in both groups is that while Jewish Christianity places Jesus within the line of the prophets as the "true prophet," Islam identifies Muhammed as God's true prophet. An examination of the letter of James also reveals how its theological perspective is in harmony with some perspectives of Islam. The one God is the origin and source of all that exists. God is the only Lawgiver who calls upon humanity to obey and give due respect and adherence.

Within the canon of the New Testament the letter of James is a welcome reminder of how an exclusive and onesided reading of Paul's letters can lead to a distortion of the importance of ethical responsibility. For James the essence is to put "faith into action" (Jas 2:17). Observance of the Torah (Jas 1:22-27) gives direction to the faith community and brings salvation (Jas 2:12-13). Paul and James need to be read together: theology and ethics are two poles that cannot exist independently of each other.

Significance of James' Vision for the Twenty-First Century

Our study has shown that James was indeed an important figure in the context of the first-generation Christian church and that his character continued to dominate certain contexts of the church for the next three centuries. The character of James continues to be an important figure in the context of the present world and church for three reasons.

---

[10] See Hans-Joachim Schoeps, "Ebionite Christianity," *JTS* 4 (1953) 219–24.

(1) Our world has been defined as the "postmodern world." While it is often difficult to identify what exactly is meant by such a phrase, one aspect the phrase captures is the fact that no single perspective dominates the landscape. In other words, there is a celebration of diversity. James would never have embraced an attitude of relativism that would acknowledge every viewpoint as having equal importance and validity. His perspective was that of ensuring that Christianity must maintain its roots in Judaism. On the other hand, the strength of James' perspective in which he acknowledged the validity of a mission to the Jews and a separate mission to the Gentiles gave impetus to the growth of diversity within early Christianity. As we have indicated, the evidence of the first four centuries of Christianity has demonstrated diverse geographical centers with focuses upon different traditions whose authority was underpinned by a number of the early Christian apostles. In this context the character of James offers a direction for Christians faced with the reality of a very diverse religious world. He issues a challenge to remain faithful to one's roots while respecting the perspectives of others. The inherent danger in a diverse world is that one can simply throw up one's hands in despair and say that all perspectives are of equal importance. While James would never acknowledge that, he does show that it is important to be open to allow the tradition to develop and flower forth as it did through his following and understanding of the messianic direction mapped out by Jesus. Jesus Christ "the Lord of glory" (Jas 2:1 [my translation]) is the one who gives meaning and direction to one's roots and heritage. In like manner in the postmodern world, if one is to avoid falling into the trap of total relativism, a Christian sees the person of Jesus as the only one who can transcend one's traditions and give them new direction and meaning. James challenges the Christian to refocus on the role of Jesus as the direction pointer and the one who instills new meaning and life into one's traditions.

(2) James provides a special concern for the poor. This is evident in the New Testament picture that is presented of James, where Paul testifies that James asked him to take up a collection on his travels for the poor of Jerusalem (Gal 2:10). This is in conformity with the spirit of Jesus as reflected in the canonical gospels and especially in their sources. His life was oriented to responding to the needs of the poor, the marginalized of society. The letter of James reflects this same spirit. In line with Jesus, James promises the poor that they will inherit a kingdom (compare Luke 6:20 and Jas 2:5). In the spirit of the prophets James promises that God will champion the cause of the poor because they have no one to stand up for them (Jas 5:1-6). The letter of James provides an insightful definition of religion that challenges the believer to embrace a social concern as its very foundation

(Jas 1:27). This is certainly an appeal that resonates with our twenty-first-century world. More and more people are being challenged to come to awareness of the injustices within society and of the suffering of the voiceless and marginalized. More than ever we are called to interface with the morality of our world. The letter of James points the way with the graphic example of discriminating between the rich and the poor (Jas 2:1-7). While the discrimination was based upon wealth, it also provides a marvelous challenge to the reader to evaluate the ways she/he discriminates against others in daily interactions. Both the character of James in the New Testament and the author of the letter of James were concerned with providing the boundaries for the social order that delineated those who were followers of Jesus. An essential value that is still relevant today is that of preserving the dignity of every human being and not discriminating against anyone for whatever reason.

(3) From the above, the challenge the author of James provides for the twenty-first century is to take seriously one's foundational values. The integration of a life of authentic faith with action is at the heart of the gospel message and James. As James of Jerusalem was concerned about the values his community held, so too does the letter of James show concern for the faith and life of its communities. James of Jerusalem and James of the letter were both concerned with real-life issues and how their communities interfaced with these issues on a daily basis. The challenge James of Jerusalem sets before the Christian reader today is to treasure his/her identity as a Christian and to hold onto the vision that fosters that identity. The mission of James was to call his fellow believers to remain firm within the boundaries of their religious society, which ultimately traces its origin back to Jesus of Nazareth. James of Jerusalem is without doubt the true heir of Jesus of Nazareth.

APPENDIX A

Synoptic Chart
Matthew 12:46-50; Mark 3:19b-21; 31-35; Luke 8:19-21

Matthew 12:46-50	Mark 3:19b-21; 31-35	Luke 8:19-21
	Then he (Jesus) went home; and the crowd came together again, so that they could not even eat. When his family heard it, they went out to restrain him, for people were saying, "He has gone out of his mind" . . .	
While he was still speaking to the crowds, his mother and his brothers were standing outside, wanting to speak to him. Someone told him, "Look, your mother and your brothers are standing outside, wanting to speak to you." But to the one who had told him this, Jesus replied, "Who is my mother, and who are my brothers?" And pointing to his disciples, he said, "Here are my mother and my brothers! For whoever does the will of my Father in heaven is my brother and sister and mother."	Then his mother and his brothers came; and standing outside, they sent to him and called him. A crowd was sitting around him; and they said to him, "Your mother and your brothers and sisters are outside, asking for you." And he replied, "Who are my mother and my brothers?" And looking at those who sat around him, he said, "Here are my mother and my brothers! Whoever does the will of God is my brother and sister and mother."	Then his mother and his brothers came to him, but they could not reach him because of the crowd. And he was told, "Your mother and your brothers are standing outside, wanting to see you." But he said to them, "My mother and my brothers are those who hear the word of God and do it."

Synoptic Chart

Matthew 13:53-58; Mark 6:1-6; Luke 4:16-30

Matthew 13:53-58	Mark 6:1-6	Luke 4:16-30
When Jesus had finished these parables, he left that place. He came to his hometown and began to teach the people in their synagogue, so that they were astounded and said, "Where did this man get this wisdom and these deeds of power? Is not this the carpenter's son? Is not his mother called Mary? And are not his brothers James and Joseph and Simon and Judas? And are not all his sisters with us? Where then did this man get all this?" And they took offense at him. But Jesus said to them, "Prophets are not without honor except in their own country and in their own house." And he did not do many deeds of power there, because of their unbelief.	He (Jesus) left that place and came to his hometown, and his disciples followed him. On the Sabbath he began to teach in the synagogue, and many who heard him were astounded. They said, "Where did this man get all this? What is this wisdom that has been given to him? What deeds of power are being done by his hands! Is not this the carpenter, the son of Mary and brother of James and Joses and Judas and Simon, and are not his sisters here with us?" And they took offense at him. Then Jesus said to them, "Prophets are not without honor, except in their hometown, and among their own kin, and in their own house." And he could do no deed of power there, except that he laid his hands on a few sick people and	When he came to Nazareth, where he had been brought up, he went to the synagogue on the sabbath day, as was his custom. He stood up to read, and the scroll of the prophet Isaiah was given to him. He unrolled the scroll and found the place where it was written: "The Spirit of the Lord is upon me, because he has anointed me to bring good news to the poor. He has sent me to proclaim release to the captives and recovery of sight to the blind, to let the oppressed go free, to proclaim the year of the Lord's favor." And he rolled up the scroll, gave it back to the attendant, and sat down. The eyes of all in the synagogue were fixed on him. Then he began to say to them, "Today this scripture has been fulfilled in your hearing."

	(Mark cont.)	*(Luke cont.)*
	cured them. And he was amazed at their unbelief.	All spoke well of him and were amazed at the gracious words that came from his mouth. They said, "Is not this Joseph's son?" He said to them, "Doubtless you will quote to me this proverb, 'Doctor, cure yourself!' And you say, 'Do here also in your hometown the things that we have heard you did at Capernaum.'" And he said, "Truly I tell you, no prophet is accepted in the prophet's hometown. But the truth is, there were many widows in Israel in the time of Elijah, when the heaven was shut up three years and six months, and there was a severe famine over all the land; yet Elijah was sent to none of them except to a widow at Zarephath in Sidon. There were also many lepers in Israel in the time of the prophet Elisha, and none of them was cleansed except Naaman the Syrian." When they heard this, all in the synagogue were filled with rage. They got up, drove him out of the town, and led him to the brow of the hill on which their town was built so that they might hurl him off the cliff. But he passed through the midst of them and went on his way.

BIBLIOGRAPHY

I. Studies

Alter, Robert. *The Pleasures of Reading: In an Ideological Age*. New York: Simon & Schuster, 1989.

Bauckham, Richard J. *Jude and the Relatives of Jesus in the Early Church*. Edinburgh: T & T Clark, 1990.

———. "James and the Jerusalem Church." In idem, ed., *The Book of Acts in Its Palestinian Setting*. The Book of Acts in its First Century Setting 4. Grand Rapids: Eerdmans, 1995, 415–80.

———. "James and the Gentiles (Acts 15,13-21)." In Ben Witherington III, ed., *History, Literature, and Society in the Book of Acts*. Cambridge: Cambridge University Press, 1996, 154–84.

———. *James: Wisdom of James, Disciple of Jesus the Sage*. London and New York: Routledge, 1999.

Bauer, Walter. *Rechtgläubigkeit und Ketzerei im ältesten Christentum*. BHT 10. Tübingen: J.C.B. Mohr [Paul Siebeck], 1934; English: *Orthodoxy and Heresy in Earliest Christianity*. Trans. Robert A. Kraft and Gerhard Krodel. Philadelphia: Fortress, 1971.

Baur, Ferdinand Christian. *Paul the Apostle of Jesus Christ: His Life and Work, His Epistles and His Doctrine. A Contribution to a Critical History of Primitive Christianity*. Ed. Eduard Zeller. Trans. Allan Menzies. 2nd ed. London: Williams and Norgate, 1876.

Berger, Peter L., and Thomas Luckmann. *The Social Construction of Reality: A Treatise in the Sociology of Knowledge*. Garden City, NY: Doubleday, 1966.

Bernheim, Pierre-Antoine. *James, Brother of Jesus*. London: SCM Press, 1997.

Betz, Hans Dieter. *Galatians: A Commentary on Paul's Letter to the Churches in Galatia*. Hermeneia. Philadelphia: Fortress, 1979.

Bockmuehl, Markus. "The Noachide Commandments and New Testament Ethics: With Special Reference to Acts 15 and Pauline Halakhah." *RB* 102 (1995) 72–101.

Brooks, Stephenson H. *Matthew's Community: The Evidence of His Special Sayings Material*. JSNTSup 16. Sheffield: Sheffield Academic Press, 1987.

Brown, Raymond E. *The Death of the Messiah: From Gethsemane to the Grave: A Commentary on the Passion Narratives in the Four Gospels.* 2 vols. New York: Doubleday, 1994.

———. "The Epistle (Letter) of James." *An Introduction to the New Testament.* ABRL. New York: Doubleday, 1997, 724–47.

Brown, Raymond E., et al., eds. *Mary in the New Testament.* Philadelphia: Fortress; New York, Ramsey, and Toronto: Paulist, 1978.

———. *Peter in the New Testament.* Minneapolis: Augsburg; New York: Paulist, 1973.

Buchanan, George W. "The Role of Purity in the Structure of the Essene Sect." *RevQ* 4 (1963) 397–406.

Cadbury, Henry J. "The Speeches in Acts." In Frederick John Foakes Jackson and Kirsopp Lake, eds., *The Beginnings of Christianity, Part 1: The Acts of the Apostles.* Vol. 5: *Additional Notes to the Commentary.* London: Macmillan, 1933.

Callan, Terrance. "The Background of the Apostolic Decree (Acts 15:20, 29; 21:25)." *CBQ* 55 (1993) 284–97.

Cameron, Ron. *Sayings Traditions in the Apocryphon of James.* HTS 34. Philadelphia: Fortress, 1984.

Cargal, Timothy B. *Restoring the Diaspora: Discursive Structure and Purpose in the Epistle of James.* SBLDS 144. Atlanta: Scholars, 1993.

Carroll, Lewis. *Alice's Adventures in Wonderland.* Books of Wonder. New York: William Morrow & Co., (1866) 1992.

———. *Through the Looking-Glass and What Alice Found There.* Books of Wonder. New York: William Morrow & Co., (1872) 1993.

Chester, Andrew, and Ralph P. Martin. *The Theology of the Letters of James, Peter, and Jude.* New Testament Theology. Cambridge: Cambridge University Press, 1994.

Chilton, Bruce, and Craig A. Evans, eds. *James the Just and Christian Origins.* NovTSup 98. Leiden: Brill, 1999.

Chilton, Bruce, and Jacob Neusner. *Judaism in the New Testament: Practices and Beliefs.* London: Routledge, 1995.

———. *The Brother of Jesus: James the Just and His Mission.* Louisville: Westminster John Knox, 2001.

Culpepper, R. Alan. *Anatomy of the Fourth Gospel: A Study in Literary Design.* Philadelphia: Fortress, 1987.

Davids, Peter H. "Palestinian Traditions in the Epistle of James." In Bruce Chilton and Craig A. Evans, eds., *James the Just and Christian Origins.* NovTSup 98. Leiden: Brill, 1999, 33–57.

Davies, W. D. *Paul and Rabbinic Judaism.* London: SPCK, 1948.

———. *The Setting of the Sermon on the Mount.* Cambridge: Cambridge University Press, 1964.

Dibelius, Martin. *Studies in the Acts of the Apostles.* Ed. Heinrich Greeven. Trans. Mary Ling. London: SCM Press, 1956.

Dodd, Charles Harold. *Historical Tradition in the Fourth Gospel.* Cambridge: Cambridge University Press, 1963.

Douglas, Mary. *Purity and Danger: An Analysis of Concepts of Pollution and Taboo.* London: Routledge & Kegan Paul, 1966.

Dressler, H. "Hegesippus." *New Catholic Encyclopedia.* Washington, D.C.: The Catholic University of America, 1967, 6:994.

Dunn, James D. G. *Unity and Diversity in the New Testament: An Inquiry into the Character of Earliest Christianity.* Philadelphia: Westminster, 1977.

———. "The Incident at Antioch (Gal 2.11-18)." *JSNT* 18 (1983) 3–57.

Elliott, John H. *The Elect and the Holy: An Exegetical Examination of 1 Peter 2:4-10 and the Phrase basileion hierateuma.* NovTSup 12. Leiden: Brill, 1966.

———. "The Epistle of James in Rhetorical and Social Scientific Perspective: Holiness-Wholeness and Patterns of Replication." *BTB* 23 (1993) 71–81.

———. *What Is Social-Scientific Criticism?* Guides to Biblical Study. Minneapolis: Fortress, 1993.

———. *1 Peter.* AB 37B. New York: Doubleday, 2000.

Farmer, William, R. "James the Lord's Brother, According to Paul." In Bruce Chilton and Craig A. Evans, eds., *James the Just and Christian Origins.* Leiden, Boston, and Köln: Brill, 1999.

Feldman, Louis. *Jew and Gentile in the Ancient World: Attitudes and Interactions from Alexander to Justinian.* Princeton: Princeton University Press, 1993.

Fitzmyer, Joseph A. *The Gospel According to Luke I–IX.* AB 28. New York: Doubleday, 1981.

———. *Luke the Theologian: Aspects of His Teaching.* New York and Mahwah, NJ: Paulist, 1989.

Francis, Fred O. "The Form and Function of the Opening and Closing Paragraphs of James and 1 John." *ZNW* 61 (1970) 110–26.

Gammie, John. "Paraenetic Literature: Toward the Morphology of a Secondary Genre." *Semeia* 50 (1990) 41–77.

Goodman, Martin. *Mission and Conversion: Proselytizing in the Religious History of the Roman Empire.* Oxford: Clarendon Press, 1994.

Hartin, Patrick J. "James: A New Testament Wisdom Writing and Its Relationship to Q." D.Th. Dissertation. University of South Africa: Pretoria, 1988.

———. "James and the Sermon on the Mount/Plain." In David J. Lull, ed., *SBLSP* 28. Atlanta: Scholars, 1989, 440–57.

———. *James and the Q Sayings of Jesus.* JSNTSup 47. Sheffield: JSOT Press, 1991.

———. "'Come Now, You Rich, Weep and Wail . . .' (James 5:1-6)." *JTSA* 84 (1993) 57–63.

———. "Call to be Perfect through Suffering (James 1,2-4): The Concept of Perfection in the Epistle of James and the Sermon on the Mount." *Bib* 77 (1996a) 477–92.

———. "The Poor in the Epistle of James and the Gospel of Thomas." *HvTSt* 53 (1997) 146–62.

————. *A Spirituality of Perfection: Faith in Action in the Letter of James.* Collegeville: The Liturgical Press, 1999.

————. "Poor." *Eerdmans Dictionary of the Bible.* Ed. David Noel Freedman. Grand Rapids: Eerdmans, 2000, 1070–71.

Havener, Ivan. *Q: The Sayings of Jesus.* Wilmington: Michael Glazier, 1987.

Hays, Richard B. "Christology and Ethics in Galatians: The Law of Christ." *CBQ* 49 (1987) 268–90.

————. "Have We Found Abraham to Be Our Forefather According to the Flesh? A Reconsideration of Rom 4:1." *NovT* 27 (1985) 76–98.

————. "Justification." *The Anchor Bible Dictionary.* New York: Doubleday, 1992, 3:1129–33.

Hoppe, Leslie J. "Nazirite." *Eerdmans Dictionary of the Bible.* Ed. David Noel Freedman. Grand Rapids: Eerdmans, 2000, 951.

Jeremias, Joachim. *Jerusalem in the Time of Jesus: An Investigation into Economic and Social Conditions during the New Testament Period.* Philadelphia: Fortress, 1969.

Jervell, Jacob. "James the Defender of Paul." In idem, *Luke and the People of God: A New Look at Luke–Acts.* Minneapolis: Augsburg, 1972, 185–207.

Jones, F. Stanley. "The Martyrdom of James in Hegesippus, Clement of Alexandria, and Christian Apocrypha, including Nag Hammadi: A Study of the Textual Relations." *SBLSP* 29. Atlanta: Scholars, 1990, 322–35.

Klijn, Albertus Frederik Johannes. "The Study of Jewish Christianity." *NTS* 20 (1973/74) 419–31.

Koester, Helmut. *Introduction to the New Testament.* Vol. 2: *History and Literature of Early Christianity.* Philadelphia: Fortress; Berlin and New York: Walter de Gruyter, 1982.

————. *Ancient Christian Gospels: Their History and Development.* Philadelphia: Trinity Press International, 1990.

Lüdemann, Gerd. "The Successors of pre-70 Jerusalem Christianity." In E. P. Sanders, ed., *Jewish and Christian Self-Definition.* Philadelphia: Fortress, 1980, 1:161–73.

MacDonald, Dennis R. *The Homeric Epics and the Gospel of Mark.* New Haven: Yale University Press, 2000.

Malherbe, Abraham J. *Moral Exhortation: A Greco-Roman Sourcebook.* Philadelphia: Westminster, 1986.

Malina, Bruce J. "Wealth and Poverty in the New Testament and Its World." *Int* 41 (1987) 354–67.

————. *The New Testament World: Insights from Cultural Anthropology.* Rev. ed. Louisville: Westminster John Knox, 1993.

————. *The New Jerusalem in the Revelation of John: The City as Symbol of Life with God.* Collegeville: The Liturgical Press, 2000.

Malina, Bruce J., and Richard L. Rohrbaugh. *Social-Science Commentary on the Synoptic Gospels.* 2nd ed. Minneapolis: Fortress, 2003.

Massebieau, Louis. "L'Epitre de Jacques est-elle l'Oeuvre d'un Chrétien?" *RHR* 32 (1895) 249–83.

McKnight, Scot. *A Light among the Gentiles: Jewish Missionary Activity in the Second Temple Period.* Minneapolis: Fortress, 1991.

———. "A Parting within the Way: Jesus and James on Israel and Purity." In Bruce Chilton and Craig A. Evans, eds., *James the Just and Christian Origins.* Leiden, Boston, and Köln: Brill, 1999, 83–129.

Maynard-Reid, Pedrito U. *Poverty and Wealth in James.* Maryknoll, NY: Orbis, 1987.

Meier, John P. *A Marginal Jew: Rethinking the Historical Jesus.* Vol. 1: *The Roots of the Problem and the Person.* New York: Doubleday, 1991.

Metzger, Bruce M. *The Canon of the New Testament: Its Origin, Development, and Significance.* Oxford: Clarendon Press, 1987.

Mirecki, Paul. "Gnosticism, Gnosis." *Eerdmans Dictionary of the Bible.* Ed. David Noel Freedman. Grand Rapids: Eerdmans, 2000, 508–509.

Neusner, Jacob. *The Idea of Purity in Ancient Judaism.* SJLA 1. Leiden: Brill, 1973.

———. "History and Purity in First-Century Judaism." *HR* 18 (1978) 1–17.

Neyrey, Jerome H. *Honor and Shame in the Gospel of Matthew.* Louisville: Westminster John Knox, 1998.

Painter, John. *Just James: The Brother of Jesus in History and Tradition.* Minneapolis: Fortress, 1999.

Penner, Todd C. *The Epistle of James and Eschatology: Re-reading an Ancient Christian Letter.* JSNTSup 121. Sheffield: Sheffield Academic Press, 1996.

Perdue, Leo G. "Paraenesis and the Epistle of James." *ZNW* 72 (1981) 241–56.

———. "The Wisdom Sayings of Jesus," *Forum* 2 (1986) 3–35.

———. "The Social Character of Paraenesis and Paraenetic Literature." *Semeia* 50 (1990) 5–39.

Powell, Mark Allan. *What Is Narrative Criticism?* Minneapolis: Fortress, 1990.

Rhoads, David. "The Letter of James: Friend of God." *CurTM* 25 (1998) 473–86.

Rhoads, David, Joanna Dewey, and Donald Michie. *Mark as Story: An Introduction to the Narrative of a Gospel.* 2nd ed. Minneapolis: Fortress, 1999.

Riegel, Stanley K. "Jewish Christianity: Definitions and Terminology." *NTS* 24 (1977/78) 410–15.

Robbins, Vernon K. "Writing as Rhetorical Act in Plutarch and the Gospels." In Duane F. Watson, ed., *Persuasive Artistry: Studies in New Testament Rhetoric in Honor of George A. Kennedy.* Sheffield: JSOT Press, 1991, 142–68.

Sanders, E. P. "Jewish Association with Gentiles and Galatians 2:11-14." In Robert T. Fortna and Beverly R. Gaventa, eds., *The Conversation Continues, Studies in Paul and John in Honor of J. Louis Martyn.* Nashville: Abingdon, 1990, 170–88.

Schmidt, Thomas E. "Taxation, Jewish." *Dictionary of New Testament Background.* Eds. Craig A. Evans and Stanley E. Porter. Downers Grove, IL, and Leicester, England: InterVarsity Press, 2000, 1163–66.

Schoeps, Hans-Joachim. "Ebionite Christianity." *JTS* 4 (1953) 219–24.

Smith, Dwight Moody. *John Among the Gospels: The Relationship in Twentieth-Century Research.* Minneapolis: Fortress, 1992.

Snell, Daniel C. "Taxes and Taxation." *The Anchor Bible Dictionary.* Ed. David Noel Freedman. New York: Doubleday, 1992, 6:338–40.

Spitta, Friedrich. "Der Brief des Jakobus." In idem, *Zur Geschichte und Litteratur des Urchristentums.* Göttingen: Vandenhoeck & Ruprecht, 1896, 2:1–239.

Tannehill, Robert C. *The Narrative Unity of Luke-Acts: A Literary Interpretation.* Vol. 2: *The Acts of the Apostles.* Philadelphia: Fortress, 1994.

Taylor, Vincent. *The Gospel According to St. Mark: The Greek Text with Introduction, Notes, and Indexes.* London: Macmillan, 1952.

Trebilco, Paul R. *Jewish Communities in Asia Minor.* Cambridge: Cambridge University Press, 1991.

Vielhauer, Philipp. *Geschichte der urchristlichen Literatur. Einleitung in das Neue Testament, die Apokryphen und die Apostolischen Väter.* Berlin and New York: Walter De Gruyter, 1975.

Wachob, Wesley Hiram. *The Voice of Jesus in the Social Rhetoric of James.* SNTSMS 106. Cambridge: Cambridge University Press, 2000.

Wall, Robert W. "James as Apocalyptic Paraenesis." *ResQ* 32 (1990) 11–22.

Wansbrough, Henry. "Mark III. 21—Was Jesus Out of His Mind?" *NTS* 18 (1971/72) 233–35.

Ward, Roy Bowen. "James of Jerusalem in the First Two Centuries." *ANRW* II,26.1. Berlin and New York: Walter de Gruyter, 1992.

Yamauchi, Edwin M. "Gnosticism." *Dictionary of New Testament Background.* Eds. Craig A. Evans and Stanley E. Porter. Downers Grove, IL, and Leicester, England: InterVarsity Press, 2000, 414–18.

II. Texts

Aland, Barbara, et al. *Nestle-Aland: Novum Testamentum Graece.* 27th rev. ed., 2nd printing. Apparatum criticum novis curis elaboraverunt Barbara et Kurt Aland una cum Instituto Studiorum Textus Novi Testamenti Monasterii Westphaliae. Stuttgart: Deutsche Bibelgesellschaft, 1994.

———. *The Greek New Testament.* 4th rev. ed. In cooperation with the Institute for New Testament Textual Research, Münster/Westphalia. Stuttgart: Deutsche Bibelgesellschaft/United Bible Societies, 1994.

Apostolic Fathers. Vol. I. I Clement, II Clement, Ignatius, Polycarp, The Didache, Barnabas. Trans. Kirsopp Lake. LCL. Cambridge: Harvard University Press, 1965.

Apostolic Fathers. Vol. II. The Shepherd of Hermas, The Martyrdom of Polycarp, The Epistle To Diognetus. Trans. Kirsopp Lake. LCL. Cambridge: Harvard University Press, 1970.

Augustine, *De diversis quaestionibus LXXXIII Liber Unus.* 76 [*MPL* 50:89].

Barnard, Leslie William, trans. *St. Justin Martyr: The First and Second Apologies.* ACW 56. New York and Mahwah, NJ: Paulist, 1997.

Charles, Robert H., ed. *The Apococrypha and Pseudepigrapha of the Old Testament in English with Introduction and Critical and Explanatory Notes to the Several Books.* Oxford: Clarendon Press, 1913.

Charlesworth, James H., ed. *The Old Testament Pseudepigrapha.* Vol. 1. *Apocalyptic Literature and Testaments.* Garden City, NY: Doubleday, 1983.

―――. *The Old Testament Pseudepigrapha.* Vol. 2. *Expansions of the "Old Testament" and Legends, Wisdom and Philosophical Literature, Prayers, Psalms, and Odes, Fragments of Lost Judeo-Hellenistic Works.* London: Darton, Longman & Todd, 1985.

Cullman, Oscar, trans. "The Protevangelium of James." In Wilhelm Schneemelcher, ed., *New Testament Apocrypha: Gospels and Related Writings.* Rev. ed. Cambridge: James Clarke & Co.; Louisville: Westminster John Knox, 1991, 1:414–39.

Eusebius. *The Ecclesiastical History.* Trans. Kirsopp Lake and J.E.L. Oulton. 2 vols. LCL. Cambridge: Harvard University Press; London: William Heinemann, 1953–57.

Evans, Craig A., and Stanley E. Porter., eds. *Dictionary of New Testament Background.* Downers Grove, IL, and Leicester, England: InterVarsity Press, 2000.

Freedman, David Noel, ed. *Eerdmans Dictionary of the Bible.* Grand Rapids: Eerdmans, 2000.

―――. *The Anchor Bible Dictionary.* New York: Doubleday, 1992.

Hedrick, Charles W., trans. "The (Second) Apocalypse of James (V,4)." In James M. Robinson, ed., *The Nag Hammadi Library in English.* 3rd ed. New York: HarperCollins, 1990, 269–76.

Hock, Ronald F. *The Infancy Gospels of James and Thomas.* The Scholars Bible. Santa Rosa, CA: Polebridge Press, 1995.

Josephus. *The Life, and Against Apion.* Vol. 1. Trans. H. St. J. Thackeray. LCL. London: William Heinemann; Cambridge: Harvard University Press, 1961.

Josephus. *The Jewish War.* Vols. II–III. Books I–VII. Trans. H. St. J. Thackeray. LCL. London: William Heinemann; Cambridge: Harvard University Press, 1956–57.

Josephus. *Jewish Antiquities.* Vols. IV–IX. Books I–XX. Trans. H. St. J. Thackeray, Ralph Marcus, and Louis H. Feldman. LCL. London: William Heinemann; Cambridge: Harvard University Press, 1961–65.

Koehler, Ludwig, and Walter Baumgartner, eds. *Lexicon in Veteris Testamenti Libros.* Leiden: Brill, 1958.

Lambdin, Thomas O., trans. "The Gospel of Thomas." In James M. Robinson, ed., *The Nag Hammadi Library in English.* 3rd ed. New York: HarperCollins, 1990, 126–38.

Layton, Bentley. *The Gnostic Scriptures. A New Translation with Annotations and Introductions.* Garden City, NY: Doubleday, 1987.

Layton, Bentley, ed. *Nag Hammadi Codex II,2-7.* Vol. 1. Leiden, New York, Copenhagen, and Köln: Brill, 1989.

Liddell, Henry George, and Robert Scott. *An Intermediate Greek-English Lexicon.* 7th ed. Oxford: Clarendon Press, 1968.

Liddell, Henry George, and Robert Scott. *A Greek-English Lexicon.* Revised and Augmented by Henry Stuart Jones and Roderick McKenzie. 9th ed. with Revised Supplement. Oxford: Clarendon Press, 1996.

Louw, Johannes P., and Eugene A. Nida. *Greek-English Lexicon of the New Testament Based on Semantic Domains.* Vol. 1. New York: United Bible Societies, 1988.

Luther, Martin. *Luther's Works: Word and Sacrament I.* Vol. 35. Ed. T. Backmann. Philadelphia: Fortress, 1960.

Martinez, Florentino García, ed. *The Dead Sea Scrolls Translated: The Qumran Texts in English.* Trans. Wilfred G. E. Watson. Leiden: Brill, 1994.

McKenzie, John L. *Dictionary of the Bible.* London and Dublin: Geoffrey Chapman, 1966.

Metzger, Bruce M. *A Textual Commentary on the Greek New Testament.* New York: United Bible Societies, 1975.

New Revised Standard Version of the Bible: Catholic Edition. Nashville: Thomas Nelson, Catholic Bible Press, 1989.

Plutarch's Lives, Vols. I–XI. Trans. Bernodotte Perrin, LCL. London: William Heinemann; Cambridge: Harvard University Press, 1959.

Rahlfs, Alfred, ed. *Septuaginta. Id est Vetus Testamentum graece iuxta LXX interpretes.* Duo volumina in uno. Stuttgart: Deutsche Bibelgesellschaft (1935) 1979.

Robinson, James M., ed. *The Nag Hammadi Library in English.* 3rd ed. New York: HarperCollins, 1990.

Schneemelcher, Wilhelm, ed. *New Testament Apocrypha.* Vol. 1: *Gospels and Related Writings.* Vol. 2: *Writings Relating to the Apostles: Apocaplyses and Related Subjects.* Rev. ed. Cambridge: James Clarke & Co.; Louisville: Westminster John Knox, 1991, 1992.

Schoedel, William R. "The (First) Apocalypse of James (V,3)." In James M. Robinson, ed., *The Nag Hammadi Library in English.* 3rd ed. New York: HarperCollins, 1990, 260–68.

Suetonius, Vols. I–II. Trans. J. C. Rolfe, LCL. London: William Heinemann; Cambridge: Harvard University Press, 1951.

Vielhauer, Philipp, and Georg Strecker. "Jewish-Christian Gospels." In Wilhelm Schneemelcher, ed., *New Testament Apocrypha.* Vol. 1: *Gospels and Related Writings.* Rev. ed. Cambridge: James Clarke & Co.; Louisville: Westminster John Knox, 1991, 134–78

Williams, Francis E., trans. "The Apocryphon of James [I,2]." In James M. Robinson, ed., *The Nag Hammadi Library in English.* 29-37. 3rd ed. New York: HarperCollins, 1990, 29–37.

Wright, R. B., trans. "Psalms of Solomon." In James H. Charlesworth, ed., *The Old Testament Pseudepigrapha.* Vol. 2: *Expansions of the "Old Testament" and Legends, Wisdom and Philosophical Literature, Prayers, Psalms, and Odes,*

Fragments of Lost Judeo-Hellenistic Works. London: Darton, Longman & Todd, 1985.

Zerwick, Max. *Analysis Philologica Novi Testamenti Graeci.* 3rd ed. Rome: Pontificii Instituti Biblici, 1966.

III. Commentaries on the Letter of James

Barclay, William. *The Letters of James and Peter.* The Daily Study Bible. 2nd ed. Philadelphia: Westminster, 1960.

Davids, Peter H. *The Epistle of James: A Commentary on the Greek Text.* NIGTC. Grand Rapids: Eerdmans, 1982.

Dibelius, Martin. *James: A Commentary on the Epistle of James.* Hermeneia. Rev. Heinrich Greeven. Trans. Michael A. Williams. Ed. Helmut Koester. Philadelphia: Fortress, 1976; English Translation of *Der Brief des Jakobus.* 11th rev. ed. Göttingen: Vandenhoeck & Ruprecht, 1964.

Hartin, Patrick J. *James.* SP 14. Collegeville: Liturgical Press, 2003.

Johnson, Luke Timothy. *The Letter of James.* AB 37A. New York: Doubleday, 1995.

Laws, Sophie. *A Commentary on the Epistle of James.* BNTC. London: Adam & Charles Black, 1980.

Martin, Ralph P. *James.* WBC 48. Waco, TX: Word, 1988.

Mayor, Joseph B. *The Epistle of St. James. The Greek Text with Introduction, Notes and Comments, and Further Studies in the Epistle of St. James.* 3rd ed. 1913. Reprint. Grand Rapids: Zondervan, 1954.

Wall, Robert W. *Community of the Wise: The Letter of James.* The New Testament in Context. Valley Forge, PA: Trinity Press International, 1997.

INDEX